Explaining Crime

Explaining Crime

A Primer in Criminological Theory

Hugh D. Barlow and David Kauzlarich

ROWMAN & LITTLEFIELD PUBLISHERS, INC.
Lanham • Boulder • New York • Toronto • Plymouth, UK

Published by Rowman & Littlefield Publishers, Inc.
A wholly owned subsidiary of The Rowman & Littlefield Publishing Group, Inc.
4501 Forbes Boulevard, Suite 200, Lanham, Maryland 20706
http://www.rowmanlittlefield.com

Estover Road, Plymouth PL6 7PY, United Kingdom

British Library Cataloguing in Publication Information Available

Library of Congress Cataloging-in-Publication Data

Barlow, Hugh D.
  Explaining crime : a primer in criminological theory / Hugh Barlow and David Kauzlarich.
    p. cm.
  Includes bibliographical references and index.
  ISBN 978-0-7425-6509-8 (cloth : alk. paper) — ISBN 978-0-7425-6510-4 (pbk. : alk. paper) — ISBN 978-0-7425-6511-1 (electronic)
  1. Criminology. 2. Crime. I. Kauzlarich, David. II. Title.
HV6018.B367 2010
364.01—dc22   2009031112

∞™ The paper used in this publication meets the minimum requirements of American National Standard for Information Sciences—Permanence of Paper for Printed Library Materials, ANSI/NISO Z39.48-1992.

Printed in the United States of America

Contents

Preface

This short book is derived from our larger work, *Introduction to Criminology*, 9th edition (Rowman & Littlefield, 2009). We have organized and written this text with one goal in mind: to provide readers with a concise and highly accessible review of major criminological theories. Designed primarily for use in undergraduate courses on crime and deviance theory, we have tried to keep students at the forefront of the writing process. Thus, we have developed both discussion questions and suggested activities for each chapter in the hope of raising the level of student engagement with the material. Further, as in our main criminology text, we have included several references to popular music and film to animate some of the theoretical concepts found throughout the book. We have also included an epilogue that provides students with concrete concepts to facilitate the application of criminological theory to a variety of crimes.

We are indebted to many colleagues, students, reviewers, and the staff at Rowman & Littlefield for providing the support necessary to produce this text. Chief among these helping hands are Alan McClare, our editor, Karen Ackermann, production editor, and Evan Wiig, editorial assistant. Many colleagues have also directly or indirectly aided in our efforts. We especially thank Jeff Ferrell, Ron Kramer, David Friedrichs, and Dawn Rothe, whose intellectual insights made this a better book. Graduate sociology students Josh Lucker, Michael Leber, and Eva-Sophia Clark also lended assistance to this book.

This book is dedicated to our partners, Sandy and Lavender, and to our children, a constant source of love and inspiration.

1

The Basics of Criminological Theory

Criminologists study how, why, when, where, and under what conditions crime, criminality, and victimization occur. Like any academic discipline, there are a variety of ways criminologists think about and research causality. Some scholars of crime seek to map out crime in its relationship to social environments, such as the economy, in institutions such as schools and families, and in group dynamics, while others focus on individual decision-making processes. Criminologists have created and tested dozens of theories (and many more variants of formal theories) in order to better understand, explain, and hopefully do something about crime in the real world. Such study and theorizing is not as straightforward and simple as it may sound. The truth is that there is a lot going on with crime, and criminological theories try to find out what exactly these things are.

Let's start with a classroom example. Occasionally we ask our students at the beginning of our criminology classes the difficult question "What causes crime?" In response, it is not uncommon for students to identify things such as poverty, dysfunctional families, racism, peer pressure, laziness, and the lack of good jobs. When probed to elaborate, some argue that if people can't find a good job, they can't make the bills, and so they decide to commit crimes (for example, steal money or sell drugs) to get by. Other students say that when parents fail to provide rules and guidelines for their children's behavior, there can be no accountability, let alone discipline, and therefore kids will be more likely to get into trouble because they do not fear punishment. Criminologists have found that while both of these lines of reasoning have merit, they do not capture the real working dynamics or root causes of crime commission. Because crime is complicated, there are no easy answers. In the explanation of crime, as in real life, things are often easier said than done.

Attempts to explain why people violate rules is not new, and what we now call criminology dates back to the middle of the eighteenth century. The pioneers in the area of theoretical criminology were trained in a variety of disciplines. Cesare Beccaria (1738–1794) and Jeremy Bentham (1748–1832) were philosophers and students of law; Cesare Lombroso (1835–1909), regarded as the founder of criminology, was a physician and surgeon; Raffaele Garofalo (1851–1934) was a professor of law and a magistrate; Enrico Ferri (1856–1929) was a criminal lawyer and member of the Italian parliament. Although people from many disciplines continued to make important contributions to the field over the years, theoretical criminology found its primary academic home in departments of sociology, although it is ever more closely associated with criminal justice departments as well.

The basic goal of **theory** is *explanation*. Explanations are important because they help us figure out why things are the way they are, and they suggest what might be done to change things. In this sense, criminological theory's main job is to render crime more understandable. This simple way of conceptualizing theory reflects the diversity of applications that theories have in criminology. Every academic discipline has theory, for it drives basic questions about the subject matter. Indeed, theory is inescapable in virtually all aspects of life and human activity. Without it "we would be lost in space and time" (Pfohl, 1985: 10). Sometimes theories are found in places not obvious to the casual observer. For example, when preparing to cross a busy street one considers how best to do so by evaluating the flow of traffic versus the distance needing to be traveled. When parenting, decisions are made about the proper balance to strike between the discipline and support of a child. When you made your decision to enroll in college, your understanding of the value of education in the marketplace and in your vision of the future helped determine your course of conduct. In all of these cases, theories have instructed the decision making by helping to make sense out of a situation and to provide options and rationales for action. Theories exist in a wide range of popular culture contexts, such as sports (there is plenty of theory behind baseball, football, golf, hockey, basketball, running, and almost every other sport) and theories of music instruction (how notes, rhythms, chords, and harmonies can be meaningfully organized). Card and casino games have plenty of mathematical theories that apply to player strategies (e.g., card counting in blackjack, probability play in poker); and there are even theories about theories, known as metatheories.

Criminology, the study of lawmaking, lawbreaking, and the reactions to crime, is a rich field of study with many ideological, intellectual, and methodological disagreements. This partially explains why there are several dozen theories in the field, all of which will be reviewed in this text. Many of the theories attempt to explain why certain people commit crime. Other theories attempt to explain why some places have higher crime rates than others, or the social conditions under which crime rates rise and fall. There is also a group of theories in criminology that endeavor to explain lawmaking, the process by which certain behaviors or people are labeled criminal. Still other criminological theories attempt to shed light on the purpose of criminal justice itself, victimology, and the politics of crime and justice.

If the purpose of criminological theory is to explain crime, how do criminologists judge its success and value? Surely a theory should be logical, testable by research, and defensible in the face of criticism, but let's consider some less obvious criteria for evaluating the quality of a theory:

The theory should shed light on the topic under study. Imagine yourself in a dark room. What do you see? Now flip on the light switch. Can you see things more clearly? Are things that were otherwise not in view now visible? A good theory should function like a light switch. Of course, the brighter the light it triggers the better. As you will see in later chapters, some theories cast more light than others.

Theory should specifically point out the relationships between variables. A variable is anything that changes or can have different values. Theories specify how relevant variables are logically linked to the problem in need of explanation. For example, a few theories of crime hold that economic status is linked to crime because of shifts and changes in the unemployment rate. A theorist adopting this approach would have to specify how changes in the independent variable (unemployment rates) impact the frequency and distribution of crime (the dependent variable). More generally, a good theory correctly predicts the outcomes produced by changing circumstances.

Theory should be helpful in guiding research and future theoretical developments. To some, theory for itself is surely a stimulating intellectual exercise, but theory is especially meaningful when it can be articulated and applied in the real world. Although it is true that theories have an indirect influence on many aspects of criminal justice policy and practice, often the actors (lawmakers, police officers, judges, etc.) are not cognizant of the academic versions of theory and therefore not necessarily informed of the potential or substantiated drawbacks discovered in the academic community. Alternatively, some theorists we have talked to care little about the "practical" side of their work, choosing to instead leave those matters to others. Yet, putting theory to work in the real world is, overall, a vitally important part of criminology (Barlow, 1995).

Theories should hold up under empirical scrutiny. Flip through any major criminology journal and you'll likely find articles that in some way attempt to gauge the veracity and explanatory power of a theory. Such tests are important in any academic discipline, as theories that have been consistently

shown to be weak should be reworked or eschewed in favor of better explanations. However, caution should be used when discussing whether or not
a study or group of studies has actually "proven" or "disproved" a theory. In
the social sciences, such absolutism is difficult to achieve, and instead, studies can either be said to have "supported" or "not supported" a theory.

Theories should be parsimonious. Anything said in wordy or complicated
ways is typically less useful than things said in a straightforward and simple
manner. One of the reasons undergraduate students often dislike theory is
because it seems unclear and abstract. The effort to explain many variables
and their relationships, thereby increasing the scope of a theory, often
comes at the sacrifice of parsimony. As we shall see, theories differ considerably in how well they balance the tension between parsimony and scope,

In addition to considering how we can judge the quality and usefulness
of theories, we also need to think about the goals of theory more generally.
One of these is that a new theory should be able to shed a *different* sort of
light on the topic under study than those previously applied. In this vein,
several criminological theories are *oppositional*. Such theories develop from
an explicit critique of existing modes of explanation. In the late eighteenth
century, for example, Classical theory (reviewed in chapter 2) introduced
the notion of rational choice and, in the process, rebuked supernatural
explanations of crime. In like manner, Edwin Sutherland introduced his
theory of differential association through a critique of earlier theories that
held that poverty was a major cause of crime. More recent theories reviewed
in this book, such as postmodernism and feminism, are also oppositional,
for they include fundamental critiques of other explanations of crime as a
central step in advancing their own arguments.

Another function of theory is to guide social and criminal justice policy.
If there is a need to convince anyone that crime is a highly significant social
problem, consider that in the United States alone billions of dollars are
spent each year on governmental crime and criminal justice programs and
institutions. Moreover, each year there are millions of victims of crime and
the fear of crime can be paralyzing for people whether they have been victimized or not. The large amount of films and televisions shows based on
crime and criminal justice themes also suggests that there is a long-standing
and significant interest in crime (see box 1.1). Perhaps the most compelling—and to some extent controversial—film on crime in recent years is
Michael Moore's *Bowling for Columbine*, which is summarized in box 1.2.

CHARACTERISTICS OF THEORY

Before we examine particular theories of crime and criminality, it is helpful
to consider how they differ. There are four main ways to classify theory:

Box 1.1.   Crime in Film

For many years the American public has been fascinated with crime. Some of this interest may be because the fear of crime is so widespread. It may also be because people enjoy thinking about others taking chances that they themselves would never consider. Strong interest in crime is also reflected in popular culture, as there are literally thousands of television shows, films, and songs that in one way or another relate to crime or criminal justice.

Regarding crime films, Nicole Rafter (2000: 141) writes in *Shots in the Mirror: Crime Films and Society* that the reason for their popularity is often tied to the nature of the heroes:

> Viewers delight in watching characters who can escape from tight spots and outsmart their enemies, all the while tossing down scotch and flibbing jibes. Good-guy heroes please us by out-tricking the tricky, tracking down the psychos, solving impossible mysteries. Bad-guy heroes appeal by being bolder, nastier, crueler, and tougher than we dare to be by saying what they want, taking what they want, despising weaklings, and breaking the law with impunity.

Our examination of the all-time highest grossing films in the United States reveals that at least a quarter of them contain some kind of crime theme. The same is true with the American Film Institute's Top 100 Films of the American century. Organized crime films seem especially popular, as movies such as *GoodFellas, Scarface,* and *The Godfather* series rank high in both popular and critics' lists.

Rafter (2000) proposes that crime films not only reflect society's interest in rule breaking but that they also provide a way to frame the causes of crime as well. For example, if films depict someone committing a crime because of an addiction to hard drugs, viewers may come to believe that this is a cause of crime in the real world. As you read through the following chapters, keep a crime movie or two in mind and see if any of the academic explanations are similar to those provided in the films.

(1) by level of analysis, (2) paradigmatic structure, (3) range of explanation, and (4) by causal locus. We shall review each of these classifications in turn.

Levels of Analysis. Some theories deal mainly with large-scale social patterns such as social change or the social, economic, and political organization of society. Crime is viewed as a property of whole groups of people rather than as a property of individuals. Because they focus on how societies are organized, these theories usually relate crime to social structure. They are called **macro level theories**, but this does not mean they lack relevance for the everyday lives of individuals. Rather, such theories attempt to make sense of the everyday behavior of people in relation to conditions and trends

Box 1.2. *Bowling for Columbine* as Pop Criminology

Michael Moore's Oscar-winning film, *Bowling for Columbine*, is regarded by many as one of the most powerful nonacademic treatments of real-world crime to date. In the film, Moore raises fundamental questions about the relationship between social inequality, opportunity, and violence in the United States by exploring destructive individual, corporate, state, and special-interest-group practices and how they contribute to both interpersonal and social injury. Moore frames crime, especially gun violence, as the result of many factors, including youth alienation, racism, and poverty. He draws attention to the high level of gun violence in the United States by providing a series of powerful images, interviews, stories, and biographies. Among the more poignant of these are:

- An interview with musician Marilyn Manson about those who blame him for the Columbine shootings and similar forms of violence.
- Chilling video that until recently had only been viewed by the parents of children killed or injured at Columbine. The video shows dozens of students panicked during the assault by Klebold and Harris.
- Juxtaposing the U.S. government's bombing of an aspirin factory in Kosovo on the same morning that Eric Harris and Dylan Klebold slaughtered thirteen people at Columbine High School. Predictably, Moore argues, then-President Clinton only defined one of those actions as violent.
- Taking two young men—one in a wheelchair and the other with a bullet still embedded in his chest, who were shot by Klebold and Harris—to Kmart corporate headquarters to demand that the company stop selling handgun ammunition. After the predictable corporate neutralization of the situation, Moore and the two young men return a few days later with the media in tow to again demand some action. Several days later Kmart announces the phasing out of the selling of such ammunition.
- The story of a woman who left her son to live with her brother because she was forced to work two jobs under Michigan's "welfare to work" program. Her son took a loaded handgun from his uncle's dwelling and then shot and killed one of his first-grade classmates.
- Moore implies that if the state of Michigan's policy was not so strict, the boy would have been with his mother and unable to access a firearm.
- Media obsession with the reporting of violent crime. Using the case of the first-grader shooting, Moore shows how media agents frame stories without consideration of the effects of poverty on individual decision making and behavior. In another instance, Moore asks a field reporter what would be more attractive: covering a "guy with a gun" or a "baby that is drowning." The reporter picked the former.
- A friendly Moore randomly opening the doors of homes in Toronto and asking the residents why they really weren't scared when he appeared.

- Moore and sociologist Barry Glassner comfortably standing at the corner of Normandy and Florence in Los Angeles. They are unable to see the famous "Hollywood" sign because of massively thick air pollution. Moore asks a cop standing by if he could arrest the people responsible for poisoning his lungs. After a mumble or two, the cop walks away.

While Moore's film does not represent anything close to an academic breakthrough in the study of crime, it does present a number of compelling visual portraits of victims and offenders that encourages viewers to think about the causes and consequences of crime and violence. And while Moore has come under fire for the film's political slant, there are those in criminology who see this as unproblematic, as many theories of crime reflect ideological beliefs, as we explore later in box 1.3.

that transcend the individual, and even the individual's neighborhood and community. A macro level analysis might also include the study of the social origins of criminal definitions as well as how their enforcement affects group life, including crime itself. Some macro level theorists are interested in why certain events and people are labeled criminal and others not; other scholars look into the process of constructing criminal definitions itself—among scientists, perhaps, or on the street or in the courtroom.

Some other theories focus on the ways individuals interact with others and with the groups to which they belong. These are called **micro level theories**, and most share an interest in the way social interaction creates and transmits meanings. They emphasize the social processes by which people and events become criminal. For example, as people move from situation to situation, they are confronted with all sorts of messages, rules, and expectations, some of which are not obvious. Through a process of sending, receiving, and interpreting messages, individuals help construct the social reality of which they are a part.

Figure 1.1 provides one way to think about levels of analysis through concentric circles. Criminality is at the center, and around it are some of its influences, such as peer group associations and broader social forces such as the economy.

In reality, some theories do not neatly fit into these categories, while others seem to bridge the two levels. Laub and Sampson (1988), for example, predict that structural factors such as household crowding, economic dependence, residential mobility, and parental crime influence the delinquent behavior of children through their effects on the way parents relate to their children day by day. Sociological theories that attempt to explain

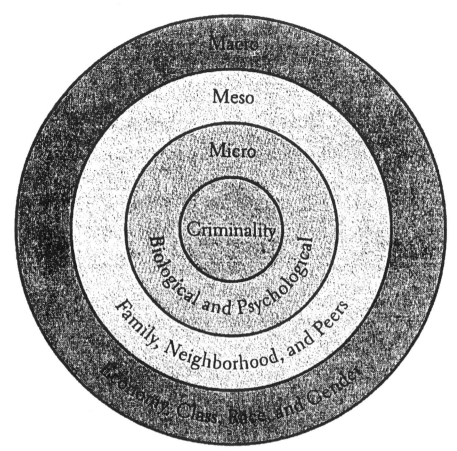

Figure 1.1.   Levels of Analysis, Crime, and Criminality

"micro-macro" dynamics between individuals and society often take this approach. Indeed, it is a daunting but important task to explain how larger social forces shape institutions and groups and ultimately find expression in the interactions of everyday life.

Paradigms and Criminological Theory. **Paradigms** are broad assumptions and presuppositions about the nature of social life (*ontology*) and how knowledge is to be gained about social life (*epistemology*). Paradigms are far more fundamental than theories or perspectives—they are indeed the foundation upon which theories are built. There are two basic paradigms in criminology: the **positivist paradigm** and the **social constructionist paradigm**. While some have argued that there are also Marxist, postmodernist, and feminist paradigms, we see these approaches as multidimensional. That is, they combine elements of both the positivist and constructionist paradigms.

The positivist paradigm holds that crime can be known and explained through the scientific method. Crime is considered an objective condition, or social fact, that can be analyzed and understood as an independent phenomenon, regardless of differing ideas about its development and constitution (Michalowski, 1985). A positivist theory of crime asks questions such as "What are the concrete cause(s) of crime?" and "How can crime be controlled or reduced?"

In contrast, the social constructionist paradigm does not assume the objective existence of crime. It emphasizes instead how crime, law, and criminal justice are differently defined and conceptualized by social actors. Thus, the term *social constructionist*. To these theorists, crime is not an objective condition, nor is the law, the criminal, or the criminal justice system. Criminologists operating from the social constructionist paradigm might build theories to explore questions such as "Who defines crime and for what purpose?," "How and why are labels attached to certain people and to certain acts at particular moments in time?," and "What are the consequences of the application of labels to people and groups over time?"

General and Restricted Theories. Another important way that theories differ is in the range of phenomena they try to explain. **General theories** are meant to explain a broad range of facts. They are also not restricted to any one place or time. A general theory of crime, for example, is one that explains many (if not all) types of crime and can be applied to a variety of social and historical settings.

Although some theories in criminology purport to explain all or most crime, few really do meet a sufficiently generalizable level of analysis to satisfy crucial questions of causality or correlation. Sometimes this results in the production of **restricted theories**, explanations designed to apply to a narrower range of facts. A restricted theory of crime might apply to one type of crime or to various types under a limited set of circumstances. Most modern theories in criminology are regarded as restricted, but the development of general theory remains an important goal, and some recent efforts are promising.

Distant and Proximate Causes. Causation is not a simple concept, especially in the social and behavioral sciences. Think about your own behavior for a moment. Right now you are reading this book. How and why you are reading could probably be explained in many different ways; in other words, various causes might be at work. Some of the causes are closer or more immediate—called **proximate causes**—while others are more **distant**, or *background,* **causes**. A proximate cause might be that your professor just assigned this chapter to be read before your next class, which is tomorrow. An even more proximate (and perhaps more powerful!) cause might be that your parents just told you that they would buy you a new car if you got an "A" in your criminology class. A more distant cause is the expectation that you will follow your mother's footsteps and become a lawyer. An even more distant cause may lie in the fact that a university education is a requirement for many professional careers and increasingly for other jobs as well.

You look out the window and notice that a friend is not cracking the books like you. No surprise, since she's not a college student. But then you wonder why not. Because you know her you comfortably reject personal explanations based on her intelligence, her drive, and her commitment to getting ahead, and start thinking about background factors. You remember that neither of her parents has a university education; you recall that she has four brothers and sisters and that only her father works outside the home, as a house painter. You remember that one of her brothers is disabled and that a few years ago the father had an accident and was out of work for two years. You start thinking about other university students you know and about high school friends who never went to college or dropped out.

Even though it is only a small sample of people, you begin to see patterns. You realize that a university education is explained by a combination of proximate and distant causes, some of which relate to the individual, some to the community and larger society, and some to the social situations people move in and out of in the course of their lives. You recognize, as well, that some causes seem to have a direct impact while the effect of others is more indirect, working through their impact on something else. Some causes are both direct and indirect. For example, the impact of poverty on behavior may be indirect through its effects on family relationships and direct through its impact on opportunities and access to them.

IDEOLOGY AND CRIMINOLOGICAL THEORY

The way criminologists visualize their field and its subject matter reflects their particular set of beliefs and values. These beliefs and values—called ideology—affect decisions about what to investigate, what questions to ask, and what to do with the knowledge gained. The intrusion of ideology is a normal aspect of the academic enterprise, and the study of crime is no exception. There are a number of competing ideological perspectives in criminology: conservative, liberal, and critical. The latter approach includes feminist, Marxist, postmodernist, cultural, and peacemaking theories, which we review more fully in chapter 6.

Conservative Criminology. **Conservative criminology** is identified with the view that criminal law is a codification of moral precepts and that people who break the law are somehow psychologically or morally defective. Crimes are seen as threats to law-abiding members of society and to the social order on which their safety and security depend. The "right" questions to ask about crime include: "How are morally defective persons produced?" and "How can society protect itself against them?" The causes of crime are located in the characteristics of individuals. The solution to the crime problem is couched in terms of a return to basic values wherein good wins over evil. For example, consider Gottfredson and Hirschi's (1990) self-control theory, a moderately conservative explanation of crime discussed later in this text. According to this theory, individuals with low self-control are most likely to commit crimes. The traits associated with low self-control include: short-time perspective; low diligence, persistence, and tenacity; a tendency to be "adventuresome, active, and physical"; a tendency to be "self-centered, indifferent, or insensitive to the suffering and needs of others"; and a tendency to have "unstable marriages, friendships, and job profiles" (Gottfredson and Hirschi, 1990: 91). The major cause of low self-control, according to the authors, is "ineffective parenting," a claim that has much more support in conservative than liberal circles. Until well into the twentieth century, most criminological thinking was conservative. In lay circles, the conservative view enjoyed a considerable boost during the Reagan and Bush years, and to some extent continued to enjoy popularity throughout the Clinton and Bush administrations.

Liberal Criminology. **Liberal criminology** began to emerge as a force during the late 1930s and early 1940s, and it has remained dominant ever since. The most influential versions of liberal criminology explain criminal behavior either in terms of the way society is organized (social structure) or in terms of the way people acquire social attributes (social process). *Social structure* theories include strain theory, cultural transmission theory, and conflict theory. Strain theory argues that when people find they cannot achieve valued goals through socially approved means, they experience stress and frustration, which in turn may lead to crime. Cultural transmission theory draws attention to the impact on individuals of the values, norms, and lifestyles to which they are exposed day to day. Delinquency and crime are learned through exposure to a criminogenic culture, a culture that encourages crime. According to conflict theory, society is characterized by conflict, and criminality is a product of differences in power exercised when people compete for scarce resources or clash over conflicting interests.

Social process theories include associational theory, control theory, and labeling theory. Associational theories assert that people become criminal through close association with others (family members, friends, coworkers) who are criminal. Control theory asserts that crime and delinquency result "when an individual's bond to society is weak or broken" (Hirschi, 1971: 16). More room is allowed for individual deviance when social controls are weak. Labeling theory suggests that some people become criminals because they are influenced by the way other people react to them. People who are repeatedly punished for "bad" behavior may eventually accept the idea that they are bad, and their subsequent behavior is consistent with that identity.

Critical Criminology. Liberal criminologists locate criminogenic forces in the organizational and routine social processes of society, yet they do not call for any change in its basic economic, cultural, or political structure. **Critical criminologists** (sometimes called *radical criminologists*) generally do. From a Marxist theoretical perspective, crime and criminal justice have reinforced and strengthened the power of the state and the wealthy over the poor, working class, and developing world. To some Marxists, crime and criminality are the products of the exploitative character of monopoly capitalism, and efforts to control crime are poorly disguised attempts to divert attention from the crimes committed by the state, corporations, and capitalists. While Marxism is but one school of thought within critical criminology, the overall approach has largely been shaped by Marx's ideas, such as his call to work for social justice, encapsulated in his dictum: "The philosophers have only interpreted the world in various ways; the point, however, is to change it" (quoted in Tucker, 1978: 143).

Feminist theories in criminology focus on how gender relations and patriarchy constitute and impact the nature, extent, and distribution of crime, responses to crime, and victimization. Theoretical criminology, like most academic areas, has historically been male-centered, sexist, and either ignorant or dismissive of issues related to gender inequality and discrimination. Since the 1970s, however, there has been a substantial increase in the study of the gendered nature of the causes and consequences of crime, although the extent to which more radical forms of feminist criminology have impacted mainstream criminology is considerably less than that of liberal forms of feminism.

Another critical criminological approach is postmodernism, which employs notions of chaos and unpredictability in the understanding of crime and questions conventional ideas about the value of science in explaining crime (Ferrell, 2003; Henry and Milovanovic, 2003). Postmodernism is clearly an oppositional theory and is really a loose collection of "themes and tendencies" that include the rejection of scientific methods, the notion of Truth, and the legitimacy of the state (Schwartz and Friedrichs, 1994). Criminological postmodernism also sensitizes us to the power of words, especially the so-called crime speak, which is how through language we think about and define the "reality" of crime and justice (Arrigo, 1998; Borkin, Henry, and Milovanovic, 2006; Henry and Milovanovic, 1996; 1999). For example, the phrase "war on crime" suggests more a more militaristic than humanist strategy to reduce crime.

Critical criminology has also given rise to what is known as peacemaking criminology. Peacemaking criminologists theorize on how to bring victims, offenders, and communities together in the harmonious resolution of conflict. Borrowing heavily from the ideas of humanist thinkers such as Jane Addams and Mohandas Gandhi, this perspective holds substantial applicability to crime and criminal justice policy, most notably in the form of restorative justice.

All of these ideological positions—conservative, liberal, and radical/critical—can be found in the various theories reviewed in the next several chapters. As you can see, there is much variety within theories of crime, and in the real world of criminology, political ideology is partly responsible for this (see box 1.3). But, there is much variety in lots of things. Consider, for example, tactics used in sports. Just as there are different ways to catch fish, pitch a baseball, or hit a golf ball, there are different ways to approach the study of crime. Further, not all theories of crime (like baseball pitches) are suitable at all times or in all places. What pitcher would only have one pitch in his repertoire? What angler would only have one lure? And what golfer would use a putter on the tee? The same holds true with theories of crime,

---

Box 1.3. Political Ideology and Criminologists' Theoretical Preferences

A survey of criminologists lends considerable support to the notion that political ideology is related to theoretical preferences. In Walsh and Ellis's (1999) survey of 138 scholars of crime, 70 identified themselves as liberal, 35 as moderates, 23 as conservative, and 10 as radical.

The study found that criminologists who regarded themselves as more politically conservative or moderate were more likely to favor theories that focus on low self-control and poor disciplinary practices as important causes of crime. Liberals were more likely to favor theories that focus on environmental factors that lead to crime, such as economic and educational inequality. Critical/radical criminologists were even stronger in their belief that these factors are important in the understanding of crime. Moreover, while radicals supported mostly Marxist and conflict theories, conservatives supported theories that do not implicate larger social factors in the causes of crime. Not surprisingly, those claiming to be liberal or moderate "fall in between" radical and conservatives (Walsh and Ellis, 1999: 14).

The authors indicate that it is unclear whether political ideology causes theoretical preference or whether theory influences a person's ideology. This is an interesting question, for if only ideology causes theoretical preference, to what degree can criminology be "scientific"? If, however, certain theories are found to be supported in the research and this causes a change in ideology, does this mean that the discipline is more "objective" and committed only to the searching of truth? Unfortunately, the answers to these questions are not easy, but what this study points out is that indeed criminology is (and perhaps has always been) "highly fragmented" by political ideology (Walsh and Ellis, 1999: 14).

as criminologists have devised a number of different theories to explain what causes crime. But as you will discover, the large number of theories in criminology is not necessarily negative, as crime itself is widely variable, changing both in time and space.

Another reason that there are so many criminological theories is that crime is an immensely variant phenomenon. From a strictly legalistic standpoint, crime includes a huge range of offenses, from property crimes like burglary and theft to violent crimes such as murder, rape, and assault. Criminologists also study white-collar crimes, which involve the violation of trust in the context of work. Examples of such crimes include embezzlement, environmental contamination, violations of worker safety laws, and genocide. With such a variety of behaviors that fall under the label "crime," you can see that it is a daunting task to try to intelligently explain the causes and correlates of these various behaviors. But this is exactly what many criminologists attempt to do.

The fact that there are numerous criminological theories is also reflected in the sheer complexity of the behaviors and actions under study by criminologists. If it is criminal behavior to be explained, must behavior more generally also be explained? If so, we are asking ourselves to accomplish a feat that scholars in all sorts of disciplines (e.g., biology, psychology, sociology, philosophy) have studied for centuries. It should come as no surprise that many theories of crime do in fact owe intellectual debts to other fields of study, since criminology is perhaps one of the more interdisciplinary fields of academic inquiry today. Yet the goal of explaining why humans behave the way they do is still elusive. This is in part due to the fact that there are so many different aspects of the human and social condition that need to be considered as potential factors that contribute to behavior and whether or not there are unique causes of criminal behavior.

CHAPTER SUMMARY

The main purpose of theory is explanation. Criminologists create, test, and apply theories in order to understand the nature, extent, definition, and consequences of crime. Theories should be able to shed light on an understudied or poorly understood problem, specify the relationship between variables, guide criminal justice policy, be economical, and hold up to empirical scrutiny. Theories are classified by their level of analysis, paradigmatic assumptions, causal focus, and scope. Macro theories deal with large-scale social patterns; micro theories focus on the interaction of individuals and on the manner in which meanings are created and transmitted in social situations. General theories explain a broad range of facts; restricted theories apply to a narrower range of facts. A general theory thus subsumes more restricted theories. However, the development of general theory is extremely difficult, and most modern theories in criminology are regarded as restricted. Paradigms structure how theorists go about viewing the world in a fundamental way. The social fact paradigm assumes the objective existence of social phenomena, while the social constructionist perspective guides the investigation of subjective, interactive, and definitional processes.

Theories reflect the values, beliefs, and academic disciplines of those who propose them. Conservative criminological theories explain crime in terms of the moral or psychological defectiveness of individuals. Liberal theories explain crime in terms of normal social conditions and processes that characterize group life. Critical theories explain crime in terms of the exploitative character of capitalist society, patriarchy, or modernism. Crime is an immensely complex and variant phenomenon, and there are equally complex and variant attempts to explain it.

KEY TERMS

critical criminologists
conservative criminology
distant causes
general theories
liberal criminology
macro level theories
micro level theories
paradigms
positivist paradigm
proximate causes
restricted theories
social constructionist paradigm
theory

DISCUSSION QUESTIONS

1. Scholars treasure the function and importance of *theory*, but this word is generally not considered to be exciting or valuable outside of academic circles. Why might this be and how can the perception be changed?
2. Why is the concept of "levels of analysis" crucial to theorizing about crime? Do you think that one level of analysis is more popular than others in the general public's thinking about the causes of crime?

3. Paradigms represent fundamental starting points for the understanding of any social scientific phenomenon, including crime. To what extent do you see either of the paradigms being more helpful and accurate than the other?
4. Some scholars believe that crime is political in all sorts of ways. Given the role of ideology discussed in this chapter, how do you see politics framing or entering into discussions of the causes of crime and crime control policy?

ACTIVITIES

1. Search the Republican, Democratic, and Green Party websites for the word "crime." Compare and contrast the different policies and approaches on these websites to the liberal, conservative, and radical theoretical perspectives on crime.
2. Watch Michael Moore's film *Bowling for Columbine* and identify the ideological components of the film as well as the extent to which attention is given to the three levels of analysis. Is Moore's analysis of crime more political than scientific?
3. Conduct an informal poll and ask people about their opinion on the causes of crime. Analyze their responses, looking for the presence of ideological assumptions and bias.

2

Classical and Rational Choice Theories

Perry Ferrell, former lead vocalist of the band Jane's Addiction, sings of a simple rationale for shoplifting in the song "Been Caught Stealing": Why pay for something if you can just take it? Indeed, why not do things that give you pleasure as long as you won't get in too much trouble for it? This kind of reasoning has intrigued criminologists, and whole theories of crime have been developed around the idea that people are rational because their behavior is a result of their quest to maximize pleasure and minimize pain. This is a fairly popular way of thinking about crime, as the phrase "it comes down to individual choice" is a comment we have heard many times from our criminology students. The logic behind this statement is that although environmental conditions can affect a person's views and behavior, ultimately an individual makes a choice to act, including in ways that are criminal. Therefore, the individual should be at the center of attention when attempting to explain the causes of crime. Modern criminological theory is no stranger to this line of reasoning, although it is not simply a matter of focusing on the person to the exclusion of all background factors. The **rational choice theory** of decision making predicts that individuals think about the expected rewards, costs, and risks of alternative actions and choose actions best suited to their goals. If such an explanation has merit, it should be revealed not only in the choice to commit crime but also in the choice to commit one kind of crime rather than another and in the decision to direct crime against one victim rather than another. Before we discuss the foundations of rational choice theories, read box 2.1 and consider the idea of rationality as it applies to attending a college class.

Box 2.1.   How Rational Is Coming to Class?

Think for a moment about your decision to attend a particular class meeting. Using rational choice theory, we would expect that this decision was based on your perception of the rewards and costs of doing so. What are some of the more immediate factors you might consider? Surely it would seem beneficial to come to class if the instructor rewards attendance, bases exams on lectures, or makes the class interesting. Some costs might be that you are tired and could use the sleep, you don't find the class interesting, or you think that the material to be covered in a particular class won't make much of a difference in your grade.

As college professors, we have noticed that attendance in our classes follows an interesting pattern. The first few weeks of class tend to have better attendance rates than those weeks in the middle of the semester. We also find that attendance peaks in a class right before an exam, while it decreases the class session immediately after the exam. Friday classes are almost always the most poorly attended unless an exam is being given. From your experience, how do you think such patterns can be explained through rational choice theory?

There may be larger, less immediate costs and benefits that enter into the equation as well. Perhaps you are so committed to the goal of graduating from college that you are willing to sacrifice being understimulated or poorly rewarded in a particular class. Even though you might have little to gain from attending the class, you might think that not doing so would increase the risk of failure in some way. On the other hand, a person may not be all that committed to school and so the thought of missing an important class is not that big of a deal. Further consider that many college students work outside of class and have dependent family members, and that on some days work and family may have to take precedence over school. Consider further that every hour you spend in the classroom is an hour you are not earning a wage. Students seem to be willing to justify that cost by thinking that in the long run, a college education will help them make more money. These are only a few things that could enter into the decision-making process involved in coming to class. Can you think of others?

Also, rare is the person who actually sits down with pencil and paper and meticulously calculates the overall costs and benefits of going to a class, or of engaging in criminal behavior for that matter. Further, costs and benefits are bounded by space and time, and their relativity only underscores the fact that their salience can vary from individual to individual and context to context.

For further reading on the relativity of rationality in criminal decision making, consult Greg Pogarsky's (2002) "Identifying 'Deterrable' Offenders: Implications for Research on Deterrence," *Justice Quarterly* 19(3): 431–532.

CLASSICAL THEORY

The end of the eighteenth century in Europe was a time of great transformation. As the Industrial Revolution motored on, populations swelled; people moved from the country to the city; worked for wages rather than for themselves or rent; and a new political economy, capitalism, acted to fundamentally restructure the more simplified arrangements of barter exchange and feudalist social organization. On the political level, the traditional authority of monarchies was under attack as political radicals, some of whom were philosophers and scholars involved in the Enlightenment intellectual movement, championed the ideas of democracy, rationality, and free will. Intellectuals began to view people's behavior as motivated by their rational choice, not as a result of some supernatural or demonological force. The view of human nature was that people possessed free will and were guided by a sort of cost/benefit analysis; thus, it was proposed that people choose their own destiny rather than being forced by circumstance or demons into action. Previously popular supernatural explanations of behavior lost their popularity rather quickly in the wake of the Enlightenment (Pfohl, 1985).

Cesare Beccaria and Jeremy Bentham, both products of this new intellectual movement, were among the first European scholars to write on issues pertaining to crime and criminal justice. Their writings were not only directed toward explaining crime but also on how a rational, fair, and democratic criminal justice system could be designed. The so-called **Classical School** had two main foci: (1) a program for changes in the administration of justice, and (2) a limited theory of crime causation.

Regarding the relationship between the state and the control of its citizens, Beccaria (1993: 9) wrote that: ". . . every act of authority of one man (sic) over another, for which there is not an absolute necessity, is tyrannical. It is upon this then that the sovereign's right to punish crimes is founded." Essentially, Beccaria and Bentham subscribed to the philosophy of **utilitarianism**, which holds that policies and deeds, particularly those associated with the government, should provide the greatest good for the greatest number of people. Applying this reasoning to law, Bentham (1973: 162) wrote:

> The end of law is, to augment happiness. The general object which all laws have, or ought have, in common, is to augment the total happiness of the community; and therefore, in the first place, to exclude, as far as may be, every thing that tends to subtract from that happiness: in other words, to exclude mischief.

The reasoning of Becarria and Bentham is compatible with common-day notions as the presumption of innocence, judicial neutrality, and proportionality in sentencing. They were opposed to the torture of prisoners and capital punishment. Further, Classical School scholars emphasized that punishment was a "necessary evil" and only justifiable if based on reasonable, humane, and rational processes. More specifically, Bentham (1973: 162) believed that punishment should not be given when it is:

1. *Groundless* (the act is not really mischievous)
2. *Inefficacious* (ineffective as a deterrent)
3. *Too expensive* (where the trouble it causes exceeds the benefits)
4. *Needless* (where the crime may be prevented or dissolved in some other way)

Bentham and Becarria also emphasized that punishment should be proportional to the harm caused to *society*, not tailored to the individual victim's preferences or the particular qualities of the individual offender. This approach is encapsulated in the commonly used phrase "let the punishment fit the crime." In this way, Classical theory's main focus is on the crime, not the offender. All persons were assumed to be operating under the same kind of rationality.

Classical School scholars also provided a rough theory of crime causation. They believed that criminal behavior resulted from the rational calculation of costs and benefits associated with the criminal act. The idea that people are *hedonistic* (pleasure seeking) guided their work. A central prediction stemming from this idea is that people would be more likely to commit a crime if the pleasure (perceived benefits) from the behavior outweighed the pain (perceived costs). Classical School thinkers thought that the most likely "cost" in the equation would be detection, apprehension, and punishment.

Not just any old punishment will do, they said. The threatened punishment for criminal behavior was thought to work best as a deterrent if it was (a) certain, (b) proportionate to the harm caused by the crime, and (c) swiftly imposed. If these conditions were met, it would mean an individual would be less likely to commit a crime if s/he knew that they would be caught and punished (certainty) soon after committing the crime (swiftness), and if the punishment mirrored the seriousness of the crime. Beccaria and Bentham considered severity to be the least important deterrent.

It is conventional to distinguish between two classes of potential offenders who may refrain from crime because they fear punishment:

1. People who have directly experienced punishment for something they did in the past. If these people refrain from future criminal activity because they fear being punished again, this is *specific deterrence*.

2. People who have not experienced punishment themselves but are deterred from crime by the fear that they might get the same punishment experienced by others. This is *general deterrence*.

The distinction is important because the deterrent effect of experienced punishments may be quite different from that of threatened punishments. When a judge hands down a sentence and tells the offender, "This ought to make you think twice next time," the judge is thinking of the penalty as a specific deterrent; if the judge says, "I intend to make an example of you," the penalty's general deterrent value is being emphasized. Box 2.2 explores some modern-day research on the topic of deterrence.

Box 2.2. Modern-day Research on Deterrence

Over two hundred years have passed since Bentham and Beccaria laid the foundation of the deterrence theory of punishment, and their ideas are still relevant today. During that time a conventional wisdom emerged that punishment deters if it is certain, swift, and reasonably severe, but modern science has not confirmed that wisdom.

The inability of the scientific community to substantiate—or reject—the conventional wisdom (and political belief) that punishment deters crime must be difficult for many people to understand. Most of us can think of anecdotal illustrations of deterrence, from our own personal experience perhaps or from hearing about other people who refrained from committing a crime because they were fearful of the consequences. But serious researchers find that the complexities of the subject present formidable obstacles to developing conclusive answers (Cohen-Cole, Durlauf, Fagan, and Nagin, 2006; Gibbs and Firebaugh, 1990; Pratt, Cullen, Blevins, Daigle, and Madenson, 2006; Stafford and Warr, 1993). This is not to say that there has been *absolutely* no support in the literature of deterrence theory. Limited support of deterrence has been found in the areas of auto theft (Di Tella and Schardrodsky, 2004), drunk driving (Davey, Freeman, Palk, Lavelle, and Rowland, 2008; Piquero and Paternoster, 1998; Walker, 1998), luggage theft (Trivizas and Smith, 1997), and crime trends more generally (D'Alessio and Stolzenberg, 1998).

Most surprising, perhaps, is the fact that more than fifty years of research has yet to uncover a deterrent effect for capital punishment (Archer and Gartner, 1984; Bailey, 1998; Cochran, Chamlin, Mitchell, and Smith, 1994; Peterson and Bailey, 1991). There is no good research that supports the oft-heard claim that there would be fewer murders if more killers were executed rather than sent to prison. Murders are often unplanned, spur-of-the-moment attacks, and alcohol is usually a factor in them. But even among hardened criminals who may think about risks in planning their crimes (Horney and

Marshall, 1992), fear of punishment does not seem to be a major factor in their decisions (Cromwell, 1999; Shover, 1999; Wright and Decker, 1994; 1997).

On balance, the threat of formal punishments is much less worrisome to potential offenders than the threat of informal punishments imposed by relatives, friends, coworkers, or other close acquaintances (Cullen, 1994; Tittle, 1980; Paternoster, Saltzman, Waldo, and Chiricos, 1983 and 1985; Braithwaite, 1989). The average law-abiding citizen is probably more concerned about losing a good job, being ostracized by friends and coworkers, and alienating family members (Shoham, 1970). Pogarsky (2002: 432) reminds us that some people are acute conformists, so that moral inhibition or worries over social isolation "may so effectively inhibit conduct that considerations of cost and benefit are not even brought into play."

One criminologist has argued that punishment may backfire under certain circumstances, and this may explain the lack of a deterrent relationship between crime rates and punishment (Sherman, 1993). Sherman suggests that if punishment is seen as unfair or excessive, an attitude of "defiance" emerges. This defiance undermines any deterrent effect the threat of punishment might have had. It can also undermine any lingering respect for the law—a consideration in the sentencing of youthful and first-time offenders. Such a reaction has also been noted by Gilligan (1996) in his research on incarcerated murderers, and to some extent by Tittle (1995).

To summarize, deterrence clearly does not score high marks as the basis for a sentencing policy and crime control. Yet the lack of strong evidence does not mean that deterrence theory is disproved. The prospect of swift, certain, and relatively severe punishment may deter some individuals from committing crimes under some circumstances. The difficulty is figuring out who those individuals are and which circumstances count. Still, rather than reject the deterrence doctrine, more research on these complex issues would seem the more prudent course. It would also seem appropriate for politicians, judges, and other court officials to refrain from claiming that harsher punishments will deter crime. The bulk of deterrence research simply does not support this claim.

Beccaria and Bentham's ideas have greatly influenced criminal justice policy both in the United States and abroad. Some of their views on the causes of crime and the criminal justice system have in a sense "stood the test of time," as deterrence and rational choice models of decision making are popular with the general public and many people working within the criminal justice system. But while seemingly related policies like "three strikes and you're out" and long mandatory minimums for minor offenses are often said to be guided by Classical theory, they in actuality may be inconsistent with the original theory, especially if the punishment is too harsh for the crime. Ironically, the Classical School's emphasis on due process (such as fair trials and the right to appeal) is not as popularly supported in the United States.

THE ECONOMIC MODEL OF CRIME

Economists have advanced more contemporary formulations of the classical view (Cherry and List, 2002; Cornwell and Trumbull, 1994), and chief among them is Gary Becker's (1968) work on crime, which was cited when he received the Nobel Prize for Economics in 1993. Many complicated models have been developed (Baltagi, 2006), but they all share certain key ideas. First, the approach assumes that individuals *choose* to commit crimes. Second, it is assumed that people choose the same course of action when confronted by the same alternatives. This is rationality as economists use the term. The choice itself is guided by maximization of satisfactions, or "utility."

Individuals evaluate possible activities according to utility. The utility of a crime is the expected gain weighed against the probability of being caught and convicted and the monetary costs, real and foregone, if convicted. When the expected utility of a criminal act is greater than the utility of a noncriminal alternative, the economic model predicts that the crime will be selected.

The classical model of criminal behavior assumes that crime follows a calculation in which the perceived rewards, costs, and risks of alternative actions are compared. In itself this is a bold assumption because it not only implies that people are capable of making such calculations but also that they have the information necessary to do so.

Economists who develop models of criminal behavior often ignore noncriminal alternatives, concentrating instead on variations of estimated costs and benefits associated with crimes. The likelihood of a particular crime (robbery, for instance) is then calculated in terms of variations in the probabilities of arrest, conviction, and imprisonment and in the economic losses (offenders' gains) for robbery, compared with other predatory property crimes. If the gains from robbery are small compared to the risks and costs, but the gains from burglary are greater, then a person acting rationally and voluntarily would choose to commit burglary.

Some authors who believe in a more limited rationality temper the assumption that choice making is a fully rational exercise—a key assumption of the economic model and also implied in the writings of Beccaria and Bentham. It is argued, for example, that most people cannot know all the information necessary to evaluate all possible actions, but rather they reflexively react to opportunities that arise in ordinary situations (Pratt, 2008; Trasler, 1986: 20).

The limited rationality view holds that behavioral choices arise in people's lives routinely, and some involve decisions to commit crime. These choices are structured by several factors, including the social distribution of opportunities and access to them; the knowledge, past experiences, and capabilities of individuals; the conditions that characterize and are created by the social situations in which individuals find themselves; and the measures taken by victims and authorities to prevent them. Individuals within the boundaries created by these factors make behavioral decisions. The chosen actions are rational to the extent that they are purposive (conscious and goal-oriented) and reasonable (efficient, economical) in light of goals and alternatives. It is not necessary to assume that criminals carefully plan and execute their crimes or use the most sophisticated techniques (Ward, Stafford, and Gray, 2006). Rational choice theories need only assume that some minimal level of planning or foresight occurs (Clark and Felson, 2004; Hirschi, 1983; Wright, Caspi, and Moffitt, 2004). Of course, whether or not an offender fears arrest or prosecution is crucial to the decision-making process. Box 2.3 reviews some research on this subject.

Box 2.3.   The Possibility of Arrest

Many who violate the law may actually spend little time contemplating the risks of crime. Several studies have found strong evidence of the insignificance of arrest and punishment in criminal decision making (Shover and Honaker, 1992; Tunnell, 1992, 2000; Wright and Decker, 1994, 1997). Interviews with forty-six persistent property offenders found that the majority gave little or no thought to the possibility of arrest and confinement. Here are some typical comments:

> Q. Did you think about getting caught?
> A. No.
> Q. How did you manage to put that out of your mind?
> A. [I]t never did come into it. . . . It didn't bother me.

Another subject said:

> A. I wasn't worried about getting caught or anything, you know. I didn't have no negative thoughts about it whatever.

And another said:

> A. When I went out to steal, I didn't think about negative things. 'Cause if you think negative, negative things are going to happen. . . . You just, you just put [the thought of arrest] out of your mind, you know (Shover and Honaker, 1992: 5).

Another study found evidence of a similar line of reasoning:

> Q: As you did the burglaries, what came first—the crime or thinking about getting caught for the crime?
>
> A: The crime comes first because it's enough to worry about doing the actual crime itself without worrying about what's going to happen to you if you get caught (Tunnell, 1990: 37).

Retrospective interviews are not without drawbacks, not least among which is the validity of reconstructions of events long past (Shover and Thompson, 1992). It remains to be seen whether more proximal memories confirm the lack of a negative relationship between perceptions of risk and criminal activity among able offenders.

Studying *active* offenders (those not imprisoned) has several obvious advantages over studies of incarcerated persons. However, several recent studies of active burglars, robbers, and drug dealers have found that most crimes are not well planned out, but there is a tendency for incarcerated offenders to make it sound as though they are (Wright and Decker, 1994).

Criminal justice policy is often misplaced in its assumption that active criminals seriously weigh the costs and benefits of committing a crime in a way envisioned by the average American. Just like any behavior, illegal behavior surfaces within a social context. This has been called the *socially bounded decision-making process*. As Shover and Honaker (1999: 20) state:

> The lesson here for theories of criminal decision making is that while utilities and risk assessment may be properties of individuals, they are also shaped by the social and personal contexts in which decisions are made. Whether their pursuit of life as party is interpreted theoretically as the product of structural strain, choice, or even happenstance is of limited importance. . . . If nothing else, this means that some situations more than others make it possible to discount or ignore risk.

RATIONALITY AND CRIME: TWO EXAMPLES

Two examples of research on decisions by property offenders are Thomas Reppetto's (1974) study of residential burglary and robbery and Wright and Decker's (1994) study of burglars. Both studies show that offenders do have target preferences and that this was taken into account when they contemplated committing crimes. Burglars looked for unoccupied single-family homes (thus reducing the risk of being seen or heard), with easy access (thus reducing the amount of skill needed to gain entry), which appeared affluent (thus increasing the possible reward), and which were located in neighborhoods where offenders felt they "fit in" (another way to reduce the risk of being noticed) (Reppetto, 1974). At the very least, most burglars want to know *something* about the people who live in the house and the types of things the house contains (Mullins and Wright, 2003; Wright and Decker, 1994). This finding, as we shall see, is supported by research in the United States and abroad (Bernasco and Luykx, 2003).

The rationality model receives additional support from studies in England and Holland. Walsh's (1980) study of Exeter burglars found that although few burglars admitted doing much preplanning or "casing" of targets, most were very concerned about being seen and avoided entering houses likely to be occupied. A second study of English burglars is more detailed and lends further support to the rationality model while pointing to the importance of situational cues in decision making. Using videotapes of thirty-six houses seen from a passing van, Bennett and Wright (1981, 1984) asked fifty-eight convicted burglars to evaluate the houses as potential burglary targets. Most of the burglars were very experienced, so there is no indication whether the findings would apply to occasional thieves or beginners. Although there was considerable variation in target choice, the burglars strongly agreed about certain blocks of houses or about one or two specific homes. When the authors grouped evaluations according to risk, reward, or skill factors, the authors found that the burglars most frequently mentioned risk of being seen or heard as the decisive consideration. Reward factors became more important than those connected with skill only when given as reasons to disregard a target. A house may not be worth burglarizing regardless of how easy it is to enter. Interestingly, a more recent study found that decision making may be significantly different in the daytime versus the night (Coupe and Blake, 2006). The authors found that more affluent targets with less security were more likely to be targeted in the day while lesser valued but well-guarded areas were more attractive to burglars at night.

Some of the above studies did not investigate actual criminal behavior, only what offenders said about it. For that reason they give only inferential support for the rationality model. However, a study of actual robberies of convenience stores and the crime prevention effectiveness of various security measures found that only six of eighteen measures were significantly related to the frequency of being robbed, and only two of these in the expected direction: stores with space around them and those with only one employee on duty were robbed more often (Calder and Bauer, 1992). It is also true that criminals might not evaluate situational cues about ease of access and neighborhood surveillance all the time, especially when they are "desperate for money, feeling impulsive or bloody-minded, or simply too lazy" (Bennett and Wright, 1981: 16; Shover and Honaker, 1992; Wright, Caspi, and Moffitt, 2004).

It is important to remember that a full-fledged theory of criminal decision making needs to address not just the crime itself, but also the offender's initial involvement in crime. Such a theory must also account for decisions to continue and to terminate criminal activity (Cornish and Clarke, 1986a, 1987; Matsueda, Kreager, and Huizinga, 2006). Traditionally criminology has been more concerned with background influences such as social structure and prior experience and less with situational and transitory influences, which may influence certain types of criminal activity even more significantly.

CRIME DISPLACEMENT

Whenever criminally motivated persons decide not to commit a crime or avoid certain victims in favor of others, the substitution is commonly referred to as **crime displacement**. Five types of displacement have been identified:

- *Temporal displacement.* Here, an offender substitutes one time of day, week, or even season for another.
- *Spatial displacement.* An offender substitutes one street, neighborhood, area, or region for another.
- *Target displacement.* An offender substitutes an easier, less risky, or more rewarding target in the same location.
- *Tactical displacement.* An offender substitutes one modus operandi (method of operation) for another.
- *Type of crime displacement.* One type of crime is substituted for another, usually one that is less risky or more easily performed (Hakim and Rengert, 1981).

Displacement is important for two reasons. First, the rationality model predicts its occurrence. The idea is that criminals generally take advantage of or seek the best criminal opportunities—those with the greatest rewards at the least risk and cost. Second, displacement is important because it is one of the potential costs of crime prevention efforts. For example, when criminal opportunities are reduced by police surveillance or other "target-hardening" measures, the net result may be an increase in crime in another place. Criminally motivated individuals simply move to the "safer" areas to commit crime. Therefore, one community may benefit from crime prevention efforts while another may suffer because of them. It should be kept in mind, however, that oftentimes offenders take big risks for very small gains (Wright, 2000). This is partially explainable by the need to support a drug habit or a strong desire to continue "partying." It can also be understood as an irrational, sensual, or thrill-seeking activity not readily understandable to the outside viewer (Katz, 1988).

Research on crime displacement is sparse because it is extremely difficult to measure substitution behavior as it occurs. At the least, one would need to show that one criminal event occurred and some other did not because the offender changed his or her mind after evaluating the situation. Criminologists often infer displacement from studies of spatial or temporal changes in the volume of crime or by asking offenders if, when, and why they made substitutions. Most studies are further limited because they focus only on temporal or spatial displacement.

Spatial displacement is probably quite limited because "criminals prefer to operate in known territory" (Bernasco and Luykx, 2003; McIver, 1981: 32). This in itself is a sign of rationality, for familiarity reduces an offender's risk of being caught and may contribute to successful completion of the crime (Wright and Decker, 1994). Nevertheless, some studies show that police crime prevention efforts resulted in "spillover" effects: Crime rates increased in neighborhoods adjacent to areas with more concentrated police enforcement. However, displacement is more likely to occur with property crimes, not with crimes of violence. The latter may be relatively impervious to displacement pressures because they are more likely to be spur-of-the-moment and tend to occur at the criminals' homes, near local bars, and so forth.

English studies lend tentative support to the displacement argument, at least for some crimes. When steering locks were introduced in new British cars as a target-hardening measure, the rates of auto crime did not drop significantly. Apparently many thieves turned their attention to the abundant older cars that did not have steering locks. In addition, determined thieves could quickly learn how to overcome the devices. This suggests that displacement brought about by changes in skill factors is probably limited to amateur and opportunistic thieves. However, a similar program in West Germany had the effect of dropping the overall rate of car theft because *all* cars were equipped with the device (Felson, 1998; Mayhew, Clarke, and Hough, 1992).

A third British study surveyed the impact of installing closed-circuit television in some London subway stations (Mayhew et al., 1979). Generally, stations with the greatest volume of traffic experienced more robberies and other property crimes. After authorities installed television cameras in high-traffic stations, the volume of robberies declined there but increased dramatically in stations without TV surveillance. On the other hand, other thefts declined throughout the subway system during the three-year test period. This finding suggests that an offense-specific spatial displacement took place rather than any general displacement. Apparently robbers took the new surveillance into consideration, merely changing location. Other, perhaps less committed or less experienced thieves, were apparently more likely to view the TV cameras as evidence of a more concerted law-enforcement effort. Reacting to this perception, offenders reduced their activity, at least for a time.

Displacement is thus not an inevitable result of crime-prevention efforts such as target hardening (Clarke and Felson, 1993; Weisburd, Wyckoff, Ready, Eck, and Hinkle, 2006; Welsh and Farrington, 1999). Prostitution is another case in point. A study showed that increased police enforcement in a North London suburb did not cause prostitutes to move elsewhere (Matthews, 1986). Studies by Clarke and Mayhew (1988) of the effects of detoxification of the British gas supply on suicide rates showed marked decreases in suicides and no evidence that suicide-prone individuals were shifting to other means. Finally, the introduction of motorcycle helmets in various countries has apparently had the unintended consequence of reducing motorcycle thefts (presumably because thieves must carry a helmet with them), but there is no evidence that similar forms of crime, for example, auto theft, have increased as a result (Mayhew, Clarke, and Elliott, 1989).

It is unlikely that many offenders substitute new crimes for old when the calculus of risks, costs, and benefits changes. Income tax evaders, shoplifters, and employee thieves will not become burglars, con artists, and robbers. Some professional or habitual criminals may respond to such changes by increasing their skills and directing their energies only toward the most lucrative targets. They may become better criminals in the process, and they may also become more dangerous—willing to take greater risks, combining into more formidable groups, or increasing their willingness to use deadly force when confronted.

Those criminals most likely to shift from one crime to another, and least likely to continue a given line of crime in the face of increased risks and costs, are the less skilled but more experienced opportunistic offenders. They take advantage of easily accessible opportunities. They are unlikely to increase their efforts and risks in search of less hardened targets with which they may be unfamiliar or which may be too far from home. These are speculations, although a study of decision making among property offenders lends them credence (Tunnell, 1992: 149). Considerably more work must be done in both theory and research to untangle the complexities of displacement.

OPPORTUNITY AND ROUTINE ACTIVITY THEORY

Let us now consider how the nature and distribution of opportunities for crime influence criminal activity and shape the contours of crime for specific groups of people.

It will help to think of crime as an event. Crime is not an event until it has occurred, for an event is an occurrence or happening. A criminal event occurs when a situation fortuitously brings together factors that facilitate it. Advocates of a situational approach look at crimes that have occurred and ask what things came together to make them happen.

Crimes differ in so many ways that any attempt to identify basic elements that all criminal events share would probably be doomed from the start. The **situational crime prevention** approach, sometimes referred to as crime opportunity theory, is based on ten principles:

1. Opportunities play a role in causing all crime.
2. Crime opportunities are highly specific.
3. Crime opportunities are concentrated in time and space.
4. Crime opportunities depend on everyday movements of activity.
5. One crime produces opportunities for another.
6. Some products offer more tempting crime opportunities.
7. Social and technological changes produce new crime opportunities.
8. Crime can be prevented by reducing opportunities.
9. Reducing opportunities does not usually displace crime.
10. Focused opportunity can produce wider declines in crime (Clarke and Felson, 1993; Felson and Clarke, 1998: v–vi).

If there is a common element in all events, criminal or not, it is opportunity. An opportunity makes an event possible; a criminal opportunity makes a crime possible. One cannot rob a bank without the opportunity to do so—without the existence of banks. Notice, however, that banks provide not only criminal opportunities, but noncriminal ones as well. In fact, the purpose of most things is not crime, but their existence creates criminal opportunities. A functionalist would say that the above principle is a "latent dysfunction" of otherwise useful objects and institutions.

One version of opportunity theory is known as **routine activities theory**, which holds that there are three essential elements of a crime: (1) a motivated offender, (2) a suitable target, and (3) the absence of a capable guardian (Clarke and Felson, 1993; Felson, 1998). Therefore, the basic proposition of the theory is that "the probability that a violation will occur at any specific time and place . . . is . . . a function of the convergence of likely offenders and suitable targets in the absence of capable guardians" (Cohen and Felson, 1979: 590). If any one of these elements is lacking, a criminal event will not occur. A routine activity is any recurring and prevalent goal-seeking activity. Work is a routine activity, but so are sex, child rearing, eating, going to the movies, and vacationing. Much crime is also routine activity.

Notice above that no mention is made of "capable" offenders, those able to "pull crimes off" (though they may later be caught). In fact, much crime is unsuccessful, making the distinction between completed and uncompleted crime an important one for theory and research. Indeed, the law has long recognized the distinction, treating attempted crimes less severely than completed ones. From the situational point of view the distinction is interesting, because it prompts one to compare attempted and completed crimes in order to establish the differences and to establish which elements account for the outcomes.

Technological change makes new activities possible, and some will be labeled criminal if those in authority accept that they should be (see Michalowski and Pfuhl, 1991). The U.S. government is obviously concerned: It has changed many of its money bills now that advanced computers, software, and copying machines have made counterfeiting easier, and all bills now contain a metal strip embedded within the paper.

Consider what many people now take for granted: electronic fund transfer. Not long ago this computer-based service was known and used only by banks and large corporations. Now the automatic teller machine (ATM) is familiar to virtually everyone. Those with personal computers may also take advantage of home banking services. With the spread of electronic fund transfer has come growth in criminal abuse. Some types of crimes resulting from this newer technology include unauthorized use and fraud. Of course, the growth of personal computers has opened up many opportunities for crime as well. Such crimes include identity theft, fraud, embezzlement, and blackmail. It is also true that contacts between people have become easier via chat rooms, instant messaging, social networking sites, and email. Thousands of arrests, for example, are made each year of adults soliciting sex from minors and running or viewing child pornography websites.

Felson (2002) offers a more detailed description of the impact of social change on crime in his book *Crime and Everyday Life*. He shows why it is that the United States maintains high crime rates by focusing on crime as an event rather than on the number and motivations of criminals. He concludes that crime has changed, as there have been changes in where people live and work, where and when they interact, the type and storage of goods and services that are available, and the movement of goods and people. For example, as cities became more dispersed, with more and more people living in single-family homes and in the suburbs, and more and more property being spread over large and larger space, it also became more difficult for people to control their environment and prevent crime. Cities that had previously been "convergent," bringing people and property together, became "divergent," spreading them apart. Work organizations and schools also became bigger, drawing thousands, often from miles away. People can less readily monitor their own families under such circumstances, let alone the activities of strangers. Both informal and formal social control, it can be argued, is therefore hampered.

Another way of looking at routine activities is to think of the locations where crimes are likely to occur. Where would you expect handgun crimes to occur most often? Your answer will depend on the routine activities of typical offenders and victims and on the relationship between the two. Thus, handgun crimes involving relatives are most likely to occur in the home; those involving strangers are most likely to occur on the street. Urban structure has an impact on violent crime, and within that context the kinds of lifestyles (routines) people follow significantly affect their chances of being assaulted, robbed, or raped: people who go to bars, work, go to class, or go for a walk or drive at night are more likely to be victimized (Kennedy and Forde, 1990). Similar findings have been discovered in studies of elderly theft-homicide victimization (Nelsen and Huff-Corzine, 1998), homicide more generally (Caywood, 1998), sex worker victimization (Surratt, Inciardi, Kurtz, and Kiley, 2004), burglary victimization (Tseloni, Wittebrood, Farrell, and Pease, 2004), and gender differences in all forms of criminal victimization (Felson, 2002).

CHAPTER SUMMARY

Classical theorists created a theory of justice and a simplified theory of the causes of criminal behavior. The theory of justice was based on utilitarian philosophy that prized a democratic and rationally designed system of punishment and deterrence. The primitive theory of crime causation held that individuals are fundamentally hedonistic and that they will pursue a course of action if the outcome is perceived to offer more pleasure than pain. Many of Beccaria and Bentham's ideas remain quite popular today.

Modern-day rational choice theories of crime assume that criminals think about their crimes before doing them. Much research supports this basic contention, although the extent to which offenders are actually weighing all or even most pertinent factors involved in a crime is probably small. The central message of opportunity-rationality theories is, first, that crime cannot be understood apart from the nature and distribution of opportunities for both criminal and noncriminal behavior. Second, when criminals find themselves in situations in which they have opportunities to commit crime, the decision to do so or not to do so is a rational one.

The routine activity approach brings rationality and opportunities together to explain the distribution of crime in time and space. Advocates of the approach argue that the everyday activities of people influence the convergence of criminally motivated individuals and suitable, unguarded, criminal targets. In this vein, social and technological changes can dramatically affect the nature, extent, and distribution of crime and victimization.

KEY TERMS

Classical School
crime displacement
rational choice theory
routine activities theory
situational crime prevention
utilitarianism

DISCUSSION QUESTIONS

1. To what extent do you think people actually think through the costs and benefits of a behavior or action before doing it? In other words, is there always, or even mostly, a rational reason for why people make the decisions they do?
2. Do you agree with the basic idea of Bentham and Becarria that punishment is a necessary evil? In what situations do you see punishment being effective for certain types of crimes and not others?
3. What are some examples of public policy or policing activities that could cause a large degree of crime displacement?
4. Just how important do you think opportunity is compared to offender motivation and the absence of a capable guardian when crime occurs? In what situations can you think of in which crime results without these three variables present?

ACTIVITIES

1. Write down all the costs and benefits of your attendance at the next meeting of your criminology class. Does this list bear any resemblance to why you may or may not come to a class without writing up such a list?
2. Listen to the song "Been Caught Stealing" by Jane's Addiction. Analyze the lyrics and report on the extent to which they are consistent with the overall approach of Classical or rational choice theory.
3. Develop a list of all the "target hardening" or crime prevention strategies and tactics you use to protect yourself and your property from victimization. To what extent do they really limit the opportunity to become victimized in the face of a motivated offender and the lack of a capable guardian?

3

Biological, Psychological, and Evolutionary Theories

It is not uncommon for consumers of popular television shows to get the impression that crimes, especially those that are violent, are committed by individuals with psychological, neurological, or biological abnormalities. However, the disproportionate emphasis placed by the media on strange and morbid crimes such as serial murder does not reflect the reality that relatively few crimes are gruesome, let alone violent. Criminal homicide, for example, makes up less than 1 percent of all reported crime, and serial murder but a fraction of all homicides. Yet, as one watches the latest example of serial murder in the news, it is tempting to say that the killer was someone "going mental," or as rock legend Ozzy Osbourne sings in the song "Crazy Train," "crazy." While most criminologists look to environmental factors to explain crime, there is a tradition within the field that has focused on the biological and psychological causes and correlates of crime. This chapter reviews several of these classical and contemporary theories.

The birth of criminology as *science* is usually traced to nineteenth-century Europe. By the latter half of that century the scientific revolution was well under way. The armchair philosophizing of the Classical theorists was grudgingly giving way to the logic and methodology of science. Observation, measurement, and experimentation are the basic tools of the scientific method, and their use in the study of human behavior heralded the development of disciplines now taken for granted—biology, anthropology, psychology, sociology, political science, and statistics. Thus was born the age of **positivism**, and crime was placed under the microscope of science. Theories now had to be spelled out, quantified, and falsifiable.

In this chapter we examine classic and contemporary theories of crime that have been influenced by the positivism of natural science. While most criminologists are not formally trained in the hard sciences, important contributions to theories of crime have come from physical anthropologists, biologists, behavioral psychologists, and evolutionary theorists.

POSITIVISM AND EARLY CRIMINOLOGY

The notion that crime could be studied through the methods of science was established early in the nineteenth century by two authors whose work earned them an honored place in the annals of criminology. Working independently, Adolphe Quetelet (1796–1874) and Andre´-Michel Guerry (1802–1866) compiled the first criminal statistics and used them to make predictions and comparisons about crime. Others soon followed suit, and these early ventures into social statistics became a model for the later work of Emile Durkheim. "For the first time in history," Leon Radzinowicz (1966: 35) has observed, "crime became thought of as a social fact molded by the very environment of which it was an integral part." This was an important break with the Classical theorists, who viewed criminal behavior as stemming from the exercise of free will in the pursuit of pleasure.

A major impetus to the rise of positivism was Charles Darwin's work on animal evolution. Darwin's followers argued that human behavior is largely determined by Homo sapiens' position on the evolutionary scale and by the ongoing battle for survival. However, the specific impact of these forces on an individual was considered a matter for empirical investigation.

Positivism is not without its critics. The objections to positivism are varied, but primarily they consist of the argument that the so-called objective depiction of "concrete facts" in the world obscures a reality that is socially constructed by the participants in it. The facts are "constructed meanings produced within specific cultural, political, and economic contexts" (Michalowski, 1988: 18). Even the nature of crime itself cannot be taken for granted.

The debate about positivism versus social constructionism is unlikely to be resolved in the near future, and it is certainly possible for both to live side by side and for criminology to profit from their contributions to our knowledge and thinking about crime. Gibbs (1988: 4) makes an important point, however: How else are scientific theories about crime to be assessed, if not by testing their predictions against a body of empirical data? This was the great insight of the early positivists, although there was actually very little research going on during this period (Garland, 1985b: 128).

BIOLOGY AND THE SEARCH FOR THE CRIMINAL TYPE

Influenced by positivism, early criminologists were convinced that they could uncover the causes of criminal behavior if they could apply the methods of science to the study of human beings. Deviance, they believed, was caused rather than chosen (Pfohl, 1985). The major figure was Italian physician Cesare Lombroso. Like many of his contemporaries, Lombroso believed that criminals must be different from law-abiding people in some important way. The problem was to find out how they differed, and the search for the criminal type consumed much of his career.

As a physician attached to the army and later to prisons and asylums, Lombroso examined thousands of individuals. Profoundly influenced by the evolutionary doctrine, he searched for physiological evidence of the link between deviant behavior and biological forces. In 1870 he claimed a triumphant discovery: In his view, many of the criminals he had studied were **atavistic**—biological throwbacks to a more primitive evolutionary state. Such "born criminals" could be identified by five or more physical stigmata, or anomalies: an asymmetrical cranium, a receding chin, a low forehead, large ears, too many fingers, a sparse beard, protruding lips, low sensitivity to pain, and deformities of the eye.

But the born criminal was not the only type Lombroso identified, nor did he argue that criminal behavior was solely the result of biological forces. He distinguished other categories of criminals, including insane criminals (idiots, imbeciles, alcoholics, degenerates), criminaloids (those with less-pronounced physical stigmata and degeneracy, but pulled into crime by situation or environment), and criminals by passion (those who were neither atavistic nor degenerate, but drawn into crime by love, politics, offended honor, or other intense emotions).

Though the core of his theory was biological, Lombroso recognized the importance of precipitating situational and environmental factors. He mentioned poverty, emigration, high food prices, police corruption, and changes in the law as nonbiological determinants of criminal behavior (Wolfgang, 1961: 207). However, it remained for one of his followers, Enrico Ferri, to undertake serious investigation of the impact of environmental factors (see Sellin, 1937).

Lombroso and his followers had a tremendous impact on the emerging field of criminology. Especially important was the impetus their work gave to research on the individual criminal offender. For more than fifty years, scholars concentrated their efforts on describing and classifying criminals and on distinguishing them from noncriminals (for a critical analysis of this movement, see Garland, 1985b).

Many felt that such research would identify traits and characteristics peculiar to criminals. Anthropologist Earnest A. Hooton did one monumental study (1939). He studied 13,873 male criminals from ten different states, as well as 3,023 individuals regarded to be noncriminals. His study claimed to show that criminals are organically inferior to noncriminals, though Hooton did not admit that environmental factors could be precipitating influences. Most controversial was his claim that certain types of crimes are committed by certain physical types of individuals: Tall, thin men tend to commit murder and robbery; short, heavyset men are prone to commit assault and sexual crimes; and men of small frame commit theft and burglary. It sounds ridiculous now, especially as one recognizes that the main differences between most assaults and most murders is the presence of a corpse, and a major difference between one type of stealing and another is the presence of an appropriate opportunity.

William H. Sheldon conducted another major study of the relationship between body type and criminality in the early and mid-1940s. Sheldon (1949) studied a sample of 200 young men, many of whom had previous involvement in juvenile delinquency. Sheldon examined each subject in great detail, noting each person's body type, temperament, recorded or reported delinquency, basic family history, and mental and physical health. In his book *Varieties of Delinquent Youth*, three pictures are presented of each of the men from back, front, and side views along with capsule summaries of their life history. Sheldon categorized the young men's body forms into three basic types: endomorphic (soft and round), mesomorphic (muscular and athletic), and ectomorphic (slender and fragile). While many of his subjects' physiques were not entirely classifiable into one of the above categories, Sheldon concluded that, overall, **mesomorphs** have a higher likelihood of being involved in crime because of their higher level of physical power and aggressiveness. Although Sheldon's research, like Hooton's, is now dismissed by most criminologists because of its questionable methodology and logical contradictions, Sheldon and Eleanor Glueck (1955) found some support for Sheldon's findings in their comparison study of 500 delinquents and 500 nondelinquents. Despite the shortcomings of the biological approach represented in the above studies, there are still serious scholars who argue that biological characteristics such as body type predisposes individuals to commit crimes (see Wilson and Herrnstein, 1985).

The search for biological correlates of criminal behavior was largely discontinued in the United States during the 1950s and 1960s, partly because studies of human behavior in general were increasingly coming under the influence of the social and behavioral sciences, but also because the necessary research became too costly. There were also many people who simply believed that its focus on pathology was inaccurate (Pfohl, 1985). Although a few Scandinavian scholars (e.g., Christiansen, 1977a) organized their

Box 3.1. Physical Appearances and Criminality

Modern-day criminologists have little use for the idea that criminals share similar physical attributes. The exception to this is that it is well known that in many Western societies people of color are more likely to be portrayed as criminal by the media. Numerous scholars, such as Barlow, Barlow, and Chiricos (1995), Greer and Jewkes (2005), and Weitzer and Kubrin (2004) have shown that media images often imply that criminals "look a certain way." As professors with many years of experience in college classrooms, we have heard similar suggestions from students. For example, we have heard that someone "looked like a child molester or serial murderer." We have even been told by a student that her former professor at a different university went to the Federal Bureau of Investigation's (FBI) website containing pictures of "The Ten Most Wanted" so that students in his class could compare the suspects' physical similarities and differences. Modern-day criminologists have all but abandoned the search for physiological signs of criminality, but that doesn't seem to stop the media or popular belief that some people "look like criminals."

studies around biology, U.S. criminologists essentially lost interest in it until the 1980s.

The biological perspective in criminology is by no means a unified approach. Its advocates draw on research from a variety of behavioral sciences, including genetics, physiological psychology, psychopharmocology, and endocrinology. Among the theoretical perspectives found within the biological camp are (1) evolutionary theories, which examine changing environmental conditions, (2) genetic theories, which focus on inherited traits, defects, or deficiencies, and (3) biochemical theories that focus on hormonal or chemical imbalances.

One example of the third perspective is found in Ellis's (1991) review of research on monoamine (MAO) and its relationship to criminal behavior. MAO is an enzyme that is believed to effect the transmission of impulses from one nerve to another. MAO is heavily concentrated in the brain stem, and its activity is believed to be influenced by both genes and hormones. The importance of MAO for brain functioning is well documented, and low MAO activity is thought to be associated with aggressiveness, feelings or anger and frustration, and various correlates of antisocial behavior such as defiance, poor academic performance, childhood hyperactivity, extroversion, and sensation seeking (Ellis and Walsh, 1997). These associations are modest, but Ellis believes that low MAO may be an important biological marker for criminality.

EVOLUTIONARY THEORIES

Some biologists believe that people are instinctively aggressive, basing their claim on studies of animal behavior. According to Konrad Lorenz (1971), nature gave animals an instinct for aggression for three reasons: (1) to ensure that the strongest males succeed in mating with the most desirable females, thus ensuring a kind of genetic quality control; (2) to protect the physical space, or territory, necessary for raising the young, securing food, and the like; and (3) to maintain hierarchies of dominance and through them a stable, well-policed society.

Following Lorenz and Desmond Morris—the author of *The Naked Ape*—Pierre van den Berghe (1974: 777) believes that human behavior is not "radically discontinuous from that of other species," and he advocates a biosocial approach to understanding human violence. Essentially, the argument is that humans, like animals, have predispositions to violence that are innate—that is, biologically grounded. Though conclusive proof of this is still unavailable, one promising indication is that aggression is a universal behavior pattern for a species: In humans, aggression has been observed everywhere, despite widely differing habitats, cultures, and technologies. The viewpoint receives additional support from the documented relationship between aggression and the male hormone testosterone and the discovery of "aggression centers" in the brain (van den Berghe, 1974; Bailey, 1976; Wilson and Herrnstein, 1985).

Robert L. Burgess (1979; Burgess and Draper, 1989) has drawn on evolutionary theory to explain variations in child abuse and family violence. Burgess argues that mature humans have two related problems. The first is to pass on their genes through successive generations, and the second is to protect their offspring despite limited resources. The solution is for parents to invest most in those genetic offspring who show the best prospects for surviving and reproducing and least in nongenetic relatives and/or those genetic offspring who show the worst prospects of surviving and reproducing.

The problems and their solutions will produce greater risks of abuse and neglect in families with stepchildren, in poorer families, in those with less education, in families with many children, in single-parent families, and in families whose children have mental or physical impairments. Burgess and Ellis and Walsh (1997) cite studies both in the United States and abroad that support these predictions (see also Daly and Wilson, 1988b). However, it should be emphasized that child abuse is not inevitable in families with these characteristics, and it is found in many families without them (Ellis and Walsh, 1997).

Daly and Wilson (1988a: 520) make the following observation on step-relationships and violence:

In view of the costs of prolonged "parental" investment in nonrelatives, it may seem remarkable that step-relationships are ever peaceful, let alone genuinely affectionate. However, violent hostility is rarer than friendly relations even among nonrelatives; people thrive by the maintenance of networks of social reciprocity that will make them attractive exchange partners. . . . The fact remains, however, that step-relationships lack the deep commonality of interest of the natural parent-offspring relationships, and feelings of affection and commitment are correspondingly shallower. Differential rates of violence are one result.

On a broader plane, Daly and Wilson's evolutionary psychological perspective (1988a; see also 1998) explains the male propensity for violence as the result of the ubiquitous struggle over control and propagation. As Green (1993: 32) explains it:

Wife-murder and wife-abuse represent the striving for control over the reproductive capacities of women. Killings arising out of trivial altercations aim to deter rivals from threatening one's interests; they give tangible proof that any such attempt will be met with severe punishment. The predominance of males is due to the greater need of men for additional resources with which to check rivals and attract women.

Ellis and Walsh (1997) have summarized the key points made by **evolutionary theorists** of crime that lead to the following claims about sexual assault:

- Males should be far more likely to engage in sexual assault (logic: males have more to gain because they do not become pregnant and in general have less commitment to their offspring).
- Rape and sexual assault is found in both human and nonhuman species (logic: genes contributing to rape are suspected to be present in many animal types).
- Victims of rape resist sexual attacks because it does not allow them the choice to select a mate that will help with child rearing (logic: some research supports the idea that females are far more choosier about their mates than males).
- Victims of rape should be females in their child-bearing years (logic: while the goal of rape is not to exactly reproduce, it approximates such a drive).

Theory is about explanation, and as you can see, at issue here is *why* we see these patterns in sexual assault. Research does indeed support the age/rape, resistance, and gendered nature of sexual assault patterns noted in the points above, but the question is *how to explain* these facts. As we will see in future chapters, sociological theories have very different explanations.

We should also note that genetic, evolutionary, and neurological explanations of crime continue to play some role in the modern-day search for the causes of crime (Janssen, Nicholls, Kumar, Stefankis, et al., 2005). Most theorists working in these areas agree that crime is best explained by studying how the social environment and internal physiological systems interact with one another to produce behavior (Ellis and Walsh, 1997; Jeffery, 1994). For example, it is quite true that the brain develops in concert with environment. Any changes in the functioning of the brain, then, may be related to behavior, including criminal behavior. This means that the nutritional content of food, adverse chemical interactions caused by drug use, and brain trauma or disease may be involved in criminal decision making (Jeffery, 1994). Additionally, some recent genetic studies of twins and adoptees have found some evidence of a hereditary element of criminality, although the correlations are small and many of the studies have major methodological limitations (Gottfredson and Hirschi, 1990; although see Ellis and Walsh, 1997). In sum, however, even biological and evolutionary theorists of crime understand that it is a serious mistake to ignore the role of the social environment in providing the context, opportunity, and motivation for much crime.

BIOSOCIAL THEORIES

Advocates of the biological perspective in criminology have been swimming against the tide for many years. However, James Q. Wilson and Richard Herrnstein (1985) helped spark renewed interest in the relationship between biology and criminal behavior. The tide hasn't turned, by any means, but a healthy interest in biological correlates of crime has emerged (Linns, 2004; Fishbein, 1990). Studies of chronic delinquents have found that, when compared with less delinquent youths, the chronic offenders are more likely to suffer from minor birth defects, to have abnormal electrical activity in the brain, or to suffer from various other neurological defects (Buikhuisen, 1988). These correlates of chronic delinquency are believed to influence behavior through their impact on the socialization process. They impede a child's ability to learn and to develop attitudes consistent with self-control, deferred gratification, and restraint. The interaction between biology and social environment lies at the heart of the biosocial perspective.

Biology and Environment. Wilson and Herrnstein take a **biosocial approach.** They argue that certain constitutional factors, some of which are genetic, predispose people to commit crimes, but also that these predispositions are influenced by social forces as well as by the individual's own personality. In their view, neither biology nor environment alone is sufficient to explain why some people commit crimes and others do not, or why some people commit more crime than others. There is certainly no "crime gene," which means there is no "born criminal" (1985: 69; Ellis and Walsh, 1997). However, Wilson and Herrnstein (1985: 103) emphasize that biological factors cannot be overlooked:

> The existence of biological predispositions mean that circumstances that activate criminal behavior in one person will not do so in another, that social forces cannot deter criminal behavior in 100 percent of the population, and that the distribution of crime within and across societies may, to some extent, reflect underlying distributions of constitutional factors. . . . [C]rime cannot be understood without taking into account individual predispositions and their biological roots.

These theorists infer the existence of biological influences from two observations. First, Wilson and Herrnstein's reading of the research shows that street crimes such as murder, robbery, and burglary are committed by young males who are disproportionately African American and possibly of lower intelligence. The most striking difference is observed for sex: Males are up to fifty times more likely to commit crimes than are females. Second, there is a large body of research suggesting something biologically distinctive about the "average offender." The typical male offender, in their view, is more muscular than other people and is likely to have biological parents who are (or were) themselves criminal.

Wilson and Herrnstein review a vast amount of research to help substantiate their claims, but how exactly are biological forces thought to influence criminal behavior? The authors are more cautious on this point, as well they might be, since many of the findings they review can be explained by other theories. However, their answer seems to rest in the impact biological factors have on (1) the things people consider rewarding; (2) the ability (or desire) of people to think about rewards and punishments that might come in the future; and (3) the ability of people to develop internal, moral constraints—the "bite of conscience." Aggressive drives and needs are dominant in males; younger and less intelligent people are more inclined to be impulsive, to want rewards now rather than later; and the cognitive skills involved in the development of conscience grow with age and are positively related to intelligence. People who are aggressive, impulsive, opportunistic, and less constrained by conscience are at greatest risk of committing crimes.

Intelligence and Crime. One of the most enduring arguments found in scientific and popular literature is that antisocial behavior is more likely among people with low intelligence. There is little disagreement that intellectual defects are heritable (Fishbein, 1990), and much of the research on intelligence and crime has concluded that boys with lower aptitude are more likely to become involved in delinquency and crime (Hirschi and Hindelang, 1977).

When a certain group of people is found to have disproportionate involvement in crime, the natural inclination is to look for things the people have in common and then attribute the criminal behavior to these things. This is the sort of reasoning that has linked intelligence to the disproportionately high rates of violent crime among African Americans compared with whites (Hindelang, 1978; Hindelang, Hirschi, and Weiss, 1979). To some, if African Americans consistently score lower on intelligence tests than whites, it is a short—but incorrect—step to conclude that African Americans are less intelligent because they are black (Fraser, 1995; Jensen, 1969). The rates of serious crime among African Americans are then explained as a result of biological differences in intelligence or aptitude.

The words "race," "intelligence," and "crime," are controversial in terms of meaning and measurement. Sociologists, for example, do not give any credence to the idea that race has any biological meaning. Rather, race is considered a pure social construction. Environmental differences such as neighborhood, upbringing, economic conditions, schools, nutrition, and discrimination could well account for most if not all of the difference in measured intelligence between African Americans and whites. Further, it is well known that the very methodology of intelligence tests is discriminatory, much like the ACT and SAT tests, and it really measures exposure to the racially dominant culture's (i.e., white culture) language, tastes, hobbies, and artistic interests (Fraser, 1995).

Perhaps the most controversial statements on the relationship between intelligence and crime are rooted in Richard Herrnstein and Charles Murray's (1994) book *The Bell Curve*. The authors argue that an "extensive research literature" shows that low IQ is a risk factor for criminal behavior. Claiming that differences in behavior result from differences in the characteristics of individuals (the classic psychological perspective), as well as differences in their circumstances (the sociological perspective), Herrnstein and Murray write that low intelligence may encourage crime in a variety of ways.

First, they argue, low IQ may be associated with failure at school and work, which in turn causes frustration and perhaps resentment toward society and its laws. Second, it is claimed that a person with low IQ is more inclined to look for immediate gratification and tends to discount far-off risks such as arrest and incarceration. Third, the contention is made that a person with low IQ finds it harder to comprehend the moral and civil reasons for not hurting others and obeying rules.

While acknowledging that most people with low IQ are law-abiding, Herrnstein and Murray maintain that the average intelligence of offenders is around ten points below that of nonoffenders, and that offenders with lower IQs commit crimes more often as well as more serious crimes. Citing research from abroad as well as self-report data from the United States, the authors conclude that individuals with the cognitive disadvantage implied by low IQ have higher rates of crime even when socioeconomic factors, family structure, and education are taken into account.

On the other hand, Herrnstein and Murray recognize that the changes in aggregate crime rates experienced in the past several decades cannot be explained by variations in intelligence. Large or sudden movements in crime rates are due to social forces rather than personal characteristics, yet these same forces nevertheless "may have put people of low cognitive ability at greater risk than before" (Herrnstein and Murray, 1994: 251). For example, while the downward shift in the age population due to the baby boomers coupled with more permissive child-rearing practices may have enhanced the risks of criminal involvement among all adolescents and largely accounts for the increased crime rate of the 1960s, Herrnstein and Murray would argue that the criminogenic impact of these forces was greatest among individuals with lower IQs.

Despite the convictions of the authors, the intelligence-criminality puzzle remains to be solved (Guay, Ouimet, and Proulx, 2005). For one thing, if cognitive disadvantage explains criminal behavior, how do we then explain the many varieties of white-collar crime, which are often committed by individuals with college degrees and require higher degrees of forethought, skill, and political capital? Nor is it clear how constitutional and environmental factors come together to influence criminal behavior.

PERSONALITY AND AGGRESSIVE TEMPERAMENT

To say that people have an innate predisposition toward violence does not mean they will be violent, nor does it explain different levels and types of violence. Furthermore, as Green (1993: 32) points out, "Most men proclaim their 'fitness' for progenitorship in non-violent ways." The actual display of aggression is affected by triggers and inhibitors, controls that may be innate but also may be learned or situational.

Some psychiatrists believe that humans develop internal inhibitors during early childhood. According to Sigmund Freud, the individual psyche is composed of three parts: the ego, the id, and the superego. Behavior is motivated by those drives that are innate: the sex drive, the aggression drive, and even the death drive. These make up the id. As one develops and interacts with others, the superego emerges. This part of the psyche consists of social ideals and rules that are internalized through socialization. Finally, the ego strikes a balance between the demands of the id and the constraints of the superego.

The aggressive drive is expressed as violence, Freudians believe, when disturbances occur within the psyche. Mulvihill and Tumin (1969: 460–61) put it this way:

> The id may overflow with violent drives: the individual hates too much, enjoys pain too much, or wants to destroy himself. Sometimes the id is just too much for the ego to control, and the individual breaks out into violent behavior. . . . Alternatively, the superego may be extremely overformed or underformed. If the superego tries to quash all expression of dislike or hatred, and to quell all fantasies about violence, the individual may build up a greater and greater reserve of unfulfilled desire, until he can no longer control himself. Then he becomes violent. If the superego is underdeveloped, the individual simply sees nothing wrong with violence; he will use it whenever the occasion seems to call for it. In the underdeveloped superego, we are not dealing with a "sick" man at variance with his environment; we are rather dealing with a sick environment which has encouraged violence as the "normal" mode of response.

Some psychiatrists locate the seeds of emotional disturbance in parent-child relationships. It is suggested, for example, that the "love bonds" between parent and child are important to regulating the aggressive drive and that destructive behavior is prevented by the formation of stable human relationships in early childhood (Chodorkoff and Baxter, 1969). By the same token, excessive physical disciplining undermines these bonds and, further, teaches youngsters that there is a place for violence in relationships. Although psychiatrists may have much to tell about aggression and violence among those who are "disturbed" or "sick," their work is not helpful in understanding types of violence for entire populations and societies. Indeed, some people question the applicability of the psychiatric approach to even extreme forms of aggression. They point out that violent offenders do not suffer from mental disorders as a rule. Summarizing the findings of investigations into mental disorders among murderers, psychiatrist Donald Lunde (1970: 93) argues:

> I cannot emphasize too strongly the well-established fact that mental patients, in general, are no more murderous than the population at large. While it should not be surprising to find that psychotic killers have been previously hospitalized for treatment of psychosis, the incidence of psychosis among murderers is no greater than the incidence of psychosis in the total population. Furthermore, the percentage of murderers among former mental patients is actually slightly lower than that among persons who have never been in a mental hospital. Crimes committed by the mentally ill tend to receive disproportionate publicity, which reinforces a widespread myth about mental illness and violence.

FRUSTRATION-AGGRESSION THEORIES

The **frustration-aggression hypothesis** was first advanced in the 1930s by psychologists at Yale University. Originally, the hypothesis asserted that "the occurrence of aggressive behavior always presupposes the existence of frustration, and . . . the existence of frustration always leads to some form of aggression" (Dollard et al., 1939: 1). Frustration arises whenever something interferes with an individual's attempt to reach a valued goal.

It was soon recognized that this early statement of the frustration-aggression relationship required modification to accommodate the complexities of real life. Even though the impulse for aggression may be strong following some frustrating experience, the actual display of aggression may be inhibited by internal or external controls. Further, frustrations may be cumulative, one experience adding to another, and they may remain potent over a long period of time. It is now known that people evaluate frustrating experiences differently, according to whether they are arbitrary or unreasonable, for example. Finally, socialization teaches people how to respond to frustrations, and since the content of what is learned varies considerably from group to group and from society to society, the reactions to frustration can be expected to vary. In short, aggressive actions are not an automatic consequence of frustration, nor is the relationship between the two a simple one. As we will discuss in chapter four, Robert Agnew has

---

Box 3.2. Falling Down

The film *Falling Down*, starring Michael Douglas, revolves around the main character's "mind snap" and subsequent aggressive criminal behavior. Douglas plays the role of Bill, an average man who starts to lose control of himself while sitting in a traffic jam on a hot day without air conditioning. Adding to his frustration, Bill has just lost his job and is late for his daughter's birthday party. After feeling overcharged by a grocer for a soft drink, Bill stumbles upon a stash of high-powered weapons and begins an aggressive attack on various parties to exact his twisted sense of justice.

Frustration-aggression theorists would examine the precipitating circumstances of such behavior and compare Bill's response to those who are similarly situated to look for differences. Although this theoretical perspective can be helpful in understanding sudden violent behavior, sociological theories reviewed in chapter 4 can also shed light on them. For example, an interesting study by Hipp, Bauer, Curran, and Bollen (2004) tests the temperature/frustration hypothesis (an idea first offered by Quetelet [1969] almost two centuries ago) against routine activities theory. The authors conclude that the latter theory better explains property crime but that both explanations offer some support for explaining violent crime.

recently developed a more sophisticated way to explain the consequences of frustration and crime.

CHAPTER SUMMARY

The scientific foundations of criminology are traced to nineteenth-century Europe and the rise of positivism. The development of new techniques of data collection and analysis and Charles Darwin's work on evolution spurred the application of science to problems of human behavior, including criminality. The work of Lombroso, Hooton, and Sheldon represent a kind of criminology inspired by the search for the biological and physiological causes of crime.

Among the theoretical perspectives found within modern biological approaches to crime are (1) evolutionary theories, which examine changing environmental conditions, (2) genetic theories, which focus on inherited traits, defects, or deficiencies, and (3) biochemical theories that examine hormonal or chemical imbalances. Each of these perspectives has very modest empirical support and for a variety of reasons cannot be considered part of the core set of popular criminological theories today.

Biosocial theories maintain that there are important interactional effects between constitutional variables and the social environment that can lead to criminal behavior. The relationship between intelligence and crime has been a part of this theoretical tradition, but there is no clear evidence that IQ plays a substantial role in explaining either individual or structural variations in criminal involvement or crime rates in general.

KEY TERMS

atavistic
biosocial approach
evolutionary theorists
frustration-aggression hypothesis
mesomorphs
positivism

DISCUSSION QUESTIONS

1. Have you ever heard someone say that a person "looked like a criminal"? On what basis would a person make that claim? Can there be

any basis whatsoever for connecting physical appearance with crime or criminality?

2. Evolutionary theories of crime are controversial because they imply that some crimes are natural outcomes of the fact that human beings are also animals. To what extent can evolutionary theory be helpful in understanding different forms of crime, such as political corruption versus violent crime?

3. Biosocial criminologists look to both constitutional and social factors in explaining crime and criminality. To what extent is this related to the age-old "nature-nurture" debate, and where do you stand on the issue?

4. What types of crime are more easily understood as a result of frustration than others? Does aggression always, or even most of the time, follow frustration? Why or why not?

ACTIVITIES

1. Go to the FBI's "Ten Most Wanted List" and study the photos. Is there any way one could make a connection between physical appearance and criminality that is not racist, ethnocentric, or otherwise stereotypical?

2. Watch the film *Falling Down* and interpret the scenes and the main character's actions through the lens of the frustration-aggression hypothesis. Why would some people follow frustration with aggression, while others would not?

3. Take any number of online IQ tests with your classmates or friends and have each self-report on their involvement in crime. Can you see any connections between the two?

4

Social Structural Theories

In the song "Breaking the Law" Rob Halford, the lead singer of the classic metal band Judas Priest, sings about familiar human and social problems: unemployment, instability, anger, disappointment, and boredom. The connection between a person's feelings, behavior, and social institutions has been a topic of intense scrutiny in academic quarters. In sociology, theories emphasize the social aspects of human behavior, including the organization, structure, and culture of group life as well as the interactions that occur among individuals and groups. As we discussed in chapter 1, theories of crime that focus on social structure are generally macrosociological. They emphasize social conditions and patterns that transcend the immediate social situation. Theories of crime that focus on social interaction explain crime in terms of social process and are generally microsociological. They emphasize how the immediate social situation shapes the behavior of participants and is, in turn, shaped by it. This chapter focuses on social structure, the next on social process, but it should be emphasized at the outset that some theories of crime defy easy classification because they bridge the conventional distinction between structure and process. This is true of the theories we review in this chapter, especially social disorganization and Chicago School theories, and it is true of conflict theory (discussed in chapter 6). In the end, all criminological theories are saying something about the behavior of individuals, for it is the individual who makes and enforces rules or who behaves in ways that violate them. The theories are grouped in different categories to emphasize their similarities and differences and to show how they build upon each other and how they compete. Let us begin our study of structural theories with a look at the work of the eminent classical sociologist Emile Durkheim.

DURKHEIM ON CRIME, LAW, AND ORDER

Emile Durkheim is regarded by many as a founder of the sociological study of crime and law. The breadth of Durkheim's work is impressive, and it is easy to see from even a cursory examination of his scholarship that criminologists owe him a heavy intellectual debt. Indeed, two major social structural theories of crime, social disorganization theory and Merton's anomie theory, have strong and direct ties to Durkheim's work.

Durkheim was a functionalist, and so it should not be surprising to find that he was concerned with how societies attempt to regulate behavior for the purposes of stability, control, and solidarity. Law, Durkheim believed, should ideally represent the collective will of the people. What should be considered criminal, then, are behaviors that compromise and jeopardize the social order. Durkheim (1893) used the term **collective conscience** to describe widely held social values and beliefs. He reasoned that something should be made or considered criminal if it offends the collective conscience, the basic normative standards of the society. Punishment, he argued, was necessary to reaffirm the collective conscience so that all members of society would understand the wrongfulness and immorality of criminal behavior. This, he explained, increases social solidarity.

Durkheim also pointed out that crime is not abnormal because it is found in every society. Further, he argued that crime and deviance are universal because every society must have norms and every society will have someone break those norms at one time or another:

> There is no society that is not confronted with the problem of criminality. Its form changes; the acts thus characterized are not the same everywhere; but everywhere and always, there have been men who have behaved in such a way as to draw upon themselves penal repression . . . No doubt it is possible that crime will have abnormal forms, as, for example, when its rate is unusually high . . . What is normal, simply, is the existence of criminality, provided that it attains and does not exceed, for each social type, a certain level, which it is perhaps not impossible to fix in conformity with the preceding rules (Durkheim, 1938: 64–66).

Crime and deviance are also functional or socially beneficial because they provide avenues for social change. Here Durkheim meant that norm or law violation can cause people to become aware of required changes in society. Using the example of Socrates, Durkheim noted that challenges to established rules may enlighten others so that laws and norms may adapt to ever-changing social conditions:

> Nothing is good indefinitely and to an unlimited extent . . . To make progress, individual originality must be able to express itself. In order that the originality of the idealist whose dreams transcend his century may find expression, it is nec-

essary that the originality of the criminal, who is below the level of his time, shall also be possible. One does not occur without the other (Durkheim, 1938: 71).

The defiant actions of people such as Martin Luther King Jr., Rosa Parks, and even Dr. Jack Kevorkian illustrate that lawbreaking or deviance can produce social change. Of course, how positive or negative the social change is determined to be can be more a matter of opinion than fact. Box 4.1 further illustrates this point in the realm of popular music.

Box 4.1. Departing from the Norm Can Be Good

Durkheim theorized that deviance can be beneficial to society. Let's apply this reasoning to changes over the years in popular music.

Every so often watershed moments in music are sparked by the unique charisma, style, and spirit of musical visionaries. Most popular musicians are able to trace back their influences to rebels who offered up something unusual and distinct. We have talked about such influences with many musicians and read about many more. Some of the names that pop up include the influence of Louis Armstrong and Count Basie on jazz; Robert Johnson and B. B. King on the blues; Elvis Presley on blues-rock; the Beatles and the Rolling Stones on rock; The Who, Jimmy Hendrix, and Motorhead on hard rock; Patti LaBelle and Aretha Franklin on soul music and rhythm and blues; Public Enemy, Eazy-E, and Run-DMC on rap; Michael Jackson and Madonna on pop; Ozzy Osbourne on all metal genres; the New York Dolls and Motley Crue on glam metal; Nirvana and Pearl Jam on grunge; Black Sabbath and Metallica on heavy metal; the Dead Kennedys and the Sex Pistols on punk; and Green Day and Blink 182 on pop punk. What do all these folks have in common? First, they achieved some degree of success in the marketplace by offering something new and distinct. Such breakthroughs can forever change music. Second, these people challenged traditional rules and norms relating to music, whether by their style, substance, or presentation. Third, to a greater or lesser extent they helped pave the way for new artists and acted as symbolic reminders of the spirit of innovation.

Durkheim's ideas can also be applied to a variety of other popular culture subjects, such as film, television, and music videos. Regarding videos, in the early days of MTV, videos were simple and low budget, often depicting little more than images of the artists performing their songs. Over time, as the popularity of cable television and visual media in general grew, landmark videos like Dire Straits' "Money for Nothing" and Michael Jackson's "Billie Jean" set new standards for the visual presentation of music. Now, of course, some music videos are the equivalent of short films, containing complicated plots, hired actors or actresses, cameos from celebrities, and lots of capital invested in their production. Times change indeed, and often, according to a Durkheimian perspective, it is triggered by those who go beyond the norm and push the envelope.

While Durkheim made numerous contributions to criminology, perhaps the most lasting was the introduction of the concept of **anomie**. In both *The Division of Labor in Society* (1893) and *Suicide* (1897), anomie was explained as a social condition in which "normlessness" prevails. More specifically, anomie exists when systems of regulation and restraint in a society have diminished so much that individuals suffer a loss of external guidance and control in their goal-seeking endeavors. The structure regulating social relationships is disrupted, and social cohesion and solidarity are undermined. Durkheim argued that anomie is more likely during periods of rapid social change, when traditional norms prove ineffective in regulating human conduct. This structural, macrosociological approach helped explain why some areas have a higher suicide rate than others. This is important because suicide is often considered a very individual act and is perhaps more appropriately explained by psychological theories. However, Durkheim showed that suicide, as a social fact, is a phenomenon explainable by the careful study of large-scale social currents and forces. Sociologist Robert Merton was heavily influenced by the concept of anomie and used it to build a theory of crime, which we shall review in a few moments. First, let's consider what is known as the first distinct sociological theory of crime in the United States, social disorganization theory.

CRIME AND SOCIAL DISORGANIZATION

Crime and delinquency in cities have been given considerable attention in the academic community, and interest in urban problems is not low in the general public, either. One common understanding of the relationship between the city and social problems is that decaying urban environments generate high rates of crime and delinquency. Beginning in the early 1900s, sociologists at the University of Chicago published a series of studies of life in Chicago. Under the guidance of Robert Park and E. W. Burgess, these studies were designed to document the belief that problems such as crime and delinquency resulted from **social disorganization**. Simply put, social disorganization is the inability of a community to regulate itself (Bursik and Grasmick, 1995). Social organization is maintained by a group's commitment to social rules; when this commitment breaks down, social control breaks down. Members of the Chicago School and many contemporary criminologists believe that this breakdown in social control could occur through ecological changes, such as when communities experience rapid population change through social mobility and migration.

By examining voluminous data on the city of Chicago, Clifford Shaw and Henry McKay (1942) were able to confirm that certain areas of Chicago experienced relatively high rates of crime and delinquency and that these areas also showed the telltale signs of social disorganization. An area known as the *zone of transition* was found to have the highest crime rate. This zone is close to the central business district and, consequently, areas of population transition. Such areas of high crime were also characterized by overcrowding, physical deterioration, concentrations of minority and foreign-born residents, concentrated poverty, lack of home ownership, lack of locally supported community organizations, and concentrations of unskilled and unemployed workers. Further analysis showed that these areas also had other problems: high rates of infant mortality, tuberculosis, mental disorder, and juvenile delinquency (Shaw and McKay, 1942; Morris, 1958). Shaw and McKay found that as the distance from the zone of transition increased, crime rates decreased.

Shaw (1931b: 387) summarized the links between ecological change, social disorganization, and the development of "delinquency areas" as follows:

> In the process of city growth, the neighborhood organizations, cultural institutions, and social standards in practically all areas adjacent to the central business district and the major industrial centers are subject to rapid change and disorganization. The gradual invasion of these areas by industry and commerce, the continuous movement of the older residents out of the area and the influx of newer groups, the confusion of many divergent cultural standards, the economic insecurity of the families, all combine to render difficult the development of a stable and efficient neighborhood for the education and control of the child and the suppression of lawlessness.

One of Shaw and McKay's most important observations was that the relative levels of delinquency and crime in local *communities tended to remain stable over many years*, despite changing ethnic and racial composition (Bursik, 1988: 524; Bursik and Grasmick, 1993: 1995). Thus, a city area with high rates of delinquency compared to other areas would tend to remain that way, as would an area with low rates relative to another. They showed this to be true of Chicago over a period spanning several decades. Shaw and McKay argued that delinquent values and traditions were being passed from one generation of residents to another; in other words, a form of cultural transmission was taking place. In Shaw and McKay's view, the only way to combat the tendency for areas to become permanently crime-prone was to develop neighborhood organizations that could help promote informal social controls and encourage residents to look out for each other's welfare (Sampson, 1986, 1987; Stark, 1987).

Shaw and McKay and their colleagues at Chicago had a major influence on the development of sociological criminology. They not only showed how social organization and culture unite to influence social behavior but also they drew attention to the processes by which youthful residents adopt the criminal lifestyles of an area and thus reinforce them. Even though their theory is essentially a macro-level explanation of variations in group rates of crime, they clearly believed that interactions between parents and children, and between neighborhood youths themselves, helped mediate the influences of structure and culture (Bursik, 1988: 521). Indeed, Shaw spent many years helping youths find alternative solutions to their problems, and he persuaded former delinquents and crooks to help him reverse the spread of delinquent values and lifestyles. The resulting Chicago Area Project became a model for delinquency prevention efforts.

Social disorganization theory fell out of favor in the 1960s as few criminologists identified themselves with the perspective. Various reasons can be advanced for this decline in popularity. For some it was sufficient to point out that many youngsters do not become delinquent despite living in high-crime areas. Others wondered whether crime and delinquency are not a part of social disorganization rather than a result of it. Furthermore, how could one explain the emergence of highly organized, cohesive youth gangs in neighborhoods that are supposedly so disorganized? Finally, there was concern that the social disorganization model diverts attention away from the delinquency and crime of middle-class neighborhoods and from nonstreet crimes such as price-fixing and the sale of unsafe products.

If Shaw and McKay's ideas were unpopular a few decades ago, there has been a recent a resurrection of the theory (Pratt and Godsey, 2003; Martinez, Rosenfeld, and Mares, 2008; Warner, 2007) One example of this is found in Rodney Stark's "Theory of Deviant Places" (1987). Using human ecology theory and other classic Chicago School concepts, Stark's theory focuses on the following variables: density, poverty, mixed use, transience, and dilapidation. He argues that poor and densely populated neighborhoods are likely to be mixed-use, and people tend to move in and out of these neighborhoods regularly. This can result in less community surveillance, more opportunities to engage in crime, and people who are disenchanted, cynical, or apathetic about their neighborhood. Neighborhoods that are dilapidated are also often stigmatized, Stark maintains, for they signify disorder and seem attractive to those seeking deviant opportunities. Furthermore, Stark (1987: 901–2) proposes that:

- More successful and conventional people will resist moving into a stigmatized neighborhood; and
- Stigmatized neighborhoods will tend to be overpopulated by the most demoralized kinds of people and suffer from lenient law enforcement, which may increase the incidence of crime and deviance.

Many of the basic propositions of social disorganization theory have been supported by scholarly research. For example, one study found that "busy places" in neighborhoods in Seattle have higher rates of violent crime (Rountree, Land, and Miethe, 1994). A study of Chicago neighborhoods found that the higher the level of informal community social control, cohesion, and trust, the lower the rate of violence in that area (Sampson, Raudenbush, and Earls, 1997: 922). This study also found that as there is more willingness on the part of people to help others in a community, the lower the level of violence in that area. However, there is also evidence to show that even nonintimates, or those removed from a person's daily or weekly routines, can also exercise considerable control over people's involvement in crime (Bursik, 2000).

Another study using concepts from social disorganization theory has shown that there are significant community-level differences in the racial and ethnic distribution of crime and victimization, with the fundamental issue being the "embeddedness of black families in social environments with depleted resources" (McNulty and Bellair, 2003: 735). Similarly, another study of the distribution of black and white homicide rates in cities also supports this reasoning, but in a slightly different way. It may be that "the racial homicide differential is better explained by the greater resources that exist among whites than by the higher levels of disadvantage that exist among blacks" (Velez, Krivo, and Peterson, 2003). In other words, whites may have more opportunities to affect neighborhood and institutional change and therefore have increased regulatory power over their community.

Finally, we should consider how the dramatic increase in U.S. imprisonment rates over the last few decades could be negatively impacting neighborhood and community social organization. In this vein, a very interesting theoretical argument has been proposed by Rose and Clear (1998: 441):

> High incarceration rates may contribute to rates of criminal violence by the way they contribute to such social problems as inequality, family life deterioration, economic and political alienation, and social disorganization . . . (and) undermine social, political, and economic systems already weakened by the low levels of human and social capital produced under conditions such as high rates of poverty, unemployment, and crime. . . . The result is a reduction in social cohesion and a lessening of those communities' capacity for self-regulation.

In sum, this argument proposes that imprisonment takes away fathers, mothers, neighbors, and workers from the very social relationships that are needed to keep community crime rates low. For example, children are less

Box 4.2.   Do You Live in a Socially Disorganized Community?

Consider the follow questions. Do you know your neighbors? Do you say hi to them in passing? Do you ever hang out with them? Do they keep an eye on your children for you? When you are away, do they watch your house or apartment for suspicious activities? Do neighbors in your community occasionally congregate on the sidewalks or arrange for their children to play with one another? Do you know more than half of the people living in your immediate area? When problems arise, do you communicate and attempt to resolve them with your neighbors? If you answered yes to all or most of these questions, you probably don't live in a highly disorganized area. Theoretically, then, such an area would be expected to have a lower crime rate than one with less neighborhood interaction cohesion, or what Sampson, Raudenbush, and Earls (1997) call "collective efficacy."

Other more structural indicators of whether you live in a socially disorganized neighborhood are the ratio of rental properties to owner-occupied homes, how often people move in and out of your area (the transience rate), and the kinds of resources provided by the government, churches, community organizations, and recreational groups in the area. Keep in mind that a socially organized community is not necessarily one that has to be so "tight" as to smother its residents in surveillance and social control. This might be dangerous: Tittle's control balance theory, reviewed in chapter 7, maintains that people who feel overcontrolled have a tendency to seek out deviant ways of expressing themselves and their interests.

likely to be well supervised if one parent, or even an older brother or sister, is incarcerated; family members devastated by the imprisonment of one parent may move in and out of areas to be nearer to the prison; and the growth of collective-political action movements that need young, energetic members is inhibited due to overincarceration.

It has been observed by many scholars that the imprisonment boom has taken its largest toll on poor African American communities (Pettit and Western, 2004; Mauer and King, 2007). Partial support of Rose and Clear's model suggests that this way of thinking about incarceration and its effects on social disorganization are promising (Clear, Rose, Waring, and Scully, 2003).

MERTON'S ANOMIE THEORY

Emile Durkheim's notion of anomie was extended and elaborated on by Robert K. Merton (1938; 1957), who made it a central feature of a strain theory of crime. According to Merton, a state of anomie exerts pressure on people to commit crime. While all societies establish institutionalized means, or rules, for the attainment of culturally supported goals, these means and goals are not always in a state of harmony or integration. The way the society or group is organized interferes with the attainment of valued goals by acceptable means for some of its members. A condition of anomie or strain therefore exists.

Looking at the United States in the 1930s, Merton saw an inordinate emphasis on material success, which was held up as achievable by all Americans. Not all segments of society, however, could realistically expect to have material success if they followed the rules of the game. African Americans and the lower classes were routinely excluded from access to legitimate means of achievement. The acceptable routes to success—a good education, a good job, the "right" background, promotions, special skills—typically were not the routes open to them. Unfortunately, things are only marginally better today (see Farley, 2005; Feagin, 2006).

Strain is essentially the disjunction or lack of fit between socially desirable goals and the socially acceptable means to achieve those goals. Merton believes that various "modes of adaptation" are possible in response to the strain resulting from unrealized expectations: conformity, innovation, ritualism, retreatism, and rebellion. You may want to refer to figure 4.1 as we proceed to discuss each of these adaptations to strain.

Many people will *conform*, simply accepting that they will never "make it big"—unless they win the lottery! Perhaps the "bite of conscience" (Wilson and Herrnstein, 1985) holds them back from crime; perhaps they fear punishment; perhaps they have too much to lose, if not materially, then in terms of relationships with family and friends; perhaps they cannot recognize—or take advantage of—illegitimate opportunities. Merton prefers the idea that conformity reflects social acceptance of the rule of law.

Other people may engage in *ritualism*. They give up on the goals but continue to support the socially approved means. They cling "all the more closely to the safe routines and institutional norms" (Merton, 1957: 151). Imagine the platoon leader who gives up on the apparently impossible task of taking the enemy position but berates his soldiers for having dirty belt buckles, or the loyal corporate manager who gives up on being promoted himself but punishes his subordinates for not "playing the game."

Still others reject both means and goals. Such *retreatism* is an adaptation to anomic conditions in which people may even withdraw from society altogether. The inner-city heroine or crack addict is most often mentioned in this context. The drug-using, antiestablishment "hippies" of the 1960s and the short-lived commune movement also come to mind. On the other hand, some people substitute new sets of norms and goals, and

When confronted by a disjunction between legitimate means and socially approved gains—a condition of anomie, which produces strain—people may adapt in various ways. This table summaries Merton's modes of adaptation.

Adaptation	Socially Approved Goals	Legitimate Means
Conformity	accept (+)	accept (+)
Innovation	accept (+)	reject (−)
Ritualism	reject (−)	accept (+)
Retreatism	reject (−)	reject (−)
Revellion	reject and replace (±)	reject and replace (±)

Figure 4.1. Merton's Modes of Adaptation to Anomie

Merton calls this adaptation *rebellion*. Unfortunately, the logical separation between these two modes of adaptation is unclear. For example, are the antiestablishment hippies retreatists or rebels? Can rebellion occur without retreatism?

The adaptation that Merton identifies most closely with crime is *innovation*. Innovators accept the goals, but they reject the institutional means and substitute illegal alternatives. Merton uses innovation to explain the relatively high rates of property crime among lower class and minority segments of society. Their disadvantaged status coupled with the high cultural priority given to material success as a goal for all makes high rates of crime a "normal outcome" for those segments of society. Box 4.3 provides another way to understand the various modes of adaptation when applied to actors in higher education.

Box 4.3. Possible Modes of Adaptation to Strain by Students and College Professors

Merton's strain theory speaks not only to crime but deviance as well, which is essentially rule violation. Using the five adaptations to strain identified by Merton, let's consider how deviance might come about for both college students and college professors.

College Students

Let us suppose the overriding goal is to achieve very good to excellent grades in a class. What kinds of actions might be associated with the various adaptations to strain over this goal?

Conformity: Diligent, careful, meticulous reading of course materials; not skipping class and coming to every class meeting prepared; asking the professor questions when clarification is needed; visiting the professor during office hours; properly using academic sources for papers; actively participating in any group work or discussion.

Innovation: Cheating on exams; plagiarizing papers; having someone else take your exam or write your paper; relying on others' notes rather than taking them yourself.

Ritualism: Here the person just wants a passing grade, nothing more; this might be expressed by sporadic attendance and participation in the class; poor or uneven performance on exams and papers; cursory reading of course materials.

Retreatism: Dropping out of class, or perhaps college altogether.

Rebellion: Disengagement from the entire conventional higher education system; possibly embracing anti-intellectualism or intellectualism outside the confines of conventional education in the form of religious training, cults, or even home schooling.

College Professors

Now, let's think about college professors. Let us suppose the overriding goal is to be an effective teacher, productive scholar, and an active member of the community.

Conformity: Put in full work weeks; work on weekends; prepare and write own lectures; give all self-composed essay exams; carefully read all student papers; publish in peer-reviewed journals and with respectable presses; spend hours each week in committee meetings.

Innovation: Copy lectures from textbooks; plagiarize parts of papers; lie on their vitas (an academic resume); not read papers but give grades anyway; exaggerate the time and energy put into community work; steal student work (as in the film *D.O.A.*).

Ritualism: This professor plays by the rules for the most part, but does seek to get: promoted, well-published, elected to important university positions, excellent teaching evaluations, or academic awards.

Retreatism: A professor who is chronically late to class; communicates with students indifferently; uses dated films and lectures; seldom changes exams from semester to semester; is unavailable to students; never writes or publishes; and does little to no community service work.

Rebellion: This is the professor who subverts the dominant academic paradigm. This can be done by using unconventional teaching methods (extreme participatory pedagogies, not giving grades, allowing students control over the classroom experience) or overtly attempting to advance ideological, religious, or political agendas in class.

Although Merton never discussed these cases, it is interesting to note that his theory is sufficiently broad enough to be applied to specific roles and occupations. Such applications of Merton's theory are becoming more common among criminologists who study white-collar crime.

Merton's theory of anomic strain and crime had a profound influence on subsequent structural theories despite some serious criticisms. In many ways his "theory" is merely a catalog of potential reactions to anomie: It does not tell us when to expect one mode of adaptation rather than another, or whether different segments of the population are likely to select different adaptations. Katz (1988: 358, note 9) objects that Merton's theory is unconvincing as an explanation for "vandalism, the use of dope, intergroup fighting, and the character of initial experiences in property theft as sneaky thrills."

Another line of criticism is directed at the social disorganization theory of Shaw and McKay: Too much is made of the high rates of crime officially observed among the lower classes. Even if the data are credible, the preoccupation with criminal behavior among the lower classes diverts theory and research from the behavior of other classes and from the power relations that exist between classes. More recent extensions of Mertonian strain theory, however, have been used to explain forms of white-collar crime. Kauzlarich and Kramer (1998), for example, have specifically studied how state strain brings about innovation by state and corporate organizations. They argue that state agencies use illegal means in order to achieve their operational goals, which may be financial health, legitimacy, national security, or political hegemony. For example, illegal human radiation experiments conducted by the U.S. government from 1940 to 1980 can be understood as the use of illegitimate means (violating international law and human rights) for the larger goal of winning the Cold War. In this way, white-collar crime can be understood in Mertonian terms, but this must be done by substituting the organization for the individual as the unit of analysis.

Another limitation of Merton's theory is that there is no explanation of why the "success ethos" is so important in the United States. Indeed, Messner and Rosenfeld (2000) maintain in their **institutional anomie theory** that the larger U.S. *culture*, not simply its structure, prizes economic success over other forms of achievement. Good parenting and good grades in school are considered less valuable because they produce no capital—that is, no direct financial benefits. More broadly, according to the theory, institutions such as the family, school, and community become visualized in economic terms, and potential informal social control mechanisms within the culture become sterile. Crime is then not so much a product of those who are unable to achieve the American Dream but those who are *locked in* to those values (Rosenfeld and Messner, 2006.) Although institutional anomie theory has only been subjected to a few empirical tests, research has generally found some support for the theory's main contentions (Bjerregaard and Cochran, 2008; Maume and Lee, 2003).

GENERAL STRAIN THEORY

Like Messner and Rosenfeld, Robert Agnew (1992; 2001) has redirected Merton's strain theory in the hope of increasing the theory's explanatory power. Unlike institutional anomie theory, however, Agnew reframes strain theory on the social-psychological or micro level of analysis. In some ways this makes Agnew's theory more similar to social process theories reviewed in the next chapter, but since Agnew's theory is rooted in Merton's work, we shall discuss it here.

Agnew's **general strain theory** (GST) starts with the assumption that negative relationships with others causes strain or stress in people's lives. Negative relationships are those "in which others are not treating the individual as he or she would like to be treated" Agnew (1992: 50). According to Agnew, Mertonian strain theory relies too heavily on the relationships that prevent the individual from reaching positively valued goals. GST, however, considers this and two other sources of strain that may lead to crime and delinquency: (1) when other individuals remove or threaten to remove positively valued stimuli that one possesses, and (2) when others present or threaten to present a person with negatively valued stimuli (Agnew, 1992: 50; 2001). Some examples might help clarify these sources of strain.

The first type of strain, the failure to achieve positively valued goals, suggests that people have in some way not met their goals, expectations, or have received unfair or inequitable outcomes in social relationships. Examples include not meeting one's expectation to earn good grades in school, financial strength from working, and fair treatment by their parents, teachers, and peers. Strain also stems from situations in which others remove or threaten to remove things that a person positively values. Think for a moment about the kinds of stressful life events we all probably encounter: the loss of partners (boyfriends, girlfriends, husbands, wives) and friends. How about when a child loses a parent? All of these negative events can place considerable stress on individuals and may trigger involvement in crime. Finally, Agnew maintains strain is also likely to develop when others present or threaten to present an individual with negative outcomes. Examples of this type of strain include a child who is abused, neglected, or otherwise criminally victimized (Agnew, 1992). The child may deal with these negative relationships by attempting to escape the environment all together (i.e., running or staying away from home) or exacting revenge upon the victimizers, who are usually family members. Further, these different types of strain can overlap:

> For example, the insults of a teacher may be experienced as adverse because they (1) interfere with the adolescent's aspirations for academic success, (2) result in the violation of a distributive justice rule such as equity, and (3) are

conditioned negative stimuli and so are experiences as noxious in and of themselves (Agnew, 1992: 59).

Agnew (2001) has more recently theorized that those negative experiences that are perceived as highly unjust, undeserved, and threatening are most likely to trigger deviant activity.

Since most people probably experience these forms of strain at some point in their lives, who is more likely to commit crime or delinquent acts because of the strain? Agnew suggests that it is those who do not *cope well* with the situations. Coping abilities, or adaptations, which moderate the effects of strain are things like the ability to "blow off," neutralize, or downplay the seriousness and/or significance of a stressful life event. For example, lowering one's standards for the accumulation of wealth or grade point average help neutralize strain. Personality traits, temperament, and social learning and bonding variables ultimately, according to Agnew, help determine whether a person's adaptation to strain is criminal or not. The theory therefore complements leading criminological theories such as social control theory and social learning theory, which we shall discuss in chapter 5. GST can also be partially integrated with social disorganization theory, as Agnew (1999) has attempted to do in order to explain community-level differences in crime rates.

Empirical tests of GST have generally confirmed that the theory has reasonably strong predictive power (Mazerolle, 1998; Moon, Morash, McCluskey, and Hwang, 2009; Slocum, Simpson, and Smith, 2005; White and Agnew, 1992). Of the several studies, two are particularly interesting because they examine the theory's ability to predict gender differences in offending (Broidy and Agnew, 1997; Mazerolle, 1998). Both found that GST did not predict the differences in overall offending very well but that it did account for some differences in violent offending by gender. Specifically, one study found that losing a parent or family member and having negative relationships with adults are more likely to be criminogenic for males but not females (Mazerolle, 1997). This provides partial support to the notion that males tend to manifest anger and strain externally while women more often manage these emotions internally. Another study of only African American youths, however, found that after controlling for prior offending and other factors, both boys and girls had similar delinquent responses to the anger and depression brought on by experiences with racial discrimination (Simons, Chen, Stewart, and Brody, 2003).

CULTURAL TRANSMISSION OF CRIME AND DELINQUENCY

As noted previously, ecological studies of crime and Merton's theory of anomie emphasized the high rates of crime officially observed among the poor. From 1940 to 1960, sociologists seemed preoccupied with explanations of criminal activity among the lower classes. Most of the theories produced in the period emphasized social structure, especially the ways in which the behavior of adolescents and young adults is shaped by the lifestyles and values to which they are exposed.

A number of theories focus on what is called the *delinquent subculture*. Any heterogeneous society is likely to have a parent, or dominant, culture and a variety of different subcultures. The dominant culture consists of the beliefs, attitudes, symbols, ways of behaving, meanings, ideas, values, and norms shared by those who regularly make up the membership of a society. Subcultures differ from the dominant culture and consist of the beliefs, values, and lifestyles shared by those members of society who belong to identifiable subgroups. For example, Goth kids, vegans, residents of a retirement community, homosexuals who have "come out," the hippies of the 1960s, and Polish Americans who belong to clubs and organizations that emphasize their common heritage are identifiable subgroups whose members share a common subculture.

Some subcultures are merely different from the dominant culture, while others are in active opposition to it. Delinquent subcultures fit neither characterization exactly. According to Cloward and Ohlin (1960: 7), a delinquent subculture "is one in which certain forms of delinquent activity are essential for the performance of the dominant roles supported by the subculture. It is the central position accorded to specifically delinquent activity that distinguishes the delinquent subculture from other deviant subcultures [such as homosexual activists]." However, even in its support of delinquent activities, a delinquent subculture may nevertheless also share aspects of the dominant culture; for example, an emphasis on material possessions or an acceptance of gender differences in social roles.

In general, then, **subcultural theories** of crime and delinquency begin with the assumption that people are socialized into the norms and values of the immediate groups to which they belong. In a sense, all people are conformists, but the values and norms with which they conform may be different from, or at odds with, those of the dominant culture, and the behaviors that result are sometimes illegal. In other words, some kinds of conformity turn out to be delinquent or criminal. So it is with the activities central to delinquent subcultures.

Cohen's Theory. One of the first sociologists to propose a subcultural explanation of delinquency was Albert Cohen (1955). In his book *Delinquent Boys*, Cohen suggests that high rates of lower class delinquency reflect a basic conflict between lower-class youth subculture and the dominant middle-class culture. The delinquent subculture arises as a reaction to the dominant culture, which is seen as discriminating against lower-class people. Told in school and elsewhere to strive for middle-class goals and to behave according to middle-class values (be orderly, clean, responsible, ambitious, and so forth), lower-class youth find that their socialization has not prepared them for the challenge. They become "status frustrated" as a result of their inability to meet middle-class standards and in reaction turn to delinquent activities and form delinquency-centered groups. Cohen describes the delinquency that results as nonutilitarian (e.g., stealing "for the hell of it"), malicious (enjoying the discomfort of others), and negativistic (taking pride in doing things because they are wrong by middle class standards).

Cloward and Ohlin's Differential Opportunity Theory. Expanding on Merton and Cohen, sociologists Cloward and Ohlin (1960) developed a theory of delinquency and youth crime that incorporates the concept of opportunity structures. The authors point out that society provides both legitimate and illegitimate opportunities for behavior, and these opportunities (whether legitimate or not) meet different kinds of needs—some help a person achieve status (and with it, membership in the middle class); others help a person achieve economic success. Not all youths aspire to the same things, and Cloward and Ohlin believe that those youth who aspire to economic success but are denied legitimate opportunities to achieve it are at the greatest risk of becoming embroiled in gang subcultures.

Cloward and Ohlin's theory is more than a rehash of strain theory because the introduction of opportunity variables enables them to explain why a particular form or type of deviance arises in response to structural strain (see Cullen, 1983: 41–45). While anomie theory predicts that strain is a motivating force behind deviance and crime, it does not explain why one form of deviance (say, retreatism) occurs rather than another. Several delinquent adaptations are conceivably available in any given situation; what, then, are the determinants of the process of selection? Among delinquents who participate in subcultures, for example, why do some become apprentice criminals rather than street fighters or drug addicts? These are distinctive subcultural adaptations; an explanation of one may not constitute an explanation of the other.

Applying opportunity theory to the world of business (conventionally thought to be a far cry from delinquency), Braithwaite (1989a: 33) shows how a criminal subculture of price fixing might arise:

> Let us imagine, for example, that the government suddenly decides to double sales tax on beer in an effort to discourage consumption. The brewing companies might find as a consequence that legitimate opportunities are blocked for them to achieve their profit or growth targets. They might get together at trade association meetings to curse the government, to begin to suggest to each other that they have no choice but to conspire to fix prices, in other words to fashion a criminal subculture which rationalizes price fixing by blaming the government for it, appealing to the higher loyalty of saving the jobs of their workers, and which evolves new criminal conduct norms for the industry.

Cloward and Ohlin identify three delinquent subcultures to which lower class youths may belong and that help structure a youngster's response to the absence of legitimate opportunities. These subcultures are criminal, conflict, or retreatist.

Criminal subcultures are characterized by illegal money-making activities and often provide a stepping-stone toward adult criminal careers. They tend to arise in slum areas where relatively well-organized age hierarchies of criminal involvement exist. This condition provides youth with adult criminal role models and encourages their recruitment into money-making crime. Also, the existence of adult roles such as "fixer" and "fence," which bridge the worlds of legitimate enterprise and crime, helps facilitate illegal money-making activities as an alternate route to economic success.

Conflict subcultures are dominated by gang fighting and other violence. They arise in disorganized slum areas with weak social controls, an absence of institutionalized channels (legal or otherwise) to material goals, and a predominance of personal failure. Violence is a route to status as well as a release for pent-up frustrations.

Finally, *retreatist* subcultures are marked by the prevalence of drug use and addiction. This subculture arises as an adaptation for some lower-class youth who have failed in both the criminal and conflict subcultures or have not successfully accessed either the legitimate or illegitimate opportunity structures. Like Merton's retreatists, they disengage from the competitive struggle for success goals.

Miller's Lower Class "Focal Concerns." The works of Cohen and of Cloward and Ohlin focus mainly on youthful gangs, and to that extent they ignore a tremendous amount of delinquency and crime that is not gang-oriented. Their work also focuses on the organization and culture of the lower class, and to that extent it may not apply to lower-class behavior in other societies.

The same observations can be made of Walter Miller's (1958) well-known study of youth gangs, a study in which he delineates the special themes or issues prominent in lower-class youth culture. The material and social deprivations that are commonplace among the urban lower class contribute to the development of special themes, or "focal concerns," as Miller calls them. Focal concerns command a high degree of emotional commitment. Among the **focal concerns** identified by Miller are "trouble" (a concern to avoid entanglements with the law), "toughness" (an ability to handle physical and emotional challenges), "smartness" (being able to con, hustle, or outwit others), "autonomy" (remaining free from domination or control by others), and "excitement" (getting kicks, avoiding the routine and the monotonous).

Some of the activities shaped by these focal concerns are delinquent or criminal, for the law reflects and supports the dominant standards of middle-class society. But even when given a choice not to engage in delinquency or crime, youngsters will often find the "deviant" activity more attractive because the norms of groups with whom they identify, as well as peer group pressures, point to it as a means of acquiring prestige, status, and respect.

Finally, let's think about another subculture theory that bears similarities to Miller's perspective. In 1967 Marvin Wolfgang and Franco Ferracuti advanced the idea that a **subculture of violence** can develop in poor urban areas. Such a subculture defines the use of physical force, aggression, and violence as appropriate and legitimate responses to a variety of social situations. Unlike Elijah Anderson's (1999) notion of the "code of the streets," Wolfgang and Ferracuti (1967) believed that the subculture of violence was widespread in some communities and revealed itself in both private and public ways.

In sum, the social structural theories reviewed thus far in this chapter purport to explain the relationship between the organization or structure of society and the behavior of its people. One problem with these theories as a whole is the almost exclusive focus on lower-class delinquency. This obviously limits the scope of the theories, and none of them was initially advanced as a general theory. Unfortunately, one of the undesirable (and probably unintended) consequences of the lower-class emphasis has been the respectability it has given the stereotypical view of crime and criminals. This view associates being criminal with being a member of the lower class. Interestingly, the considerable media publicity given to crimes by members of the middle class and especially the upper class sensationalizes their crimes, and by doing so seems only to confirm the idea that "real" crime is committed by the poor, the unemployed, and the disreputable. The misbehaviors of "real" criminals are, by definition, unsensational. We expect crime from the "criminal classes." The objection to the criminological emphasis on lower-class crime is essentially that it lends the weight of "expert opinion" to this popular stereotype. If this (i.e., the lower class) is where criminologists look to find crime, then it must be where crime really is!

A common thread runs through social structural theories of crime, a thread that explains to a large extent why they have been almost exclusively theories of lower-class crime. These theories see crime as a consequence of inequality in the distribution of material resources. Lack of economic opportunities, the social disorganization of inner-city neighborhoods, the subculture of youth gangs, and unrealized expectations of affluence are hallmarks of inequality. They are the products of a social organization that puts some people at a disadvantage in the competition for scarce resources. Crime is therefore an unexceptional consequence of economic, social, and political disadvantage.

This common thread reflects an assumption that is made about human nature: Human beings are basically good people. When they become "bad," it is because they are pushed or pulled into crime by adverse conditions. If the lot of the lower classes was improved, there would be less crime. Since food, clothing, and shelter are material resources, the bettering of conditions must begin with economic change that distributes material resources to segments of society where they are most needed. This is a major policy implication of social structural theories, but it is not as far-reaching as the implications of critical theories reviewed in chapter 6.

CHAPTER SUMMARY

This chapter has reviewed theories of crime that emphasize the relationship between crime and social structure. Emile Durkheim's work in sociology provides much of the intellectual foundation for both social disorganization theory and strain theory. As a sociologist, Durkheim was interested in the various roles that deviance and crime played in society as well as how and why deviance persists but also changes over time. Durkheim also advanced the notion of anomie in order to explain how deviance results from weakened social solidarity and control.

Following Durkheim, social disorganization theories maintain that crime and delinquency result when there is a breakdown in social control. Members of the Chicago School believed that such a breakdown could result from ecological changes, as when communities experience rapid population change through social mobility and migration. Although this theory was almost forgotten, it has recently made a major comeback in criminology. Variations of the original theory have held up well to empirical scrutiny.

Merton's strain theory posits that when people find they cannot achieve valued goals such as wealth and status through socially approved means, they experience stress and frustration, which may lead to crime and deviance. In Merton's view, the poor are especially vulnerable to strain. Merton's theory is not without its faults, however. Two important revisions of Merton's theory, Messner and Rosenfeld's institutional anomie theory and Agnew's general strain theory, have expanded upon the theory's original position. The former seeks to extend Merton's argument to the macrocultural sphere, while Agnew's theory focuses on the more social-psychological dynamics of strain.

Subculture theories of crime revolve around the idea that crime and delinquency are connected to restricted opportunities and exposure to criminogenic cultures. Cloward and Ohlin's theory focuses on differential opportunities for delinquency. Cohen's subculture theory does as well, but it is also concerned with how children from the lower class are treated in institutions such as school. Miller's theory of lower-class gangs specifies how subcultural value systems develop to provide rationales for delinquency.

KEY TERMS

anomie
collective conscience
focal concerns
general strain theory
institutional anomie theory
social disorganization
strain
subcultural theories
subculture of violence

DISCUSSION QUESTIONS

1. According to Durkheim, a certain amount of crime and deviance is functional or socially beneficial. Which crimes, if any, do not provide some form of functionality in society?
2. Shaw and McKay believed that an urban area's geography had a lot to do with where crimes most occur. Thinking of modern cities, does social disorganization theory apply equally as well today?
3. Robert Merton and those who have created more modern theories of crime based on the American Dream see crime as directly related to the pursuit of material items and financial success over things such as community building and family. Do you believe that things are continuing to move in that direction or not?
4. Agnew's strain theory suggests that those who are unable to cope with difficult or negative situations are more likely to turn to crime. In your view, what are the most important ways of coping with problems so that crime does not become attractive?
5. Are criminal subcultures as prevalent in today's society as in the past? Do people belonging to subcultures as described by Miller and others really have a greater chance of committing crime, or have technological and social changes allowed subcultures to find other ways of expressing needs and wants?

ACTIVITIES

1. Take a tour of a local area and look for signs of social disorganization. What things do you see that might be related to higher levels of crime in some areas according to the theory? If possible, consult online police statistics to see if the data supports your impressions.
2. Take an informal poll of people to see if they think, as Durkheim did, that crime is useful and functional for society (you might get some strange reactions!). If your interviewees answer negatively, share with them some of Durkheim's observations and note their reactions.
3. To better understand Merton and Agnew's theories, take an informal poll of fellow students and ask them when they are most likely to *consider* cheating or plagiarizing on a course assignment or test. Are their responses consistent with the theories?

5

Social Process Theories

Humans are social animals and for the most part we like to have friends to share our time with and to help us navigate life. We need some social support from our friends, parents, and teachers in order to develop emotionally and intellectually. For many years, social scientists have been able to show that our relationships with intimate others substantially impact our values, beliefs, and behavior. Criminologists are especially interested in the manner in which friends, parents, and teachers "teach" us lessons about obeying or disobeying rules. Some criminological theories focus on parental behavior and practices, while others cast their gaze on peer groups. Still others examine how peer, parental, and school experiences combine to push or pull someone toward criminal values and behavior.

Social process theories, the type of explanations we shall review in this chapter, recognize that not all people exposed to the same social structure engage in the same behavior, nor do people who come from dissimilar social environments necessarily behave differently. Social process theories are more microsociological, as they are concerned with how individuals acquire social attributes through interaction with others. A person's attributes are what identify a person in the eyes of others, distinguishing one person from another. When thinking about attributes it is important to keep in mind that their meaning is always contextual; how one person looks to another is always a matter of how other people in a similar situation look to that person.

Social attributes, such as being reliable or being "forward," convey messages about a person's behavior, status, and ideas. They are part of that person's social identity, and other people use them to determine how they should behave toward that individual and to distinguish that person from others. A person is not born with these attributes but acquires them through interaction with others. Criminality is a social attribute. People become criminals, and that status is confirmed when others treat them like criminals and confirmed again when people so identified actually engage in criminal behavior.

Social learning theorists owe a major intellectual debt to the ideas of the renowned social psychologist George Herbert Mead. Mead's **interactionist perspective** (sometimes called symbolic interactionism) sees human beings as *active agents* in the construction of the social world they experience. The idea is that during interaction, people construct meanings, expectations, and implications that shape everyone's behavior and thus create a certain social reality for participants. This experience influences what happens in later interactions, although each interaction creates its own social reality. Social order is therefore fluid and ever-changing.

One of the most important elements of the interactionist perspective is the idea that actions arise out of situations (Blumer, 1969: 85). Whether people are at home with their families, in school, at work, or at play, each situation presents opportunities, demands, tasks, obstacles, pleasures—and sometimes dangers—that must be taken into account and evaluated by the actor. That assessment provides people with the basis for understanding the situation and forming their actions. Essentially, the meaning of a situation for each participant derives from the actions and reactions of the other participants.

For example, how do you decide that you are in control of a situation? By how others respond to you. Or consider how you know that a situation is safe or dangerous. You can "read" the situation through the actions of others, or you can put yourself in the shoes of another and imagine how they would act and what the likely results would be. Obviously, this becomes possible only when you have prior knowledge or experience with similar situations and people. Social order is constructed as people agree on the meanings and implications of the situations they are in, and act accordingly.

THE PROCESS OF ASSOCIATION

In criminology, **social process theories** attempt to describe and explain the ways in which individuals become criminal or adopt criminal values. They deal with the links between an individual's interaction with others and that person's motivations, perceptions, self-conceptions, attitudes, behavior, and identity. Although many interactionist theories seem to place greater emphasis on the behavior of others than on the behavior of "self," the goal is the same: to explain the emergence and consequences of behavior. An underlying assumption is that criminal behavior can be explained within the same framework as any other behavior. A common theme in many social process theories is that criminal behavior is learned through interaction with others.

THE THEORY OF DIFFERENTIAL ASSOCIATION

In the 1939 edition of *Principles of Criminology*, Edwin H. Sutherland forwarded what is known as **differential association theory**. According to this theory, criminal behavior patterns are acquired through processes of interaction and communication, just as are other behavior patterns. The principle of differential association accounts for the particular behavior pattern acquired through these processes: Individuals acquire criminal behavior patterns because they are exposed to situations in which the learning of crime outweighs the learning of alternative, noncriminal behaviors. Sutherland wanted it clearly understood that criminal behavior was not the result of biological or psychological pathology, but rather was one possible outcome of normal interactive processes. In their daily lives, people are participants in a variety of group situations, in which they are exposed to the behavior and influence of others. What they "pick up" in these situations helps shape their own behavior. When a person is more involved with delinquent or criminal groups, he or she is more likely to become delinquent or criminal as a result. The theory as a whole consists of the following nine propositions:

1. Criminal behavior is learned.
2. Criminal behavior is learned in interaction with other persons in a process of communication.
3. The principle part of the learning of criminal behavior occurs within intimate personal groups.
4. When criminal behavior is learned, the learning includes (a) techniques of committing the crime, which are sometimes very complicated, sometimes very simple; (b) the specific direction of motives, drives, rationalizations, and attitudes.
5. The specific direction of motives and drives is learned from definitions of the legal codes as favorable or unfavorable.
6. A person becomes delinquent because of an excess of definitions favorable to violation of law [the principle of differential association].
7. Differential association may vary in frequency, duration, priority, and intensity.
8. The process of learning criminal behavior by association with criminal and anticriminal patterns involves all of the mechanisms that are involved in any other learning.

9. While criminal behavior is an expression of general needs and values, it is not explained by those general needs and values, since noncriminal behavior is an expression of the same needs and values (Sutherland and Cressey, 1974: 75–77).

Figure 5.1 illustrates the process of differential association. Box 5.1 discusses how principles of differential association theory can be used to understand the idea that music affects behavior.

Three important observations should be made about this theory. First, the theory of differential association purports to explain noncriminal as well as criminal behavior. Noncriminal behavior emerges because of an excess of definitions unfavorable to law violation. Thus, if a child spends a great deal of time interacting intensely with people whose behavior and ideas stress conformity to the law, the child is likely to grow up a conformist (in terms of the law, at least).

Second, the theory can be used to explain variations in group rates of crime as well as individual criminality. Although the theory focuses on how

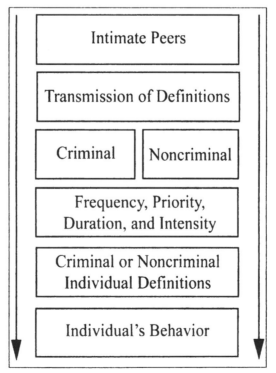

Figure 5.1   The Process of Differential Association

Box 5.1.   Connections between Music and Differential Association Theory

Every once in a while a musician or band attracts the attention of those who would never be their fans. This is most often the case when the artist's style or lyrics receive widespread press coverage because they are seen by mainstream audiences as especially obscene, pornographic, offensive, or dangerous. It is the latter concern that is most interesting to discuss from the perspective of differential association theory.

One early example that illustrates the fear in some quarters about corrupting the morals of youth stems from a performance that would surely now would be considered conservative. By the time Elvis Presley made his third appearance on the *Ed Sullivan Show* (a very popular 1950s mainstream variety television program), Presley's gyrations and hip shaking were deemed so risqué that the cameras were aimed above the waist so audiences wouldn't have to be exposed to his shaking lower body movements. Elvis's style was shocking to older generations but attractive to younger folks, and sometimes the former tried to "protect" the latter from the sensuous messages sent by Presley for fear that they would imitate him or adopt casual attitudes about sex.

Fast-forward fifty years and compare this to the now infamous 2004 Super Bowl halftime fiasco between Justin Timberlake and Janet Jackson. As they performed a highly sexualized dance, Timberlake tore some fabric from Jackson's chest and exposed her bare breast to millions of live viewers. It is unclear if the stunt was planned, but reactions to it ranged from laughter and ambivalence to shock and outrage. MTV, which produced the miniconcert, was told by the National Football League that they would never work together on a show like this again. Citing decency regulations, the Federal Communications Commission threatened MTV along with CBS, the television station that aired the halftime show, with fines and other penalties for the incident.

Some social control agents (especially parents and teachers) have in other instances tried to prevent kids from getting the "wrong" message by attacking artists' music. Heavy metal artists such as Ozzy Osbourne and Judas Priest were early targets of such attacks in the 1980s; in fact, both were unsuccessfully sued over the content of their lyrics. Marilyn Manson has been vilified by many as a modern-day devil who encourages youth to be disobedient, anarchist, hedonistic, and violent. He was singled out by some as encouraging the views that lead to the 1999 Columbine school shooting. Rent Michael Moore's film *Bowling for Columbine* to view Manson's reaction to those who blamed him for that kind of violence. Several years ago Ice-T and his band Body Count was accused of encouraging youth violence against law enforcement officers in his song "Cop Killer." Led by police officers, a whole social movement sprung up against him and his music. More recently, Eminem has been accused of encouraging homophobia, sexual assault, and misogyny in his lyrics.

The connection we are trying to make here is that there appears to be a widely held popular belief that listening to music and watching musical

performances can affect not only the attitudes of the young but also their behavior. This is not dissimilar to the underlying logic of differential association
theory. Let's think further on this. When you were a younger teenager, some
of you might have been told by your parents to avoid contact with certain
people. Parents often do this because there is something about another kid
they don't like and they are concerned that this person may negatively influence your values, attitudes, and behavior. Put more simply, the rationale is
that parents don't want their kids "hanging out with the wrong crowd." Essentially this is a Sutherlandian argument, as it assumes that frequent and intense
interactions with others might directly affect your attitudes and behavior. A
similar line of reasoning applies to the possible effect of the media on beliefs.
Clearly many people believe that indeed the media can negatively influence
children, as regulatory bodies that govern the content of television shows,
films, and CDs all have some form of rating system designed to alert parents
to adult content, such as the use of profanity, violence, sex, or illegal drugs.

Of course, when Sutherland wrote differential association theory, the
world was a very different place in terms of the mass media. Children, and to
some extent adults, had less exposure to messages outside of their immediate
physical environments. Sutherland didn't give much credence to the idea that
"picture shows" could influence the formulation of definitions favorable or
unfavorable to law. This is one of the reasons he limited the theory to interactions with intimate others. In today's society, however, children and adults
alike are surrounded by mass media and access to Internet-based social networking sites such as Facebook, Twitter, and MySpace, and the possible effects
of media images on crime continues to draw scholarly interest.

individuals come to engage in criminal behavior, a compatible explanation
of variations in rates of crime for whole populations is possible. Thus, relatively high crime rates are predicted for people and places having extensive
exposure to definitions favorable to law violation, especially when there is
a high probability that such definitions will be learned by a relatively large
number of people. Shaw and McKay's delinquency areas, discussed in the
preceding chapter, would meet these criteria.

Third, the theory can applied to white-collar crime as well as traditional
street crime. Sutherland invented the term *white-collar crime*, and he soundly
criticized other theorists (like Shaw, McKay, and Merton) for failing to consider those crimes situated within the context of work. Sutherland believed
that a general theory of crime cannot be based on a class-specific model of
criminal behavior. Variables like poverty or neighborhood disorganization
are insufficient explanatory variables since people can, and do, learn criminal behavior and attitudes in any economic or neighborhood context.

It is fair to say that the theory of differential association has been very
influential in criminology. It is, after all, hard to argue with the idea that

people learn criminal ways from others. Yet few theories have been sub-ject to more criticism: The language is imprecise; the theory is untestable because major variables such as "definitions favorable or unfavorable to law violations" cannot be measured; the theory deals with the acquisition and performance of behavior and yet leaves out any mention of personal-ity traits or other psychological variables; and the theory does not explain the fact that people often respond differently to the same situation. C. Ray Jeffery (1959) observes that since crime is learned, it must first exist. What accounts for the first criminal act? How does one explain crimes that are committed "out of the blue" or by people with no prior interaction with criminals?

BEHAVIORAL LEARNING THEORIES

According to *behavioral* learning theories, people tend to repeat activities for which they will be rewarded and to avoid those for which they will be pun-ished. They also tend to copy others whom they see being rewarded. In this case the reward is experienced vicariously. The sanctioning effect of rewards and punishments may apply to any behavior. One influential modifica-tion of Sutherland's original theory has been made by Robert Burgess and Ronald Akers (1966). They argue that Sutherland's formulation does not identify the mechanism by which individuals in fact learn. Taking a social learning approach, the authors restate Sutherland's theory in terms of **oper-ant conditioning**—a view that argues a certain behavior is learned because past examples have been rewarded. Thus, people engage in crime because it has been more highly rewarded in the past than has other behavior. That some people become criminals and others do not is explained by noting that all people do not go through the same socialization process, nor are they exposed to the same nonsocial situations of reinforcement.

Another quasi-behavioral learning theory was proposed by Daniel Glaser (1956), who argued that all forms of interaction between an individual and his or her social environment be incorporated in a modified theory of *differential identification*. "A person," writes Glaser (1956: 440), "pur-sues criminal behavior to the extent that he identifies himself with real or imaginary persons from whose perspective his criminal behavior seems ac-ceptable." These people serve as behavior models, and they need not come into direct, personal contact with the individual. Hence Glaser acknowl-edges something that Sutherland did not: the possibility that portrayal of criminal roles in the mass media is linked with the adoption of criminal behavior patterns.

These modifications of Sutherland's theory have some parallels with a prominent theory that people learn violence by imitating or modeling the behavior of people they "look up to." Albert Bandura (1973) showed that the behavior of aggressive models is readily imitated by experimental subjects, whether observed in the flesh or via film. In one well-known experiment, Bandura played a film of a woman who beat, kicked, and hacked an inflatable doll. After witnessing the film, nursery school children, when placed in a room with a similar doll, duplicated the woman's behavior and also engaged in other aggressive acts.

Experiments such as these have established the existence of immediate imitation, but how enduring are the behaviors learned, and does each new situation have to be virtually identical with the one originally observed in order for similar behavior to occur? While the jury is still out on these questions, there is evidence that suggests imitated behaviors do survive over time and that people will generalize from the initial modeling situation to other, sometimes quite dissimilar, situations.

Violent behavior has its rewards. Many people learn about them quite early in life. They learn that conflicts can be won through violence, that violence can be effective as a rule-enforcing technique, and that violence helps people get their way in the face of resistance. They also discover that respectable people often reward violence used in their interest, especially against "outsiders" and people regarded as a threat. From history, they learn that violence helped make America a better place to live. Closer to everyday life, they see that successful use of violence often confers status, authority, and even riches.

This brief list by no means exhausts the rewards associated with violence. As people grow up they have many opportunities to learn that violence is rewarded. But they also learn that it has its costs. Violence is costly when used at the wrong time, in the wrong place, or against the wrong person. But since there are differences of opinion as to when the use of violence is wrong, the costs (and rewards) of violence in any given situation are perceived differently by members of different groups (Stanko, 1990). One cannot assume that because one person or group refrains from violence in a certain situation, others will too.

PEER GROUPS AND SERIOUS DELINQUENCY

The observation that association with friends who are delinquent or criminal is associated with high rates of offending is not new, but it continues to be reconfirmed in study after study (Gorman and White, 1995; Hochstetler, Copes, and DeLisi, 2002; Moon, Morash, McCluskey, and Hwang, 2009).

Recall that the associational argument states when youths are involved with delinquent friends, the association encourages further delinquency. How it does is a matter of debate, but various mechanisms are possible:

the group's power to sanction behavior of members; the social rituals that confirm membership and confer status; the role models provided by the group's leader(s); the facilitation of activities that are not easily (or successfully) performed alone. The essential idea is that the delinquency of the group influences its members, and vice versa.

It all sounds simple enough, but the issue of peer influence remains controversial. In the first place, some studies have found that seriously delinquent youths are weakly attached to delinquent peers (e.g., Chapman, 1986; also Gottfredson and Hirschi, 1990: 154–57). They are loners. Other studies have found quite the opposite, at least for youths involved in illicit drug use (Bahr, Hoffmann, and Yang, 2005; Kandel and Davies, 1991). Youths in drug-using networks display extremely strong interactive ties with peers. Second, a study of incarcerated offenders found that group members who conformed to conventional standards were more popular than less conforming members (Osgood et al., 1986). Third, at least two observational studies, one in the United States (Schwendinger and Schwendinger, 1985) and one in England (Parker, 1974), have shown that occasional and serious delinquents participate side-by-side in the same street-corner networks, and the occasionals remain sporadic offenders.

Another issue further complicates what appeared to be a simple matter. Rather than influencing a youth's propensity to commit crimes, it has been suggested that delinquent peer groups merely facilitate crime among individuals whose tendencies are already compatible with it (Linden and Hackler, 1973; Gottfredson and Hirschi, 1988). A network of delinquency-prone individuals creates and responds to criminal opportunities in its milieu. The type and frequency of criminal acts will be determined largely by that milieu. A chronic delinquent is most often a lower-class, street-corner male who keeps company with other lower-class, street-corner males. This suggests that, quite apart from the intimate interaction among peers, the social structure of lower-class, street-corner society is conducive to high rates of street crime (Barlow and Ferdinand, 1992: 60–79).

TESTING DIFFERENTIAL ASSOCIATION THEORY

Testing the original formulation of differential association is not easy, and both the methods used and the results have been inconsistent. Usually researchers infer support (or nonsupport) of the theory and do not test it directly. This is largely Sutherland's fault because he did not specify how the theory might be tested, and he left major concepts undefined. We shall now review a few studies that have attempted to test differential association.

One study involved interviewing 1,544 students in nine high schools in the Southeast (Paternoster and Triplett, 1988). The authors reported strong support for differential association. Friends' definitions of appropriate and inappropriate behavior and friends' actual behavior were significantly related to an individual's own use of marijuana, drinking behavior, petty theft, and vandalism. A study of more than 1,000 Dutch children found great support for the idea that the frequency of contact with deviant friends significantly influences definitions favorable to deviant behavior (Bruinsma, 1992). In another study, Warr and Stafford (1991) used National Youth Survey data (see chapter 2) to evaluate associational theory. They found that peers' behavior—what they actually do—was a more important predictor of self-reported delinquency than peers' attitudes about behavior.

Two tests of differential association have been conducted from data obtained from the Richmond Youth Project, a self-report survey of more than 4,000 high school students. The first study found that definitions favorable to law violation predicted delinquency more strongly than any other variable (Matsueda, 1982; Matsueda and Heimer, 1987). However, in a recent reexamination of this data, it was found that the bonds to parents and friends more strongly explained delinquency (Costello and Vowell, 1999). More specifically, the authors found that definitions favorable to law violation were shaped or mediated by other factors, especially measures of the social bond (discussed in some detail later in this chapter). (A similar finding was made by Matsueda and Anderson, 1998, and Bahr, Hoffmann, and Yang, 2005.)

Indeed, tests of differential association theory have supported the *mediation hypothesis*—the notion that larger social and structural factors shape the content and form of definitions favorable or unfavorable to crime (Heimer, 1997). This approach has been used to explain the gender differences in violent offending. A study by Heimer and De Coster (1999) found that:

- Learning violent definitions is an important predictor of violent delinquency;
- Aggressive peers and coercive discipline each has a larger effect on boys' than girls' learning of violent definitions;
- Emotional bonds to family influence girls' but not boys' learning of violent definitions;
- Accepting traditional gender definitions significantly reduces violence among girls but does not influence violence among boys; and
- Boys engage in more violent delinquency than girls in part because they learn more violent definitions and more traditional gender definitions than girls and have more previous experience with violent offending than girls.

How and with whom we associate varies in a number of ways (e.g., by age, location, gender, and time). In the case of gender, role socialization reflects larger social norms and values, which help shape definitions of socially acceptable and unacceptable behavior in everyday interaction. When combined with a consideration of structural inequality in opportunities in schools, politics, and the workplace, one can see why there are differences in criminal offending by gender.

Differential association theory can also be helpful in explaining the causes of occupational and organizational crime. Indeed, partial support of the theory has been found in studies of organizational crime (Kauzlarich and Kramer, 1998). In some respects, white-collar crime:

> may be better understood by reference to differential association than is true of conventional lower class crime and delinquency, both because of the broader range of learning options generally available to the white collar crime offender and the complex nature of the offenses themselves (Friedrichs, 1996a: 229).

However, differential association theory is not equipped to explain the larger structural and organizational elements involved in the genesis and persistence of many organizational crimes. This limitation has prompted many white-collar crime scholars to study how definitions of appropriate and inappropriate behavior are created and maintained in unique organizational climates.

For example, Vaughan's (1996) monumental study of the space shuttle *Challenger* explosion employs the notion of the **normalization of deviance**, a condition in which deviations from technical protocols gradually and routinely become defined as normative. Risky practices, which can be an outcome or a precursor to the normalization of deviance, are often caused by "environmental and organizational contingencies (which) create operational forces that shape world view, normalizing signals of potential danger, resulting in mistakes with harmful human consequences" (Vaughan 1996: 409).

SELF-CONCEPT

Most research and theorizing based in differential association theory addresses the ways in which youths, in particular, come to adopt patterns of delinquent or criminal offending. Learning, communication, and interaction are the fundamental processes by which individuals acquire their social identities. These processes are also crucial to the development of an individual's personality—motivations, ideas and beliefs, perceptions, feelings, preferences, attitudes, values, self-control, inhibitions, and awareness or sense of self. Some authors have argued that a person's sense of self, or self-concept, is a major element among the forces that control behavior.

Containment Theory. One of the first to propose a link between self-concept and criminal behavior was Walter Reckless. Reckless (1973) believes that the individual confronted by choices of action feels a variety of "pulls" and "pushes." The pulls are environmental factors—such as adverse living conditions, poverty, lack of legitimate opportunities, abundance of illegitimate opportunities, or family problems—that serve to pull the individual away from the norms and values of the dominant society. The pushes take the form of internal pressures—hostility, biopsychological impairments, aggressiveness, drives, or wishes—that may also divert the individual away from actions supported by dominant values and norms.

But not all people faced with the same pulls and pushes become delinquent or criminal. To explain why some do not, Reckless advances **containment theory**. According to Reckless (1973: 55–56), there are two kinds of containment, inner and outer.

Inner containment consists mainly of self components, such as self-control, good self-concept, ego strength, well-developed superego, high frustration tolerance, high resistance to diversions, high sense of responsibility, goal orientation, ability to find substitute satisfactions, tension-reducing rationalizations, and so on. These are the inner regulators.

Outer containment represents the structural buffer in the person's immediate social world that is able to hold him within bounds. It consists of such items as a presentation of a consistent moral front to the person; institutional reinforcement of his norms, goals, and expectations; the existence of a reasonable set of social expectations; effective supervision and discipline (social controls); provisions for reasonable scope of activity (including limits and responsibilities) as well as for alternatives and safety valves; and opportunity for acceptance, identity, and belongingness. Such structural ingredients help the family and other supportive groups contain the individual.

In Reckless's view, the inner control system, primarily self-concept, provides a person with the strongest defense against delinquency involvement. Commenting on the results of a follow-up study of white schoolboys in high-delinquency areas in Columbus, Ohio, Reckless and Simon Dinitz (1967: 517) observe:

> In our quest to discover what insulates a boy against delinquency in a high delinquency area, we believe we have some tangible evidence that a good self-concept, undoubtedly a product of favorable socialization, veers slum boys away from delinquency, while a poor self-concept, a product of unfavorable socialization, gives the slum boy no resistance to deviancy, delinquent companions, or delinquent subculture. We feel that components of the self strength, such as a favorable concept of self, act as an inner buffer or inner containment against deviancy, distraction, lure, and pressures.

The work of Reckless and his associates has not gone without criticism, but interest in self-concept and its connection with criminality has remained very much alive in some circles. One study seems to confirm the importance of favorable family experiences in protecting a child against criminogenic influences, even in slum neighborhoods. Joan McCord (1991) used case records of visits to the homes of 232 boys as well as records of their juvenile and adult criminal activity covering a thirty-year period. She found that sons of mothers who were self-confident, offered leadership, and were affectionate and consistently nonpunitive in discipline tended to escape delinquency involvement. However, McCord also discovered that a different mechanism seemed to relate to whether a child subsequently became an adult criminal: a father's behavior toward wife and children. Apparently, fathers who undermine their wives, who fight with the family, and who are aggressive "teach their sons how to behave when they become adults" (McCord, 1991: 412). Thus, juvenile crime may be more susceptible to control mechanisms, including self-concept, whereas adult crime may be more susceptible to the influence of role expectations. More recent extensions of this approach have focused on how different identities both between *and* within gender influence the process of constructing one's self and criminal offending and victimization (Giordano, Cernkovich, and Holland, 2003; Giordano, Millhollin, Cernkovich, Pugh, and Rudolph, 1999). A central finding is that although involvement in crime by both men and women is strongly influenced by their peer and intimate relationships, women are less significantly affected by these relationships than men.

Techniques of Neutralization. One interesting theoretical contribution bearing on self-concept comes from David Matza and Gresham Sykes. Matza (1964) argues that individuals are rarely committed to or compelled to perform delinquent or criminal behavior. Rather, they drift into and out of it, retaining a commitment neither to convention nor to crime. This so-called **drift theory** is also applicable to some instances of organizational crime (Braithwaite, 1989b).

In Matza's view, delinquents are never totally immune to the demands for conformity made by the dominant social order. At most they are merely flexible in their commitment to them. In a joint publication, Sykes and Matza (1957) argue that if delinquents do form subcultures in opposition to dominant society, they are surprisingly weak in their commitment to them. They show guilt and shame, though one would expect none; they frequently accord respect and admiration to the "really honest" person and to law-abiding people in their immediate social environment; and they often draw a sharp line between appropriate victims and those who are not fair game—all of which suggests that "the virtue of delinquency is far from unquestioned." In terms of the dominant normative order, the delinquent appears to be both conforming and nonconforming.

Sykes and Matza believe that in order to practice nonconformity, delinquents must somehow handle the demands for conformity to which they accord at least some recognition. In the view of these authors, delinquents handle those demands by learning to neutralize them in advance of violating them. That is, they redefine their contemplated action to make it "acceptable" if not "right." The authors identify five **techniques of neutralization** that facilitate the juvenile's drift into delinquency:

1. *denial of responsibility* ("alcohol causes me to do it; I am helpless");
2. *denial of injury* ("my action won't hurt anyone");
3. *denial of the victim* ("he 'has it coming'");
4. *condemnation of the condemners* ("those who condemn me are worse than I am"); and
5. *appeal to higher loyalties* ("my friends, or family, come first, so I must do it").

Two other techniques of neutralization have been proposed and discussed in a classic study of occupational crime (see Hollinger, 1991; Klockars, 1974; Minor, 1981). They are "defense of necessity" and "metaphor of the ledger." Defense of necessity relates to the fact that among business offenders illegal acts are seen as standard business practice and necessary in a competitive marketplace. Metaphor of the ledger relates to the idea that a person can build up "good" credit so that he or she can later do something "bad" without feeling guilty—a form of cashing in the credits.

More recently, scholars of state crime, corporate crime, and elite deviance have found strong evidence of how techniques of neutralization work (Jamieson and McEvoy, 2005; Kauzlarich, Matthews, and Miller, 2001; Piquero, Tibbetts, and Blankenship, 2005). Obviously, one of the most important things that separates victimizers from their victims is their power to exert their will. Most often, the perpetrators of state crime (e.g., human rights violations and illegal wars) do not acknowledge the degree to which their policies have caused harm. Instead, they concentrate on assessing the "effectiveness" of their policies, no matter how harmful they might be to others, to bring about desired change or to maintain positions of dominance. Injury caused by criminal domestic and international policies can also be downplayed by neutralizing reasonable categorical imperatives (e.g., do no harm) by employing bankrupt utilitarianism, that is, arguing that the ends justify the means. Further, harms are neutralized by denying responsibility, dehumanizing the powerless for purposes of exploitation, and appealing to higher loyalties (i.e., the capitalist political economy and "national security") (Kauzlarich, Matthews, and Miller, 2001; Simon, 2007; 1999).

Political policy makers attempt to "neutralize" the destructive and harmful effects of their policies, as in the long history of U.S. abuses in Latin and Central America:

> U.S. policy makers have consciously decided (1) that the U.S. is entitled to control Central America and that the peoples of Central America are obligated to acquiesce in this power exercise; (2) that violence is permissible, and policy makers can live with themselves and conclude that they are ethical/moral persons and that these policies are ethical/moral even if they involve violence; (3) that the use of violence, intimidation, and threat of violence will produce the desired effect or minimize a more negative one; and (4) that the policy of violence and control will not unduly endanger the United States, and the country will neither sustain physical harm nor suffer legal, economic, or political consequences that will outweigh the benefits achieved through this violence (Tifft and Markham, 1991: 125–26).

With respect to the historical treatment of Native Americans within the United States, "colonists quickly justified their violence by demonizing their enemies" Takaki (1993: 43). However, the transference of one's own negative tendencies to another group is not something new. While Native Americans were seen as unruly, "God-less" savages, Takaki (1993) notes that the atrocities committed by the civilized whites against the Native Americans, were, in fact, savage. It is in this light, then, that Native Americans became an enemy worthy of indiscriminate killing. In much the same manner, the indiscriminate killing of the "God-less" communists of Central America were also justified:

> [This] is a painful reality. Many of us face this reality with initial disbelief and denial, for it is difficult for us to see either the United States or ourselves as terrorists, as batterers. Terrorists and batterers are someone else. To emotionally experience, to actually witness the destruction, the horror, the reality of destabilization, starvation, torture and death by design, by public planning, is beyond our comprehension (Tifft and Markham, 1991).

Empirical evaluations of the neutralization hypothesis are scarce in part because of the difficulty of establishing what happens cognitively *before* a law violation occurs. Almost all research has looked at rationalizations after the fact, which provides at best only inferential evidence. The problem is one of establishing the causal order: neutralization before transgression.

In any case, with the exception of Agnew's (1994) study and some indirect support from Presser's (2003) interviews with violent men, the evidence is not very impressive in studies of most traditional street crimes. The absence of neutralizations, however, does not mean they might not have operated at some time in the mind of an offender. Neutralizations might arise after earlier transgressions and act as rationalizations for later ones, perhaps contributing to a "hardening" process that leads to a commitment to deviance (Hirschi, 1971: 208). Hamlin (1988: 432) goes even further and calls the prior sequencing argument "a fallacy." He argues that the motives for doing things are created during the process of legitimizing actions that have been criticized or challenged.

Furthermore, neutralization may be necessary only for certain offenders. According to one scholar, "neutralization should only be necessary when a potential offender has both a strong desire to commit an offense and a strong belief that to do so would violate his personal morality. . . . If one's morality is not constraining, however, then neutralization or rationalization is simply unnecessary" (Minor, 1980: 103–20). Topalli (2005) has even found that some offenders neutralize "being good rather than being bad." In other words, to survive on the streets and reach high status in their neighborhood, some offenders actively seek to enhance their "hard core" reputations on the street and neutralize in the opposite direction that Sykes and Matza would predict.

There may be no adequate way to disentangle the causal order problem mentioned above, even with longitudinal data, since definitional learning ("this is right to do, this is wrong," and "I'm OK, I'm not OK," etc.) occurs concurrently with rule breaking (Hollinger, 1991). Even so, neutralization theory may have received a "bum rap" from critics, especially in light of his finding that neutralization may interact with age, younger people being less likely to neutralize than older ones (Hollinger, 1991).

SOCIAL CONTROL THEORY

Like Matza and others, control theorists emphasize the episodic character of much crime and delinquency, but unlike their colleagues, they build in no assumptions about what motivates people to commit deviance. Indeed, "They assume that human beings are born free to break the law and will refrain from doing so only if special circumstances exist" (Box, 1981: 122).

The most prominent version of control theory is that of Travis Hirschi (1971). According to Hirschi, these special circumstances exist when the individual's bond to conventional, or moral, society is strong. As originally conceived, Hirschi's **social control theory** holds that this bond is based on four elements: *attachment, commitment, belief,* and *involvement. Attachment* refers to the individual's affective involvement with conventional others (e.g., parents, teachers, friends), including sensitivity to their thoughts, feelings, and desires. When that attachment is weakened, the individual is free to deviate. *Commitment* is the "rational" component in conformity. It refers

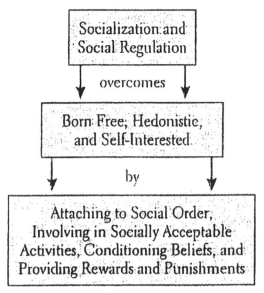

Figure 5.2. Hirschi's social control theory

to the weighing of the costs and risks of deviance in light of that person's investment, or "stake," in conformity. "When or whenever he considers deviant behavior, he must consider the costs of this deviant behavior, the risks he runs of losing the investment he has made in conventional behavior" (Hirschi, 1971: 20). The weaker the commitment to conformity, the lower the costs of deviance; hence the freer one is to deviate. Figure 5.2 illustrates the major thrust of the theory.

Hirschi defines *belief* as "a common value system within the society or group whose norms are being violated." But individuals differ in the strength of their belief in the moral validity of these social rules. If for some reason these beliefs are weakened, the individual will be freer to deviate. By including *involvement*, Hirschi suggests that deviance is in part a matter of opportunities to deviate. He argues that the more one is involved in conventional things, the less one has the opportunity to do deviant things. This is one of the weakest parts of the theory, as Hirschi himself discovered in his research with more than 4,000 California junior high and high school students. The reason is that opportunities for criminal or delinquent activities increase along with opportunities for noncriminal activities.

Both the clarity of its exposition and the many research findings supporting it have given Hirschi's control theory a prominent place in criminology. For example, one test of the theory conducted on the subject of misbehavior in school found that every measure of the social bond except involvement was shown to have significant effects in the predicted direction (Stewart, 2003). As the study's author explains, the logic goes like this:

> Students who accept and believe in the dominant set of conventional school rules will be less likely to engage in delinquent behaviors and recognize the validity of those rules for maintaining a safe school environment. Those who care about and feel supported by their teachers and friends are more likely to develop affective ties to school and display socially acceptable behavior. Those with well-defined educational goals, who invest greater effort, and display higher aspirations for status attainment may be more committed to the educational process overall. As a result, they may recognize that involvement in delinquent behavior may jeopardize their future goals (Stewart, 2003: 493).

A study by Agnew (1985), however, questions social control theory's utility as an explanation of youth crime. He studied a national sample of 1,886 male youths interviewed first in the tenth grade and again at the end of the eleventh grade. He found delinquency involvement to be remarkably stable over the two-year period, with the delinquency measured in the tenth grade accounting for 65 to 68 percent of the delinquency measured later.

In contrast, Agnew found that the social bond variables of parental attachment, school grades, and commitment explained only 1 to 2 percent of the variance in delinquency. Agnew speculates that as children grow older, the importance of the bonds discussed by Hirschi may diminish, but he does not rule out that they may be important among younger children.

Hirschi's social control theory has also been heavily criticized for overstating the importance of the social bond. A reanalysis of the Richmond

---

Box 5.2. Differential Association, Social Control Theory, and *Boyz n the Hood*

The 1991 film *Boyz n the Hood* is still regarded as one of John Singleton's best movies. The story revolves around a father (played by Laurence Fishburne) trying to shield his teenage son Tre (Cuba Gooding Jr.) from widespread crime and violence on the streets of their neighborhood in south central Los Angeles, where Singleton himself was raised. Criminologically, the film illustrates the difficulties that parents have in connecting with their children, as there is competition from peer groups over what values and beliefs are most desirable. In real life, we know that as children enter the teenage years, they begin to model their friends' behavior more than their parent(s), and sometimes regard their parent(s) as the enemy, or cops, which can further add to the distances between them. If you haven't seen the movie, watch it and think about its connection to social process theories of crime. If it's been awhile since you've seen it, give it another viewing.

Youth Project data by David Greenberg (1999) found that while social control theory has its merits, criminologists have overestimated the strength of the theory. For example, Greenberg (1999) found that (a) intimacy in communication between parent and child (a measure of attachment) is not highly correlated with delinquency, (b) a very modest negative relationship between involvement in school-related activities and delinquency, and (c) negative correlations between aspirations to attain higher levels of education (e.g., college) and delinquency are also quite small. However, another study also using the same data source found that measures of the social bond, especially belief, were the greatest predictors of delinquency (Costello and Vowell, 1999).

One final comment on this prominent theory is in order. Some criminologists contend that control theory ignores the criminal activity of career offenders, as well as the crimes of people in positions of economic and political power. The "upperworld" individual is actually freed by conventional society to engage in "indiscretions" because these are not viewed as especially disreputable, much less criminal (Hagan, 1985). Such a person may thus exhibit strong social bonds to conventional society and considerable involvement in illegal activities. Indeed, if we are to take into consideration political and state crimes, many of the offenders would be discovered to be very bonded to the social order because of their high levels of education, employment status, familial relationships, and general belief systems. While there has been some support for social control theory in studies of occupational crime (Lasley, 1988; Makkai and Braithwaite, 1991), Hirschi's version is best suited to explain juvenile delinquency, not white-collar crime.

INTERACTIONAL THEORY

Terrence Thornberry (1987) developed an **interactional theory of delinquency** that highlights the relationship between delinquency and the family, school, and peers. While attention to these factors is certainly not new, Thornberry argues that criminologists have only explored their unidirectional (one-way) qualities. His theory unites insights from social control and differential association theories, among others.

Thornberry argues that instead of simply studying how a person's commitment to school affects their belief in conventional or unconventional values, we should also consider how beliefs shape the commitment to school, which in turn may further influence beliefs, which then may further affect commitment, and so on. He explains, "Bonding variables appear to be reciprocally linked to delinquency, exerting a causal impact on associations with delinquent peers and delinquent behavior; *they also are causally effected by these variables*" (our emphasis; Thornberry, 1987: 876). Interactional theory, then,

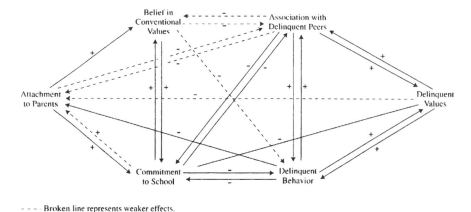

- - - Broken line represents weaker effects.
——— Solid line represents stronger effects.

Figure 5.3.   An Interactional Theory of Delinquency
Source: Thornberry (1987). Reprinted with the permission of the American Society of Criminology.

suggests that many of the variables in social control theory and differential association theory can affect one another in all sorts of ways. Again, most people would think that strong attachment to parents reduces the extent to which youths associate with delinquent peers. But is it not true that associations with delinquent peers could affect a child's bond with their parents? Is it not also the case that delinquent peers could affect delinquency, just as delinquency affects association with delinquent peers? (Matsueda and Anderson, 1998). Figure 5.3 illustrates Thornberry's theory applied to those in middle adolescence.

That the school, family, and peers have multiple and reciprocal effects is just part of the interactional theory. The second major part of the theory specifies how these variables affect people over the life course. This developmental approach, which is similar to that of Sampson and Laub's (1988; 1992) theory reviewed in chapter 7, suggests that the importance of these factors *varies by age*. For the very young, the family is the most important agent of socialization; when youths enter into middle adolescence, friends and the school become more important than before, and as the person enters adulthood, work and families of procreation (second families) become salient. All of this suggests that at different points in life, some associations more than others will be connected with our attitudes, beliefs, and behavior. It has been furthered argued that earlier delinquency has effects on later delinquency, and that low social economic status can have compounding effects (Thornberry and Krohn, 2001).

There is no doubt that the journey from childhood to adulthood is marked with change. Criminal offending is often shaped by these developmental changes, and at least one test of Thornberry's theory has been supportive (Jang, 1999; Thornberry and Krohn, 2001).

THE LABELING PERSPECTIVE

Up to this point, the focus has been on crime and delinquency as behavior and on people who commit crimes and the distinctions between them and those who do not. The questions "What causes or influences criminal behavior?" and "What factors are associated with committing crime or becoming criminals?" are underlying concerns in the work reviewed. However, the conception of crime and the criminal that underlies such questions is not the only one that has been recognized. Instead of viewing crime simply as illegal behavior and the criminal as one who engages in it, some criminologists draw attention to the behavior of other people with whom an individual interacts. Crime is a label attached to behavior, and the criminal is one whose behavior has been labeled crime. Crime is thus problematic and a question of social definitions. Nothing intrinsic in behavior makes it a crime:

> Social groups create deviance by making the rules whose infraction constitutes deviance, and by applying those rules to particular people and labeling them as outsiders. From this point of view, deviance is not a quality of the act a person commits, but rather a consequence of the application by others of rules or sanctions to an "offender." The deviant is one to whom that label has been successfully applied; deviant behavior is behavior that people so label (Becker, 1963: 9).

Labeling theory, or the societal reactions approach, gained immense popularity in the fields of crime and deviance during the 1960s. This was also about the time that the social constructionist paradigm reviewed in chapter 1 fully emerged in sociology. In its applications to the crime scene, labeling theory has been used to explain why individuals continue to engage in activities that others define as criminal, why individuals become career criminals, why the official data on crime and criminals look the way they do, why crime waves occur, why law enforcement is patterned the way it is, why criminal stereotypes emerge and persist, and why some groups in society are more likely to be punished, and punished more severely, than others. Box 5.3 describes a famous study by William J. Chambliss (1973) that vividly illustrates some of these points.

Though labeling theory gained popularity during the 1960s, it is based on the much earlier contributions of Frank Tannenbaum (1938) and Edwin Lemert (1951; 1972). Sixty years ago, Tannenbaum pointed out that society's

Box 5.3. The Saints and the Roughnecks

William J. Chambliss (1973) followed the experiences of two small-town juvenile gangs whose members were students at "Hannibal High." The youths
regularly broke the law. However, only the members of the Roughnecks were
considered delinquent by officials and repeatedly arrested. The other gang, the
Saints, largely escaped criminalization, and no members were ever arrested.

According to Chambliss, four factors played important roles in the differential response, and all related to the class position of the gang members.
The Roughnecks came from the lower class, while the Saints came from more
"respectable" upper-middle-class families.

First, the Roughnecks were more visible. Unlike the Saints, whose members
had access to cars and could escape the local community, the Roughnecks
had little choice but hang out under the surveillance of neighbors and local
authorities.

Second, the outward demeanor of the Saints deceived parents and officials.
Around authority figures, they wore masks of courtesy and obedience, and
when accused of deviant behavior, they were apologetic and diplomatic. The
Roughnecks, on the other hand, misbehaved openly and showed little regard
for social customs or the feelings of others.

Third, when responding to the gangs' misbehavior, authorities displayed
bias that favored the Saints. The Saints were characterized as typical adolescents who were merely sowing their wild oats as normal boys do.

Finally, in defining the Roughnecks as boys who get in trouble, the community reinforced the "deviance" of gang members and helped produce a
self-fulfilling prophecy so that deviant self-images promoted further deviance.
The Saints, meanwhile, remained respectable in the eyes of the community,
although in reality they continued to maintain a high level of delinquency.

Chambliss's study is one of the best examples of the importance of the labeling perspective to date. It clearly shows that "labeling, stigma and negative
self-images have a powerful impact in determining who we are and what we
become" (1999: 120).

efforts at social control may actually help create precisely what those efforts
are meant to suppress: crime. By labeling individuals as "delinquents" or
"criminals" and by reacting to them in a punitive way, Tannenbaum argued,
the community encourages those individuals to redefine themselves in accordance with the community's definition. A change in self-identification (or
self-concept) may occur, so that individuals "become" what others say they
are. Tannenbaum (17–18) described the process:

From the community's point of view, the individual who used to do bad
and mischievous things has now become a bad and unredeemable human

being. From the individual's point of view there has taken place a similar change. He has gone slowly from a sense of grievance and injustice, of being unduly mistreated and punished, to recognition that the definition of him as a human being is different from that of other boys in his neighborhood, his school, street, community. This recognition on his part becomes a process of self-identification and integration with the group which shares his activities. It becomes, in part, a process of rationalization; in part, a simple response to a specialized type of stimulus. The young delinquent becomes bad because he is defined as bad and because he is not believed if he is good. There is a persistent demand for consistency in character. The community cannot deal with people whom it cannot define. Reputation is this sort of public definition.

Even if people act in ways normally defined as good, their goodness will not be believed. Once stigmatized, they find it extremely difficult to be free of the label "delinquent" or "criminal." As Erikson (1966: 17) notes in *Wayward Puritans*, "The common feeling that deviant persons never really change . . . may derive from a faulty premise; but the feeling is expressed so frequently and with such conviction that it eventually creates the facts which later 'prove' it to be correct."

A bad reputation doesn't just affect individuals. Reuter and Rubinstein (1983) describe the experience of corporations and even whole industries (e.g., the vending machine business) whose bad reputations have lead to an increase in crime. The reason, they argue, is that when labeled crooked, respectable people do not apply for jobs or work with such businesses, leaving them open and attractive to risk-takers and criminals—a kind of self-selection is going on, "bad" places attracting "bad" people.

Societal reaction to crime and delinquency helps turn offending individuals from seeing themselves as basically "straight" and "respectable" and toward an image of themselves as criminal. Thus, some people who are reacted to as criminals come to think of themselves as criminals, or at least they participate in what becomes a *self-fulfilling prophecy*. In a study of used car fraud, one of Braithwaite's (1978) informants said, "They think because you're a used car dealer you're a liar. So they treat you like one and lie to you. Can you blame the dealer for lying back?"

The term **secondary deviation** refers to the criminal acts associated with the individual's acquired status as a criminal and his or her ultimate acceptance of it (Lemert, 1951; 1972). Secondary deviation emerges from a process of reaction and adjustment to the punishing and stigmatizing actions of significant others, such as schoolteachers, parents, and law enforcement officials. Although initially the individuals engage for a short time in deviant acts that they regard as incompatible with their true selves (suggesting the need for the techniques of neutralization discussed earlier), they eventually come to accept their new identities as deviants and are well advanced toward a career in deviance:

> The sequence of interaction leading to secondary deviation is roughly as follows: (1) primary deviation [initial acts of deviance prompted by any number of reasons]; (2) social penalties; (3) further primary deviation; (4) stronger penalties and rejections; (5) further deviation, perhaps with hostilities and resentments beginning to focus upon those doing the penalizing; (6) crisis reached in the tolerance quotient, expressed in formal action by the community stigmatizing of the deviant; (7) strengthening of the deviant conduct as a reaction to the stigmatizing and penalties; (8) ultimate acceptance of deviant social status and efforts at adjustment on the basis of the associated role (Lemert, 1951: 77).

Whether an individual moves from primary to secondary deviation depends greatly on the degree to which others' disapproval finds expression in concrete acts of punishment and stigmatization. In a later paper, Lemert notes: "While communication of invidious definitions of persons or groups and the public expression of disapproval were included [in earlier discussions] as part of the societal reaction, the important point was made that these had to be validated in order to be sociologically meaningful. Validation was conceived as isolation, segregation, penalties, supervision, or some kind of organized treatment" (1974: 457). Support for the criminogenic impact of validation comes from Shannon's (1991) famous cohort study in Racine, Wisconsin, which found that boys who experienced repeated contacts with the police were at much greater risk of chronic delinquency.

A more recent version of the theory that has been empirically supported in the literature posits that official intervention during adolescence can negatively impact educational attainment and employment opportunities in direct ways. In regard to education, children labeled as troublemakers are more likely to be harshly disciplined. They may even be suspended or expelled. This may not only create animosity toward the school system and administrators but also preclude the child from eventually landing a good job. It is theorized that this leads to reduced opportunities for legitimate ways to achieve income and status and thus raises the probability of secondary deviation as the individual does not see him or herself fitting into mainstream society (Bernburg and Krohn, 2003).

Some critics have attacked labeling theory, arguing that many of its key assumptions are not supported by the bulk of available evidence. Indeed, Wellford (1975: 342) asserts that the supposed connection between punitive reactions, changes in self-concept, and secondary deviation is "a simplistic view of behavior causation, one that stresses the explanation of intellectual as opposed to behavioral characteristics of the subject." More contemporary critics argue that the claim that changes in self-concept produce changes in behavior has yet to be demonstrated. Some prefer to view behavior as situationally determined, and thus crime may well occur quite independently of the actor's self-concept.

To be sure, labeling theory has come in for its share of criticism—perhaps even a disproportionate share—but it is far from dishonored as a theoretical perspective on crime, nor is it about to be abandoned by the field. Braithwaite's (1989) theory of reintegrative shaming (discussed in detail in chapter 7) and Sampson and Laub's (2003; 1997) continuing work in developmental criminology both take labeling theory seriously, giving it a prominent place in their theories of crime.

While differential association theory, social control theory, and varieties of strain/anomie theory are more frequently tested than labeling theory, several studies in addition to the ones mentioned above have found that labeling theory is helpful in explaining some of the dynamics involved in crime and deviance (Bernburg, Krohn, and Rivera, 2006). For example, because of the stigma surrounding being "mentally ill," people who may in fact be mentally ill might avoid treatment, keep their problems secret, or withdraw from the very audiences (friends, family) that might be able to help them improve the quality of their lives (Link and Cullen, 1983; Triplett, 2000). Criminal justice policies are also instructively viewed through labeling theory, as Triplett (2000) notes in the context of social reactions to juvenile delinquency in the 1990s. Furthermore, two studies found that while the effects of labeling theory are not as direct as the initial authors of the theory suggest, the effects of labeling are mediated through differential association (Adams, 1996; Downs, Robertson, and Harrison, 1997). Another study found that the effects of labeling were far stronger—a child's perception of teacher disapproval was highly associated with delinquency, independent of prior delinquency. However, the effects of labeling were less direct when considering a child's delinquent peer associations (Adams and Evans, 1996). Other research has found that the effects of labeling were highly significant in explaining adolescent drug use (Edwards, 1993).

CHAPTER SUMMARY

This chapter has considered the social processes by which people acquire the attributes of a criminal. A common theme running through many social process theories is that criminal behavior is learned through association with others who have criminal attributes. Edwin Sutherland's differential association theory is among the most well-known social process theories, and it has received considerable empirical support. Sutherland's theory, like several other social process theories, also draws attention to the ways in which relationships with others provide opportunities and incentives to learn criminal behavior patterns.

Self-concept theories of criminality suggest that a person's sense of self, which is grounded in the reactions of others, is an important element in the internal control of behavior. A strong self-concept is a defense against criminal influence. Neutralization theories suggest that self-respecting individuals will occasionally drift into crime or delinquency, provided they can rationalize their misdeeds so as to protect their self-image as essentially good and honest people.

Control theory, on the other hand, asserts that by nature people will tend to do whatever they want, including crime, so the important theoretical question is "What stops them?" Hirschi believes that people are less likely to become criminals the more attached they are to the people, values, and activities of conventional (i.e., noncriminal) society.

Labeling theory revolves around the idea that crime is a label attached to behavior and to people; there is nothing intrinsic in behavior that makes it a crime. Labeling theory emphasizes how the stigmatizing reactions of others may turn an individual's infrequent or spontaneous criminal behavior into persistent involvement that matches a criminal identity.

KEY TERMS

containment theory
differential association theory
drift theory
interactional theory of delinquency
interactionist perspective
normalization of deviance
operant conditioning
secondary deviation
social control theory
social process theories
techniques of neutralization

DISCUSSION QUESTIONS

1. Social process theories tend to focus on peer and family relationships as key in leading an individual to or away from crime. How important do you think family is compared to peer relationships in influencing criminal involvement?

2. Differential association theory seems very intuitive and based on common sense. Is the theory sufficiently detailed enough to provide a firm understanding of the causes of crime? If so, how? If not, what might be added to theory to make it more powerful?
3. What techniques of neutralization appear to be the most commonly used by offenders? Would you expect the neutralizations of white-collar criminals to be substantially different than those involved in traditional street crime?
4. The involvement variable in Hirschi's social control theory has been shown to be particularly weak. Why do you think this is so? Could the theory be as strong without the concept of involvement?
5. One radical implication of labeling theory is to ignore juvenile delinquency because youths often grow out of crime if they are not labeled "criminal." Is such a policy preferable or even possible given the increasingly strong movement to prosecute children as though they are adults?

ACTIVITIES

1. Sutherland placed a high value on peer relationships and crime. Think about the role your friends have played in your decision to engage in crime or not. Are there any specific moments in time that were particularly poignant in leading you one way or another?
2. Listen to the Dixie Chicks's song "Goodbye Earl," and note all of the different techniques of neutralization vocalized to justify the killing of "Earl." To what extent do the lyrics mirror the main ideas of Sykes and Matza?
3. To better understand Hirschi's social control theory, talk to your parents or legal guardians about how they tried to guide your moral and ethical development. To what extent are their responses interpretable through the Hirschi's variable "belief"?

6

Critical Theories

The lack of good jobs and homelessness are enduring social problems in the United States and in many other countries of the world. Hope that "things will get better" often hinges on the idea that financial security will bring about greater happiness. For the most unfortunate, hope might simply be for a meal or home. Many more dream of a life free from abuse, assault, and neglect. As critical theorists point out, however, forces external to the individual such as gender, economic class, and race have a lot to do with who "makes it" in any given society. Critical criminological theorists are openly critical of social forces that limit opportunities for some groups while expanding them for others.

What distinguishes critical theories of crime from other explanations is their *opposition* to—not just interest in—unequal political, economic, and social structures and relationships. The major forms of critical theories reviewed in this chapter include Marxist, left realism, feminist, postmodernism, peacemaking, and cultural criminology perspectives. Respectively, their critiques are centered on capitalism, stratification and inequality, patriarchy, modernity, war making, and monolithic understandings of crime. Critical theories of crime have roots in general sociological conflict theory.

While the social structural theories reviewed in chapter 4 consider the impact of social and economic inequities on crime, they do so only up to a point. **Conflict theory** goes a step further by seeing society shaped by conflicts among people who have competing self- and group interests. Even though at any time a society may seem to agree on basic values and goals, the existence of scarce resources and the tendency for them to be allocated unequally means that someone (or some group) is benefiting at the expense of someone else. In American society, groups at an overall disadvantage are women, minorities, and the poor. People on the "losing end" may not recognize or admit that their interests are in conflict with the interests of others, when in fact they are. Even though the struggle over scarce resources may be unrecognized or acknowledged, conflict theorists believe it is historic and ubiquitous. It usually consists of a struggle over three related things: money, power, and influence. Those who have more of them try to keep things the way they are; those who have less of them favor change so that they can obtain a bigger share. The groups with wealth, power, and influence are favored in the conflict precisely because those resources put them in a dominant position. It is the "haves" rather than the "have-nots" who make the rules, control the content and flow of ideas and information, and design (and impose) the penalties for nonconformity. Dominance means people are in a position to promote their self-interest, even at the expense of others.

Sometimes the struggle over scarce resources is blatant and bloody, but more often it is subtle and restrained. Conflict theorists point to various factors as part of the complex reasons for the restraint. For example, by controlling ideas and information, the dominant group is able to promote beliefs and values that support the existing order. In this way, the disadvantaged classes in society may develop what Marx and Engels (1947) called "false consciousness": a belief that prevailing social conditions are in their interest, when in fact they are not. Marx and Engels (1947: 39) illustrate how this happens in the case of law. Law is presented to the masses as "the will of the people," and this "juridical illusion" undermines the development of opposition and resistance among the disadvantaged. People are likely to feel uncomfortable challenging a law that they believe reflects public consensus. In reality, law reflects the interests of the ruling class, according to Marx and Engels. In like manner, contemporary feminists theorize that law is not only biased against the poor, but also against women.

A second way that the struggle over scarce resources is kept in check is through the institutionalization of conflict. Special mechanisms such as courts, tribunals, and (in modern times) arbitration and civil rights hearings are set up to settle disputes. Disputes between individuals and groups are often conflicts over the distribution of scarce resources. When institutionalized avenues of settling disputes exist, the underlying struggle tends to be moderated and obscured. Aggrieved parties in the immediate dispute are pacified if not by talk of "justice," then by the emphasis on procedures. Nowhere is this more evident than in the realm of crime, where victims often experience a complete loss of purpose as they face interminable delays and the intricacies of judicial procedure.

The *consensus* or functionalist view sees law and other political arrangements as useful for society as a whole, which justifies their existence. Conflict theorists, on the other hand, see them as useful for the dominant group(s) (i.e., the wealthy, men, and whites), and perhaps even harmful to other groups or to the larger society. Law and politics protect the interests of the powerful, who in turn resist efforts to change them. Before we examine various critical and feminist theories in detail, let's first look at an influential pluralist conflict theory, which is one source of contemporary critical criminology.

TURK'S CONFLICT THEORY

Austin Turk (1966; 1969) has developed a conflict theory of criminality, and his work illustrates many of the points made above. What makes Turk's work distinctive is his emphasis on authority and power relations rather than on economic inequality.

Turk begins by rejecting the conception of crime as behavior, arguing instead that crime is a status acquired when those with authority to create and enforce legal rules (lawmakers, police, prosecuting attorneys, judges) apply those rules to others (the "subjects" in authority relations). He then constructs a theory to explain this process of criminalization. Turk believes that criminology needs a theory "stating the conditions under which cultural and social differences between authorities and subjects will probably result in conflict, the conditions under which criminalization will probably occur in the course of conflict, and the conditions under which the degree of deprivation associated with becoming a criminal will probably be greater or lesser" (1969: 53).

Turk hypothesizes that conflict between groups is most likely when authorities and subjects disagree about a particular activity, but the actions of both groups (social norms) correspond with what they each think ought to happen (cultural norms). For example, if the authorities hold that marijuana use is wrong and refrain from using it themselves, but a group of subjects holds that marijuana use is okay and they use it, then conflict is likely because there is no room for compromise. In such a case, Turk argues, the authorities are likely to resort to coercion in order for their view to prevail. Conflict is least likely when neither authorities nor subjects act in accordance with their beliefs: Neither group is sufficiently committed to a value or belief to make an issue out of it. Other factors can affect the probability of conflict, including the degree to which subjects who resist are organized and the level of their sophistication. Conflict is more likely when norm resisters are poorly organized and unsophisticated.

Given the existence of conflict, the probability of criminalization depends on power differentials between authorities and subjects and on the realism of moves (i.e., tactical skills) employed by opposing parties. Criminalization is more likely when the power difference favors authorities and the moves adopted by resisters are unrealistic. Examples of unrealistic moves are those that: (1) increase the visibility of an attribute or behavior perceived by authorities as offensive; (2) draw attention to additional offensive attributes or violate even more significant norms upheld by authorities; and (3) increase the level of consensus among authorities, for example, by turning opposition to a particular rule into an attack on the whole system; or (4) increase the power differences in favor of the enforcers (Turk, 1969: 72).

Turk's theory has not been tested as much as other theories reviewed in this chapter, but one of the very few empirical studies found considerable support for the notion that poor organization and a lack of sophistication among norm resisters tend to produce conflict. However, the more specific claims of Turk regarding the relative importance of organization and sophistication were not well supported (Greenleaf and Lanza-Kaduce, 1995).

It should be noted that for a number of reasons Turk's theory represents one of the finest examples of theory construction in criminology. Foremost among these issues is the nature of the relationship between those who create, interpret, and enforce legal rules and those who are subject to them. Crime has no objective reality apart from the meanings attached to it, and criminality is an expression of those meanings. As Turk makes clear, the structure of authority relations must be included in a comprehensive theory of criminalization. Turk's theory focuses on authority relations and explains how it is that some people are labeled as criminals. Marxist theorists go further, casting conflicts of authority and criminal labeling within a general theory of political economy having roots in the work of Karl Marx.

MARXIST CRIMINOLOGICAL THEORY

While Karl Marx said little about crime, some criminologists, especially critical criminologists, recognize a substantial debt to this nineteenth-century scholar. Marx believed that a society's mode of economic production—the manner in which relations of production are organized—determines in large part the organization of social relations, the structure of individual and group interaction. Marx (1859: 20–21) put it this way:

> In the social production in which men carry on they enter into definite relations that are indispensable and independent of their will; these relations of production correspond to a definite stage of development of their material powers of production. The totality of these relations of production constitutes the economic structure of a society—the real foundation, on which legal and political superstructures arise and to which definite forms of social consciousness correspond. The mode of production of material life determines the gen-

eral character of the social, political, and spiritual process of life. It is not the consciousness of men that determines their being, but, on the contrary, their social being determines their consciousness.

Under a capitalist mode of production, there are those who own the means of production and those who do not. The former group is known as the *bourgeoisie* and the latter as the *proletariat*. The bourgeoisie, or ruling class, controls the formulation and implementation of moral and legal norms, and even ideas. Both classes are bound in relationship to one another, but this relationship is asymmetrical and exploitive.

This relationship affects law, and by extension, crime. Laws are created by the elite to protect their interests at the expense of the proletariat. However, the image of law promoted to the masses is one that implies democracy and consensus. For example, nearly everyone would agree that killing another without legitimate reason should be criminal. However, what are those legitimate reasons? War? Corporate violations of safety laws that result in worker deaths? Marxists might point out that even presumably simple and well-supported laws may not work in the interests of the have-nots, though they may be perceived to be a representation of the collective will of a society. In this spirit, Marxist scholars have noted:

> The fact is that the label "crime" is not used in America to name all or the worst of the actions that cause misery and suffering to Americans. It is primarily reserved for the dangerous action of the poor (Reiman, 1999: 25).

> [I]t is not the social harms punishable by law which cause the greatest misery in the world. It is the lawful harms, those unpunishable crimes justified and protected by law, the state, the ruling elites that fill the earth with misery, want, strife, conflict, slaughter, and destruction (Tifft and Sullivan, 1980: 9).

Marxist criminology probably hit its high point in the 1970s after many of Marx's early writings were translated to English and made available in the United States. The perspective is still a force in criminology, but not in its original formulation, as its applicability to the study of crime and law has been realized more fully by contemporary critical criminological scholarship. First, however, let's take a look at the classic work of the Dutch criminologist Willem Bonger.

Bonger on Crime and Economic Conditions. As previously discussed, Marx himself wrote little about crime. However, an intellectual follower of Marx, Willem Bonger, applied some of Marx's arguments to crime in capitalistic societies. In *Criminality and Economic Conditions* (published in English in 1916), Bonger observed that capitalistic societies appear to have considerably more crime than do other societies. Furthermore, while capitalism developed, crime rates increased steadily.

Under capitalism, Bonger argued, the characteristic trait of humans is self-interest (egoism). Given the emphasis on profit maximization and competition, and the fact that social relations are class structured and geared to economic exchange, capitalistic societies spawn intraclass and interclass conflicts as individuals seek to survive and prosper. Interclass conflict is one-sided, however, since those who own and control the means of production are in a position to coerce and exploit their less fortunate neighbors. Criminal law, as one instrument of coercion, is used by the ruling class to protect its position and interests. Criminal law "is principally constituted according to the will of" the dominant class, and "hardly any act is punished if it does not injure the interests of the dominant class" (1969: 379, 380). Behavior threatening the interests of the ruling class is designated as criminal.

Since social relations are geared to competition, profit seeking, and the exercise of power, altruism is subordinated to egoistic tendencies. These tendencies lead, in Bonger's view, to a weakening of internal restraint. Both the bourgeoisie and proletariat become prone to crime. The working class is subject to further demoralization, however, because of its inferior exchange position and its exploitation at the hands of the ruling class. "Long working hours and monotonous labor brutalize those who are forced into them; bad housing conditions contribute also to debase the moral sense, as do the uncertainty of existence, and, finally, absolute poverty, the frequent consequence of sickness and unemployment" (1969: 195).

In Bonger's view, economic conditions that induce egoism, coupled with a system of law creation and enforcement controlled by the capitalist class, account for (1) higher crime rates in capitalistic societies than in other societies, (2) crime rates increasing with industrialization, and (3) the working class character of official crime.

A Sampling of Marxist Criminology: 1970s to the Present. It was in the 1970s in the United States that the first systematic Marxist statements on crime began to appear. Many works by Marx (such as the *Economic and Philosophic Manuscripts of 1844*) became widely available to U.S. scholars at this time. Also adding to the appeal of Marx's scholarship was the spirit of sweeping social movements of the 1960s and the accompanying cultural and political changes that occurred at this time. Students, professors, and social activists looked to alternative literatures to help them answer big questions about social problems such as crime, racism, sexism, and war. Marxist theory is still a valuable tool for analyzing the nuances of the political economy's impact on crime and victimization, but much of the contemporary relevance of Marxian criminology is attributable to the work of David Gordon, Richard Quinney, Steven Spitzer, and William Chambliss, whose work we will now review.

According to David Gordon (1971; 1973), most crime is a rational response to the structure of institutions found in capitalistic societies. Crime is "a means of survival in a society within which survival is never assured" (1971: 59). Gordon identifies three types of crime in the United States as the best examples of this rationality: ghetto crime; organized crime; and corporate, or white collar, crime. These types offer a chance at survival, status, and respect in a society geared to competitive forms of social interaction and characterized by substantial inequalities in the distribution of social, economic, and political resources.

Involvement in different types of crime is explained by class position. Those in the upper socioeconomic classes have access to jobs in which paper transactions, large amounts of money, and unobtrusive communication are important features. Illegal opportunities are manifest in the many forms of white-collar crime. Those in the lower classes, especially those who are "raised in poverty," do not have easy access to money and nonviolent means to manipulate it. Accordingly, illegal activities tend to involve taking things by force or physical stealth. Gordon sees duality in American justice in that the state tends to ignore certain kinds of crime, most notably corporate and white-collar crime, and concerns itself "incessantly" with crimes among the poor. According to Gordon, this duality is understandable only if one views the state through the radical perspective. First of all, government in a capitalistic society exists primarily to serve the interests of the capitalist class, and preservation of the system itself is the priority. So long as power and profits are not undermined, the offenses that tend in general to harm members of other classes receive little interest. Second, even though offenses of the poor tend to harm others who are poor, they are collectively viewed as a threat to the stability of the system and the interests of the ruling class. Furthermore, an aggressive lower class is a dangerous class, and the spread of ghetto crime (conveniently identified with African Americans) to other parts of the nation's cities heightens the fears of the affluent classes who are in a position to influence policy. Gordon's critical approach provides a framework for explaining both the status of criminality and the behavior of the criminal (see also Spitzer, 1975).

Richard Quinney, one of the most prolific criminologists in the world, has written on crime from a number of theoretical perspectives, but here we will consider his Marxist theory of crime, first published as *Class, State, and Crime* in 1977. This work is really not a theory of crime causation *per se*, but a call through critique for the use of Marxist theory in the scholarly understanding of law, justice, and crime.

Quinney starts with a number of presuppositions. First, to understand the meaning of crime in capitalist society one must take into account how capitalist economics develop. By this Quinney means that to understand crime in U.S. society, we should have a sense of the historical evolution of political economy and how it instructs our everyday lives and ideas. Second, says Quinney, it is important to get a grasp on how systems of class domination and repression operate for the benefit of the capitalist class through the vehicle of the state. Here Quinney suggests that law is one weapon in the arsenal of the bourgeoisie to exploit the proletariat and to deflect scrutiny from their own harmful actions. Additionally, Quinney writes that ideas about crime and justice are created through human experiences within a capitalist society, and therefore the dominant ideology of crime reflects that bias. Justice, too, is ideological in this sense, as it is constituted through the prism of capitalist logic and interests. Crime itself, according to Quinney, is a manifestation of class struggle as well:

> Much criminal behavior is of a parasitical nature, including burglary, robbery, drug dealing, and hustling of various sorts. . . . the behavior, although pursued out of the need to survive, is a reproduction of the capitalist system (61).

Crimes such as murder, assault, and rape, he continues, often stem from those who are already "brutalized by the conditions of capitalism" (61). The solution to crime, according to Quinney and others working from this perspective, involves a fundamental restructuring of society on socialist principles (Quinney, 1979).

Quinney called criminologists on to the carpet over their role in all of this as well. Quinney viewed uncritical criminologists as tacit agents of the capitalist state, for the discipline of criminology "seeks to control anything that threatens the capitalist system of production and its social relations" (176). What Quinney meant is that by divorcing the study of crime from the study of class domination, criminologists are involved in reproducing the inequalities caused by capitalism. Many mainstream criminologists have taken issue with the claim that they are capitalist patsies because they study crime in traditional ways, but Quinney's claim is defensible from a Marxist point of view; as the old saying goes, "if you are not part of the solution, you are part of the problem" would apply. Indeed, from this perspective, the problem of crime is rooted in capitalism, and thus the study of anything else is uncritical and indirectly supportive of the system. It is therefore part of the problem because it detracts attention from the real issues.

At about the same time Richard Quinney was making his important stance in criminology, another Marxist-inspired conceptualization of crime was offered by William Chambliss (1975). Chambliss, also a highly prodigious criminologist, maintained like Quinney that the state was a tool used by the elite to control the poor and protect their own wealth, status, and privilege. If this wasn't the case, he asked, how is it that the wrongs committed by the rich, which represent just as much of a threat if not greater than traditional street crimes in terms of injury, are either not defined as criminal or are not prosecuted and punished? While in today's world it may seem there that there is more attention paid to elite crime by both the public and the state (e.g., publicity surrounding the Enron fiasco), there is hardly equity in enforcement and punishment. This is not to say that traditional street crimes such as murder and robbery should not be taken seriously, but rather if an important rationale for criminalization and punishment is the seriousness of injury, white-collar crimes (including state crimes like genocide, illegal war, and repression) must also be taken seriously. Chambliss maintained that crimes in the suites are often off the radar screen because of the elite's grip on power and their influence on those who control the creation and enforcement of law. Unless the proletariat were to achieve class consciousness—a Marxian term for the crystallization of thought by the proletariat that capitalism must end—the crimes of the elite will escape proper scrutiny. More directly, Chambliss argued that:

- Acts are criminal because it is in the interests of the ruling class to so define them.
- The lower classes are labeled criminal and the bourgeoisie is not because the bourgeoisie's control of the means of production gives them control of the state and law enforcement as well.
- Socialist and capitalist societies should have significantly different crime rates since class conflict will be less in socialist societies.

In a similar vein, Steven Spitzer (1975: 352) has maintained that people become candidates for formal social control in a capitalist society when they "disturb, hinder, or call into question" any of the following:

- capitalist modes of appropriating the product of human labor (theft)
- the social conditions under which capitalist production takes place (those unable or unwilling to perform labor)
- patterns of distribution and consumption in capitalist society (drug use)
- the process of socialization for productive and nonproductive roles (youths who refuse schooling or traditional family life)
- the ideology that supports the functioning of capitalist society (revolutionaries and other political deviants)

Because there has never been a genuine socialist society that would meet Marx's definition, it is difficult to gauge the validity of Chambliss's and Quinney's assertions that crime will be lower in communist societies. However, elements of Chambliss's first two points identified above are more amenable to empirical scrutiny, and studies based on these points have found that some but clearly not all lawmaking and law enforcement is as classist as theory suggests. In fact, later modifications of the theory by Chambliss and others clearly leaves room for such possibilities. Spitzer's theory also has both strengths and weaknesses, as some deviance is defined as such by authorities because it threatens the principles of the economic system, but the extent to which the laws are passed with this specific intent on the part of the bourgeoisie is questionable.

This points to one of the problems with early efforts in Marxist criminology: their overly instrumentalist theme. **Instrumental Marxism**, which has fallen out of favor in critical criminological circles, grants too much importance to the direct relationship between the economy and crime. The theorized supremacy of economics results in overgeneralization, as it is now commonly understood that rather than conscious capitalist interests dictating the whole content of law and the working of the criminal justice system, other interests and actors shape institutions and social structures such as criminal justice and law. Another major problem with the instrumentalist treatment of the structural sources of crime is its vision of the ruling class itself. Sometimes the image conjured up is of a small band of powerful individuals in collusion with one another to determine the destinies of all. Some early Marxists also portrayed those whose criminal actions were political as victimized prisoners of circumstance whose crimes were not their responsibility. A final tension in instrumental Marxist theory can be identified. Some adherents to the perspective are against short-term reforms of the criminal justice system because such actions would undermine the militant opposition necessary for a socialist revolution. This matter has been a source of tension between critical criminologists, as less radical scholars have argued that even small change is better than nothing. Left realists (discussed later) have grounded their integrative theory with specific attention to this issue.

As the years passed, Marxist criminology, as many theories have, began to develop into more sophisticated sets of ideas about crime and law. David Greenberg (1977), for example, developed an explanation of juvenile delinquency that focused on teenagers' exclusion from the labor market. Greenberg noted that since children and teenagers do not normally engage in "serious work," their ability to achieve status through money is difficult. Everyone knows that it is difficult if not impossible for teens to work at a place like McDonald's while in high school and make the rent. Some parents, of course, neither have the means nor the desire to buy their children all the clothes, toys, concert tickets, and cars that youths might want. Youths, then, because they are not capable of buying these items themselves, might turn to delinquency (such as theft) to upgrade their lifestyle or status. By showing how the lack of participation in a capitalist labor market might be connected to crime, Greenberg's theory adds some explanatory power to Marxist criminological theory, as many of the explanations for crime causation by earlier Marxist criminologists were somewhat crude.

Mark Colvin and John Pauly developed another influential Marxist theory of juvenile delinquency in 1983. Juvenile delinquency, they argued,

Box 6.1. Challenging Inequality through Music: The Lyrics of Public Enemy and Rage against the Machine

Public Enemy and the now defunct band Rage against the Machine were among the most commercially successful music groups to write songs that included explicit critiques of racial and economic inequality in the United States. In a study of Rage against the Machine lyrics, Finley (2002) notes that several critical criminological themes are represented in the group's lyrics, including the ideas that (a) capitalism is a source of crime, (b) crimes of the powerful are more harmful than those of the poor, and (c) the media transmits racist and classist messages about crime.

In the song "Know Your Enemy," Rage against the Machine criticizes the culture of capitalism, especially in the educational system that forces students to conform and submit to authority figures who may not themselves be sources of accurate knowledge. A similar attack on the culture of educational and political institutions in the United States is found in the lyrics to "Take the Power Back," which specifically criticizes ethnocentrism and the purified history lessons that are taught in schools. A reading of Public Enemy lyrics, particularly those from the *Fear of a Black Planet* album, also reveals the presence of critical criminological themes, especially those that are attentive to the intersection of race and class. One example of this is found in the lyrics to "Burn Hollywood, Burn," which excoriates the media's portrayal of urban blacks.

While early forms of critical criminology were silent on the issue of race (and gender), it has become increasingly attentive to the intersections of the various forms of inequality under capitalism. This is evidenced not only in individual scholarly contributions and anthologies (e.g., Barak, Flavin, and Leighton, 2001; Ross, 2009; Schwartz and Milanovic, 2000) but also by the growing collaborative efforts between the American Society of Criminology's divisions on Women and Crime, People of Color and Crime, and Critical Criminology.

begins with parenting. While this does not seem all that Marxist, they argued that parenting styles are influenced by relationships and experiences at work. First, many delinquents come from working-class families, where the breadwinners are employed in "dead end" jobs (so-called Fraction I jobs) and are subject to coercion, threats, and the possibility of dismissal at any time. Such jobs include nonunionized industrial, textile, and agricultural work. Workers in this category tend to be highly alienated from their jobs, and this tends to carry over at home. Such parents are likelier to be punitive (sometimes physically), inconsistent with discipline, and generally more abusive than parents employed in better jobs. As a result of this type of parenting, children are more likely to become alienated from their parents, and that leads to a greater likelihood of alienation at school and association with other alienated peers. Along with the disadvantages of their class position, the table then becomes set for the formulation of delinquent attitudes and behavior. Bohm (1998) has suggested that more workers today are employed in Fraction I jobs, and if Colvin and Pauly's theory is correct, we would expect to see higher rates of alienation and consequently criminal violence by juveniles. Colvin and Pauly's theory was a major contribution to critical criminology at the time, as it showed, like Greenberg's, that both cultural forces and insights from other theories of crime can be integrated into Marxist theory to form a potentially more valuable explanation of crime.

Marxist criminology matured immensely in the 1990s. Perhaps the best illustrations of this change are recent socialist feminist theories (discussed later) and Chambliss's **structural contradictions theory** (Chambliss and Zatz, 1993). Let's examine the latter now.

Rejecting theories (and to some extent his earlier work) that maintained that the capitalist mode of production exclusively determines law, and by implication crime, the new theory posits that every society attempts to resolve conflicts and dilemmas caused by fundamental contradictions. The creation of law, then, is more complicated than the ruling class plotting against the interests of the working class (see figure 6.1). The basic contradiction within capitalism is between labor and capital, and it

> produces conflicts between workers and capitalists, and for the state it creates a set of dilemmas. Should the state represent only the interests of capitalists, the conflicts will increase in intensity, with workers pitted against the state. . . . Were the state to side with the workers . . . the system would likewise collapse and a new social order would have to be constructed. Faced with this dilemma, officials of the state attempt to resolve the conflict by passing laws, some which represent the interests of capitalists and some the interests of workers (Chambliss and Zatz, 1993: 10).

This refinement of Marxist theory allows for the idea that the state has *relative autonomy* from the capitalist class. While elite interests surely shape law, they do not exclusively instruct it. Consider the example of white-collar crime. A major goal of the capitalist state has been to promote capital accumulation (corporate money making). However, there is quite a bit of regulation over business as well. Barnett (1981: 7) has argued that while this is true, the state's regulatory function "must not be so severe as to diminish substantially the contribution of large corporations to growth in output and employment." So, from this structural—rather than instrumental—Marxist view, while state regulatory agencies have been created to help protect workers (The Occupational Safety and Health Administration), the environment (The Environmental Protection Agency), and consumers (The Consumer Product Safety Commission), they cannot do anything to seriously compro-

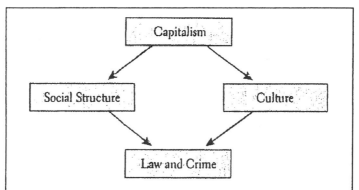

Instrumental Marxist Approach: Capitalism and capitalist interests determine the particular form of institutions, organizations, ideology, and social processes. Law is used to control the proletariat and to shield the crimes of the bourgeoisie.

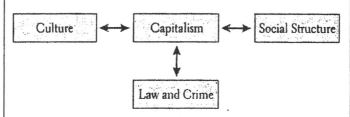

Structural Marxist Approach: Capitalism and capitalist interests shape institutions, organizations, ideology, and social processes, which then further shape the political economy of capitalism. Law and crime are strongly influenced by the interests of the economy, not simply elites conspiring to control the proletariat.

For in depth discussions of these perspectives, see Raymond J. Michalowski (1985) and William Chambliss and Marjorie Zatz (1993).

Figure 6.1. Instrumental and Structural Marxist Theories

mise an industry's basic contributions to the functional requirements of the economy (Matthews and Kauzlarich, 2000). While regulatory agencies can help protect the environment and make workplaces and commodities safer, the laws and regulations will never be so strong as to disable business from the ability to reap profits. This is seen as problematic by Marxists, as the main motivation of corporate crime can be linked to the desire to maximize profits (Friedrichs, 2009). Ultimately laws governing business will not be created or enforced if they seriously compromise principles designed to facilitate capitalist accumulation. In fact, to some Marxists, their very existence increases false consciousness, as the illusion of protection is enhanced when the "front" put up by the state seems legitimate on the surface (Pearce and Tombs, 1998).

Research by Michalowski and Carlson (1999) illustrates the enduring value of the Marxist criminology. The authors have shown that unemployment rates and new court admissions to prison can be linked to swings and qualitative changes in the U.S. economy. These changes include shifts in the productive dimension of the overall economy, the workforce, and various state interventions. Thus, periods characterized by high unemployment, deteriorating job quality, low social-welfare benefits, and a growing surplus population of young, disaffected, unemployed men will generate a greater reliance on punitive strategies than other periods in time (Michalowski and Carlson, 1999: 227). In sum, the study illustrates how discrete changes in capitalist economies affect aggregate levels of crime.

LEFT REALISM

Several years ago British criminologists Jock Young and Roger Matthews started to systematically critique some radical Marxist criminological theories. Young and Matthews proposed that the "left idealism" of the radical perspective be replaced by "**left realism**." According to Young (1986; 1997), left idealism has tended to downplay the severity of crime and the fact that it is most often intraclass and intraracial. As Matthews (2004: 9) explains:

> While not ignoring crimes of the powerful, new left realists have taken the position that the effects of street crime are both serious and real, that the criminal class is not revolutionary, and that critical (i.e., Marxian, conflict, feminist, and radical) criminologists must pay attention to it. What ties new left realism to Marxian criminology, however, is its emphasis on understanding crime within the larger political economy.

In addition, Young charges that left idealism has failed to build on past theories of criminal etiology and in consequence has failed in its theoretical mission to explain crime. For example, Young writes:

> there is no evidence that absolute deprivation (e.g., unemployment, lack of schooling, poor housing, and so forth) leads automatically to crime. Realist criminology points to relative deprivation in certain conditions as being the major causes of crime; i.e., when people experience a level of unfairness in their allocation of resources and utilize individualistic means to attempt to right this condition. . . . To say that poverty in the present period breeds crime

is not to say that all poor people are criminals. Far from it: most poor people are perfectly honest and many wealthy people commit crimes. Rather, it is to say that the rate of crime is higher in certain parts of society under certain conditions (Young, 1997: 30–31).

Young (1986: 25) believes that the central tasks of radical or critical criminology still remain: "to create an adequate explanation of crime, victimization, and the reaction of the state." The alternative realist criminology deals with that agenda while uncovering the reality of crime, "its origins, its nature, and its impact" (Young, 1986: 21). Official data and research is not rejected out of hand, nor will current definitions of crimes and their severity constrain the realist's search for this reality (Matthews, 1986: 8). Left realism emphasizes going behind appearances that pass as reality. A "central tension" in left realism is working both "in" and "against" the state. The question is this: How can the victimization and suffering of crime, especially among the lower classes, be reduced without extending the coercive and bureaucratic apparatus of the state? (Dekeseredy, Alvi, Schwartz, and Tomasceski, 2003; Matthews, 1986: 14).

Like other social structural perspectives, one of the central ideas of realist criminology leads to the lower classes. But rather than looking there only for offenders, the realists see the lower class as a victim of crime "from all sides" (Young, 1986: 23). The lower class generally, and racial minorities in particular, are doubly vulnerable to crime because they are victims of predatory street crimes as well as white-collar crimes: They are victims of the poor and the powerful (Young, 1997; 2000).

In the tradition of both left realism and strain theory, Elliott Currie (1997) has theorized about crime in so-called *market societies*. These types of societies (e.g., the United States and Great Britain) have significant economic inequality as well as a scarcity of stable and rewarding jobs. Market societies are characterized by the pursuit of personal economic gain in all facets of life. This one-dimensional motivation, Currie argues, comes at the expense of people's interest and ability to invest in powerful social, cultural, and human forces (so-called social capital), which are known to be negatively related to violence in any given society. In such societies, people have little or marginal interest in furthering their relationships with others outside their immediate group, such as the larger community or neighborhoods.

According to Currie (1997), market societies are criminogenic—they provide fertile grounds for crime to flourish—in a number of ways. First, while market economies like the United States can produce lots of jobs, many are low paying and without benefits. So, even though the unemployment rate in the United States is currently low, many people are working very hard for very little. This continues to produce economic and social inequalities that positively correlate with the overall crime rate. Second, market societies tend to have limited formal and informal social supports.

For example, the strains between family and work are profound for many working people. There is little formal support by employers or the government to provide paid parental leaves, quality universal health care, or to do something about the disintegration of neighborhoods and communities. Third, market societies often place "competition and consumption over the values of community, contribution, and work" (Currie, 1997: 161). We should therefore expect that in a "dog-eat-dog" world, people will care less about others' well-being, and not caring about other people makes it easier to victimize them. Fourth, Currie believes that it is possible that the amount of firearm violence in the United States could be reduced with more sensible gun regulation. The United States leads the advanced industrialized world in the rate of gun crime and violence—it also has the weakest national regulations on the sale and possession of guns. Finally, Currie notes that at least in the United States, the lack of alternative political discussion leads people to believe that there is nothing that can be done about social problems like crime. Crime is thus easily divorced from its larger structural roots, which in turn lessens people's ability to envision a safer and less violent society.

Left realism is surely here to stay, for it provides a richer approach to understanding the links between crime and the economy than traditional Marxist theories. In fact, the approach may soon be as recognizable as any

---

Box 6.2.   Policy Proposals of Left Realism

Left realist criminological theory has a number of clear policy implications, some of which are similar to those of Merton's strain theory (reviewed in chapter 4). Which of the following left realist proposals do you think have a good chance to reduce crime?

- Job creation and training programs
- A higher minimum wage
- Government-sponsored day care
- Housing assistance
- Teaching of entrepreneurial skills in high school
- Linking school, business, and state services
- Creating universal health care

As one of the preeminent left realists of our time notes, the perspective emphasizes the importance of making changes in the area of *social policy* more than criminal justice policy (Walter Dekeseredy and Barbara Perry, 2006; Dekeseredy et al., 2003). Do you agree?

Source: Dekeseredy (2004).

other criminological theory discussed in this text, especially given its clear practical implications (see box 6.2).

FEMINIST THEORIES OF CRIME

Feminist theory has challenged many of the biases of traditional academic disciplines, including criminology. For years criminology was very androcentric, as criminologists were mostly males studying males, either ignoring women altogether, stereotyping them, or otherwise downplaying their importance. While there are many different forms of **feminist criminology** (e.g., liberal socialist and radical) at the most basic level feminism in criminology is about centering gender and its relationship to lawmaking, lawbreaking, and reactions to crime (Iadicola and Shupe, 1998: 78; Miller, 2003). Several years ago Kathleen Daly and Meda Chesney-Lind (1988: 108) published a landmark paper on feminism and criminology in which they identified five elements of feminist thought that distinguish it from other forms of social and political perspectives. These are:

1. Gender is not a natural fact but a complex social, historical, and cultural product.
2. Gender and gender relations order social life and social institutions in fundamental ways.
3. Gender relations and constructs of masculinity and femininity are not symmetrical but are based on an organizing principle of men's superiority and social and political economic dominance over women.
4. Systems of knowledge reflect men's views of the natural and social world.
5. Women should be at the center of intellectual inquiry, not peripheral, invisible, or appendages to men.

Taken together, these points suggest that a small physiological difference at birth between males and females (that is, our sex) becomes the basis for drastically different expectations, opportunities, and socialization throughout the life course. Open almost any introductory sociology textbook and read the chapter on gender. There you will find overwhelming evidence of the significance of (a) gender role socialization (the teaching of girls to be feminine and boys to be masculine) and (b) gender inequality (the differences in political, social, and economic power, authority, and status among men and women). There is simply little doubt that in aggregate, men and women have very different social statuses.

Criminologists who take gender seriously use these larger sociological realities to help understand issues such as (a) different offending rates,

(b) differential involvement in types of crime, (c) police, prosecutorial, and judicial discretion in criminal justice, (d) institutional discrimination against women in criminal justice, and (e) differential victimization (Flavin, 1998; Miller, 2003; Stanko, 1995). This last area has played a key role in the development of criminological research and theory on domestic assault, sexual assault, child maltreatment, pornography, and prostitution. While there is considerable debate among criminologists about the impact of feminism on criminology more generally (Rafter and Heidensohn, 1997), there is little question that feminist criminology is a growing area of scholarship, and in our view, it makes considerable contributions to the understanding of crime.

There are two issues that lie at the heart of the feminist challenge to theoretical criminology: (1) whether traditional theories of crime apply to girls and women, and (2) why women offend significantly less than men (Miller, 2003). Regarding the first, it is important to examine the question of whether interactions and relationships with friends and family are qualitatively different for boys and girls. For example, research has shown that parents tend to be more controlling in some aspects of their daughters' lives but not their sons'. Instead of "control" being a gender-neutral variable, it could be that girls are subject to different forms of control, say in the monitoring of physical appearances and sex. If parents exercise control and tolerance in gendered ways, a seemingly objective measure of the social bond, such as the quality or time of "parental interaction," may be measuring different things for boys than girls. Further, how do we know there are not significant variations in the causes of offending within gender categories? To explore this question, feminist criminologists are working on new ways to understand the intersections of race and class with gender (Miller, 2004).

The second issue relates to what is known as the gender-ratio problem. The concern here is rooted in the fact that official statistics and other measures of crime indicate that men and boys are much more involved in criminal activity than girls and women. From a feminist perspective, any legitimate theory of crime must be able to address this relationship, as it is among the more universal facts about crime. We turn to one such theory now.

Gender Class Theory. As we have seen, theories of crime that focus on class relations and economic inequality owe a heavy debt to Marx and Engels. However, some criminologists believe that an adequate theory of crime requires the incorporation of a second aspect of social structure, what Messerschmidt (1986) calls *relations of reproduction.* "[I]n all societies," Messerschmidt writes, "people need to reproduce, socialize, and maintain the species. Consequently, people organize into relations of reproduction to satisfy these needs" (1986: ix).

From a socialist feminist perspective, in capitalist societies such as the United States "relations of reproduction take the form of patriarchal gender relations, in which the male gender appropriates the labor power and controls the sexuality of the female gender" (Messerschmidt 1986: ix–x). However, the domination of women as a group by men as a group is intertwined with class domination: "Women labor in both the market and the home, and suffer masculine dominance in each. But in addition, their experience in both realms is determined by their class" (1986: xi). In production and in reproduction, behavior is shaped by power relations that cut across both spheres. In the United States, "we do not simply live in a 'capitalist' society, but rather a 'patriarchal capitalist' society" (Messerschmidt, 1986: 35). One can therefore distinguish two basic groups: "a powerless group, comprising women and the working class, and a powerful group, made up of men and the capitalist class" (1986: 41).

Messerschmidt endeavored to show how interlocking class and gender relations affect both criminal behavior and its control. For example, the well-documented gap between female rates of serious crime (which are low) and male rates (which are high)—the so-called gender ratio problem we discussed above (Daly and Chesney-Lind, 1988: 119; see also Chesney-Lind and Shelden, 1992: 7–28 and Miller, 2003)—is explained in terms of the lack of female opportunities for legitimate and illegitimate activities that results from the fact that women are subordinate, "and therefore less powerful in economic, religious, political, and military institutions" (Messerschmidt, 1986: 43). On the other hand, males have power, which provides them with far more opportunities to commit crime. When class is brought into the picture, the argument is this: Lower-class males have less power, hence commit less crime, than capitalist and middle-class males, but in all social classes, males are more powerful than females. "Their powerful position allows some men to engage in crimes specifically as men to maintain their dominant position" (Messerschmidt, 1986: 45). Rape and wife beating are examples.

While socialist feminist theories of crime can be criticized for their lack of attention to race, the theory offers a more sophisticated way to think about the relationship between gender and class and how both operate to structure the nature and extent of crime and victimization.

Power control theory. John Hagan and his colleagues have developed what has become known as the *power control theory* of crime, which attempts to explain gender differences in offending. The theory focuses on the relations of girls and boys to their parents and argues that in patriarchal (male-dominated) families, male delinquency will be greater because parents encourage, support, and socialize boys into masculine roles and behaviors. Girls in patriarchal families, however, commit less crime because they are more subject to regulation by their parents and are encouraged to adopt more feminine roles and behaviors. On the other hand, girls in more egalitarian families, where each parent has equal power and status, are more likely to engage in delinquency because fewer controls are exercised over her behavior. In sum, the theory holds that: As women enter the paid labor force and assume more powerful positions in the workplace, mothers, and by extension their daughters, might become freer and less controlled. Thus, daughters could become more like sons in their willingness to take risks and their involvement in delinquency (McCarthy, Hagan, and Woodward, 1999: 762).

What makes Messerschmidt's and Hagan's work important is its improvement over other critical theories that focus on only economic inequality, and particularly its specification of how class and gender together affect crime. Even so, the approaches, specifically Hagan's, are not without critics. Meda Chesney-Lind (1987), for example, objects that Hagan's work represents a "not-so-subtle variation" of the now discredited view that "liberated" females commit more crime. The *liberal feminist* theory of crime to which Chesney-Lind is referring to here maintains that women's involvement in crime is linked to their increased opportunities in society, especially in the workplace. The argument goes like this: The women's liberation movement has pushed for equality between the sexes. The result, Adler (1975) and Simon (1975) suggested, has been a convergence of gender roles as many of the experiences and opportunities previously reserved for males (and a few "lucky" females) are open to more and more females. In Adler's terms, a "virilization" of women has taken place, and the masculine female will become less distinguishable from her male counterpart in all areas of life, including crime. The changes, because they affect home life and the socialization process, presumably will filter down to young girls. This **liberation/opportunity theory** predicts that the crime rates of women and girls will increase and broaden. Under empirical scrutiny this theory has been shown to be weak. This is partly due to the fact that females are still more likely to hold low-paying jobs that are often auxiliary to the "more important" and better-paying jobs of men. Some have suggested that many women are actually *less free* today than they were forty years ago. They are expected to contribute to family income, and yet child care facilities are woefully inadequate. This is particularly burdensome on young single mothers, many of whom are teenagers (Morris, 1987: 72).

Hagan and his colleagues have recognized the merit of such criticism by Chesney-Lind and have pointed out in a test of a revised power control theory that there is a "further possibility that changes in women's work and family experiences might affect their relationships with their sons and their sons' fathers, thus altering, and perhaps diminishing delinquency among males" (McCarthy, Hagan, and Woodward, 1999: 761). This richer, more dynamic power control theory has been to some extent empirically supported, and the revised power control theory now awaits further test.

A Sampling of Feminist Works. There are hundreds, perhaps thousands, of feminist studies and tests of theories in criminology. As with our review of Marxist criminological theories, however, we can only provide a snapshot of these works. Let's review a few that illustrate the continuing value of contemporary feminist scholarship in criminology.

Jody Miller (1998) has studied the similarities and differences between men and women robbers. Based on interview data from St. Louis, Miller found that while the *motivations* for engaging in robbery for men and women were similar, the *accomplishment* of robbery was very different. She found that (a) women robbers targeted female victims more than men, and (b) some of the women robbers used men's perceptions of women as weak and sexually available to facilitate robbing males. These differences suggest that women who commit violent crimes may do so quite differently than men because of the gendered nature of their environment, wherein "the differences that emerge reflect practical choices made in the context of a gender-stratified environment, one in which, on the whole, men are perceived as strong and women are perceived as weak" (Miller, 1998: 60–61). Other research by Miller on girls and gangs also suggests similar social processes and structures at work (Miller, 1998b). In a different vein, Lisa Maher (1997) has found evidence that women who engage in violent crime often do so to protect or defend themselves. While Miller (1998) found that the motivations for men and women to commit robbery were similar, Maher found that women often "vicced" (robbed) male clients in part because of their increased economic marginalization and vulnerability to abuse and assault on the street. Women, then, according to Maher, can clearly have different motivations than men for engaging in violent crime.

A study of the impact of gender on residential burglars by Mullins and Wright (2003) has found further evidence of this. Regardless of gender, the majority of the burglars indicated that they stole money and other items to enhance a "party" lifestyle (i.e., buying drugs, alcohol, fancy clothes, and jewelry). However, women were far more likely to report that the money gained from the burglaries would be in some way used to take care of their children. Consider the following statement:

> I needed money, cause I needed a roof over my head, food to eat, things for my baby . . . cause I needed diapers and I was broke and, you know, my hours had been cut and I didn't have the money to pay rent plus to get the baby what it needed. You know, it's gonna be cold soon, I need winter clothes for my kid.

Men rarely mentioned such problems.

Another interesting type of feminist criminological theory has developed around the relationship between masculinities and crime. Led by James

Messerschmidt (1994; 2000: 6), **structured action theory** "emphasizes the construction of gender as a situated social and interactional accomplishment. . . . Gender grows out of social practices in specific social structural settings and serves to inform such practices in reciprocal relation." Essentially, the theory suggests that when men "do" crime or violence, they are oftentimes acting out a role within a specific social context that can be related to the presentation of masculinity.

But this performance of masculinity is relative and intermittent. Obvious affronts to a boy's or man's masculinity are called *masculinity challenges*, and it is these things, such as insults and threats to a boy or man, which can give rise to the motivation to violent behavior or masculine social action (Messerschmidt, 2000). However, many threats to masculinity may not result in violent behavior.

Using structured action theory to help understand the identities of nine boys, Messerschmidt (2000: 139) notes that each of the boys, and all males presumably, construct or "do" gender differently. The difficult part is identifying who is most at risk and how to promote a "democratic manhood" in which men and boys separate violence, authority, and domination from being masculine. Closing this section with the words of Messerschmidt (1997: 185) seems appropriate. His take on the future directions of feminist criminology is consistent with ours:

> rather than conceptualizing gendered crime simplistically in terms of, for example, males commit violence and females commit theft, new directions in feminist theory enable us to explore which males and which females commit which crimes, and in which social situations.

Indeed, it is quite fair to say that criminology can only benefit from this type of analysis.

POSTMODERN CRIMINOLOGY

Like other critical criminologies, postmodern theories of crime are oppositional, only for this perspective the opposition is to modernity, or more specifically, privileged discourses (i.e., writing and speaking by the more powerful members of society) that drown out and marginalize the less powerful in society. Grounded in a critique of the notion that rationality, reason, science, and technology lead to progress (as implied by Enlightenment-era thought) **postmodern criminology** has its intellectual roots in the writings of French scholars such as Lacan, Baudrilland, Foucault, and Lyotard, whose work remains largely unread by most criminologists, even by many critical criminologists. Postmodernism openly questions conventional ideas about the value of science in explaining crime and posits that the world is chaotic and unpredictable (Ferrell, 1998; Henry and Milovanovic, 2003). According to Arrigo (2004), there are three themes of the postmodernist perspective: (1) the importance of language, (2) the notion of partial knowledge and provisional truth, and (3) deconstruction, difference, and possibility. Let us consider each of these in turn.

Criminological postmodernism sensitizes us to the power of words, especially the so-called crime speak and how the use of language is linked to how we think about and define the supposed "being" of crime and justice (Arrigo, 1998; Henry and Milovanovic, 1996; 1999). For example, a postmodern *constitutive theory* of crime offered by Arrigo (1998: 56) maintains that:

- Language is never neutral. It is encoded with multiple desires and multiple ways of knowing.
- Certain conversations about crime are valued and esteemed over others. Crime talk provides one accented or anchored representation of reality.
- There is an inherent problem when crime talk signs are reduced to perpetuate conventional criminological meanings . . . this semiotic cleansing of being . . . denies . . . the possibility for emerging alternative or replacement narratives on crime, on criminal behavior, and on the criminal law.
- Theories of crime [are the] product of coterminous forces, the subject in process and economic conditions that give rise to notions of crime.

While postmodern criminology has yet to make a significant impact on the discipline of criminology as a whole, it clearly raises important questions such as "how do we know what we think we know?" This is the second important theme of the perspective, and perhaps the most powerful. Philosophically speaking, truth is not absolute, nor is it something that can ever really exist on its own. A simple way to think about it is by picturing all of the different situations that people find themselves in as they make decisions about their lives.

While there surely may be shared statuses (e.g., race, educational level, and gender), human beings are infinitely different and, from the postmodern perspective, there is no compelling reason to assume that their behavior has the same universal cause. Lyotard (1984: 82) even goes so far as to "wage war on totality," the so-called metanarrative of grand social theories.

Postmodernist opposition to general or macro level theories of crime also stems from the idea that some "texts" or "discourses" (e.g., discussions, images) of crime are given more credence than others for no other reason than they come from people in a position of power to be heard. Such texts should be deconstructed to reveal the interests that guide them, which may, for example, be racist, sexist, or economic. This dismantling of dominant understandings of crime leaves room for the creation of *replacement discourses*, stories that have been neglected or dismissed not because they are necessarily inaccurate, but because they do not fit into the dominant paradigm. As Henry and Milovanovic (2003: 67) note, replacement discourse "is designed to displace harmful moments in the exercise of power with discourses that tell different stories about the world." An example would be busting myths about crime being primarily committed by the underclass and minorities (which would be one logical conclusion if official government statistics are the primary source of data) by placing narratives from workers and consumers victimized by wealthy corporations into the story of crime.

PEACEMAKING CRIMINOLOGY

Critical criminology has given rise to what is known as **peacemaking criminology**, a perspective that sees crime and suffering as part of the larger problem of domination caused by the unequal distribution of power in society. The perspective shares much in common with the nonviolent philosophies articulated by thinkers such as Jane Addams, Dr. Martin Luther King Jr., and Gandhi. Some peacemaking criminologists credit Zen Buddhism and Quakerism as inspirations as well (Quinney, 1991). First developed in 1991 by Richard Quinney and Hal Pepinsky, the perspective sees human existence as being characterized by suffering; crime is a most vivid example of this. Through compassion and genuine care for ourselves and others, it is maintained, the suffering can end as personal and collective awareness grows. Peacemaking criminology is therefore a criminology of "compassion and service" that seeks to eliminate suffering and therefore all crime (Quinney, 1991: x). This is done through working for peace at all levels of social and personal life.

Peacemaking criminologists see that much of criminal justice is geared toward "war making." Of course this is not a particularly novel observation, as the phrase "war on crime" is well integrated into the common vernacular in the United States. The use of the term *war* assumes that there is an enemy. The word also implies that violence is an acceptable way to resolve problems. Peacemaking criminologists, however, subscribe to the view that violence begets violence, and that war making is the least effective way to bring about justice and healing for the individual, self, and society. More specifically, violent responses to suffering undermine the ability of victims, offenders, and communities to communicate and cooperate. As Pepinsky (1999: 69) explains:

People cannot talk, listen together, and fight one another at the same time. Peacemaking is a matter of injecting doses of conversation into our social space—conversation that embraces the greatest victims and the most powerful oppressors of the moment at the same time. The sooner dialogue begins, the less likely explosive and violent relations will develop. The sooner the dialogue commences, the sooner power imbalances will be mediated, and the sooner peace will be made.

While peacemaking criminology is regarded by some as too philosophical or even metaphysical, John Fuller (2004) has identified some basic principles of the perspective that are more amenable to practice in the day-to-day criminal justice context, and perhaps life more generally:

1. *Nonviolence* (force, especially the physical variety, is counterproductive)
2. *Social justice* (fairness and equality in all aspects of social policy and social structure)
3. *Inclusion* (all stakeholders should participate in the process)
4. *Correct means* (no coercion or discrimination)
5. *Comparable knowledge* (everyone should know what's going on)
6. *Categorical imperative* (act as though it was universal law; do no harm)

As you can see, peacemaking criminology is not just theoretical, but can be applied to a number of real-life situations both in and outside of the criminal justice system. One such one way that peacemaking criminology is practiced in criminal justice is through victim-offender reconciliation programs, where a trained mediator oversees face-to-face meetings between the offender and victim. Now a fairly common practice in the United States and Australia, the idea here is that the offender is placed in the situation of actually thinking about how his/her actions have affected others. Studies have shown that victims often feel some sense of catharsis in the process, and offenders, often for the first time, are confronted with the victim's reaction to the crime. Unlike the traditional model of criminal justice where there is little to no interaction between the main participants in a crime, the hope is that "victims and offenders are able to develop creative and long-lasting resolutions to their difficulties" (Fuller, 2004). Another way that peacemaking criminology can be put into practice is through family group conferencing in the juvenile justice system, where the offender's and victim's family members discuss how the crime has impacted their lives. As with all forms of restorative justice, the hope is that the wounds from crime can be healed through genuine dialogue designed to promote forgiveness, introspection, and change.

CULTURAL CRIMINOLOGY

Over the last fifteen years a fresh perspective on crime and deviance has developed from the work of Jeff Ferrell (1995; 1999) and other scholars that challenges and moves beyond other critical theories of crime. Known as **cultural criminology**, this school of thought views crime and deviance, and the reactions to them, as dynamic and ever-changing processes linked to creating and maintaining meaning through resistance, power, and reactions to everyday conflict and dilemmas (see Ferrell, Hayward, and Young, 2008; Hayward, 2003). Unlike structural theories of crime, cultural criminology does not maintain that crime and deviance, or the reaction to them, are caused by any *one* particular social structural force (such as capitalism for Marxists or patriarchy for feminists). Rather, cultural criminologists see crime and deviance as activities constructed by individuals and groups in their everyday lives as a response to the context (both immediate and distant) in which they live and the meaning the acts have for their lives in a situated moment of time. Borrowing from cultural theories such as interactionism, labeling, and to some extent subculture explanations of crime, cultural criminologists are interested in explaining a wide range of crimes, and reactions to them, but have principally written on acts of resistance such as vandalism, stylistic crime in art and music, illegal motorcycle racing, graffiti, and some forms of youth violence, although more recent scholarship has also examined terrorism, genocide, and corporate crime (Muzzatti, 2006). Just as critical to the perspective is how power and inequality impact rule-making, law enforcement, and media images of crime. The perspective includes serious consideration of how larger structural forces such as the economy and shifts in politics and technology affect crime, both in the development of deviant or criminal labels and in the performance of norm violation. Cultural criminology is a broad theoretical perspective which has certain advantages over other critical theories because it is highly integrative and is concerned with both rule development and the violations of rules (not just one or the other, as is the case with most theories of crime).

One of the many unique features of cultural criminology is its appreciation of the role of boredom, the search for excitement, thrills, and risk-taking in crime. Extending Katz's (1988) work on sensual attractions to crime (reviewed in chapter 7), scholars such as Ferrell (2004), Presdee (2000), and Lyng (1990) have analyzed how resistance to bureaucracy, irrational rules, social control, authority, and quite simply the banality of everyday life, can provide the grounds for rule-breaking and risk-taking in a variety of forms. Presdee (2000: 47) has argued that crime can be understood as "carnival," which he defines as "a domain in which the pleasure of playing at the boundaries (social and personal) is most clearly provided for. . . . It functions as a playful and pleasurable revolution, where those normally excluded from the discourse of power may lift their voices in anger and celebration." Activities such as body modification, joy riding, S&M, raving, recreational drug taking, gang rituals, the Internet, festivals, and extreme sports, Presdee maintains, can be seen as a part of the carnival of crime. For the most part, these crimes are not "rational" in the sense that monetary gain can be achieved by their performance. Particularly important for Presdee is how media images of crime are produced, consumed, circulated, and commodified into pseudo-objective accounts and narratives about crime.

In another cultural criminology analysis, Ferrell (2004: 294) has argued that boredom resulting from alienation in the postmodern, hyper-capitalistic world can also provide the basis of forms of crime and deviance:

> So, while some die a day at a time, others seek to overturn organized boredom, here with a spray can, there with a swirling interruption of automotive traffic. And in many of these large and small revolutions there is clearly something more being sought than excitement. Excitement, it seems, is in reality a means to an end, a subset of what ultimately emerges as the antidote to modern boredom: human engagement.

Sometimes this desire for engagement takes on highly political or social organizational purposes. As Ferrell (1993; 2001; 2005) has found in his ethnographic studies of urban graffiti artists, dumpster diving, and others on the street, "crimes of style" are partly developed out of the desire to share creativity with others, individual artistic expression (which is often quashed in schools, jobs, and youth home-life) while at the same time having qualities of resistance to agencies of social control such as the police, schools, and local government.

As you can see, cultural criminologists have something unique to say about crime even though the perspective has roots in some well-known sociological theories (especially interactionism, phenomenology, the Chicago School, positive postmodernism, and Weberian theory). Cultural criminology's rejection of traditional criminological theories which rely on mechanistic, static, and rational choice based variables as well as its often poetic and richly enthnographic approach to studying crime and deviance makes the perspective intriguing and important as it certainly captures elements of crime not previously considered by criminologists.

CHAPTER SUMMARY

Critical theories of crime include Marxist, left realism, feminist, postmodernism, peacemaking, and cultural criminology perspectives. Respectively, their critiques are centered on capitalism, stratification and inequality, patriarchy, modernity, war making, and monolithic approaches to crime.

Critical theories of crime have roots in general sociological conflict theory, which sees society shaped by conflicts among people who have competing self- and group interests.

Stemming from Karl Marx's critique of capitalism, early Marxist criminological theory saw law as a tool of the bourgeoisie that is used to control the proletariat and to protect the harms committed by the elite from scrutiny. Crime was seen as a reaction of the proletariat to its oppression. This instrumentalist approach gave way to more sophisticated Marxist theories of crime, some of which maintained that economic class influences everyday activities, making crime more attractive to the economically marginalized. Other structural Marxist theories see the state as relatively autonomous from elite interests, but still a reflection of the logic of capitalism. Left realism developed out of a critique of the tendency of Marxist theory to downplay the importance of street crime and victimization. The perspective emphasizes the relationship between the nested contexts of racial, gender, and class stratification.

Feminist criminological theory developed through the critique of the andocentric nature of criminology and theories of crime. There are several different varieties of the perspective (e.g., liberal socialist and radical), but at the most basic level of analysis, feminism in criminology is about centering gender and its relationship to lawmaking, lawbreaking, and reactions to crime. Two of the most important questions raised by feminist criminologists are: (1) Do extant theories of crime apply to girls and women?, and (2) How is the tremendous gender differences in criminal offending to be explained? Studies of burglars and robbers show that while offenders may share some similarities across gender, there are notable difference as well.

Postmodern criminology has attacked the notion that an absolute truth exists about crime. The deconstruction of dominant crime stories is considered necessary to allow room for replacement discourses, which are marginalized perspectives on crime that don't fit into the dominant or publicized understanding of crime. Peacemaking criminology holds that crime is a part of human suffering, and that violence by both individuals and social institutions like the criminal justice system are equally unacceptable. From this perspective, the ultimate solution to crime is to be found in sweeping cultural changes that emphasize nonviolence and social justice in all aspects of life. Among the newest critical theories of crime, cultural criminology sees crime and deviance as an ever-changing response to the banalities and alienating features of contemporary society.

Cultural criminology approaches crime and deviance, and the reactions to them, as dynamic and ever-changing processes linked to creating and maintaining meaning through resistance, power, and reactions to everyday conflict and dilemmas. The perspective includes both macro- and micro-level analyses of crime and is unique because it considers understudied elements of life and their relationship to crime.

KEY TERMS

conflict theory
cultural criminology
feminist criminology
instrumental Marxism
left realism
liberation/opportunity theory
peacemaking criminology
postmodern criminology
structural contradictions theory
structured action theory

DISCUSSION QUESTIONS

1. Karl Marx's critique of capitalism is among the most influential intellectual projects that has informed critical criminological theories. We suspect most Americans have had very little exposure to Marx's academic theories and instead identify him only with communism. To what extent do you see value in Marx's work when applied to contemporary economic issues and crime?
2. Structural and instrumental Marxists find that laws and their enforcement favor the wealthy at the expense of the working class and poor. What are some examples of these laws and practices? Alternatively, what kinds of laws seem to be unrelated to economic status?
3. Feminist theorists have proposed alternative theories and ways of thinking about crime. Do you believe that involvement in crime has more to do with gender or other things? Are there any crimes in which gender is more likely to play a role than others?
4. Peacemaking criminology is sometimes critiqued for being too optimistic. Given what you know about the theory, do you see the perspective having a legitimate chance of influencing criminal justice system operations? Why or why not?

ACTIVITIES

1. Visit the FBI, Bureau of Justice Statistics, and U.S. Census websites and find data about state poverty levels and crime rates. Are poorer states more likely to have higher rates of crime? Interpret your findings through conflict theory.

2. Listen to the Public Enemy song "Hazy Shade of Criminal," and note the extent to which the lyrics are consistent with the perspectives offered by Marxist theorists of crime. Do you find value in the lyrics as a critical commentary on law and crime?

3. Research the band Leftover Crack and listen to their song "Burn Them Prisons Down." To what extent do the lyrics relate to conflict theory? Are the song's claims accurate?

4. Listen to and analyze the lyrics of Suzanne Vega's song "Luka." How does the artist draw the connection between domestic violence, oppression of women, and patriarchy?

7

General and Integrated Theories

Students and professors alike experience a certain degree of frustration when trying to answer the seemingly straightforward question: "What causes crime?" There is no doubt that the question is deceiving in its simplicity, as in reality, crime is an immensely complex and ubiquitous problem that varies over space and time. But when asked what the causes of crime all boil down to, as professors, we tell our students that we need to ask more questions before we even begin to pursue the answer. Such questions would be "What type of crime?," "Crime rates or individual criminal activity?," "Juvenile or adult crime?" Even after whittling down the question, the truth of the matter is that there is still much controversy and disagreement about the nature, extent, and distribution of particular types of crime, criminality. Inevitably some students get the impression that criminological theory is incapable of generalizing about crime and that the answer might just as well be, as Bob Dylan sings, "blowin' in the wind."

Such an opinion is not shared by general and integrative criminological theorists, the two major forms of theory to be discussed in this chapter. Let us first discuss general criminological theory.

The period of time from the late 1980s to the mid 1990s may very well go down in history as the time criminology finally took stock of its achievements and rediscovered general and integrated theory. **General theories** explain a broad range of facts and are not restricted to any one time or place. This does not mean that a particular general theory has to explain all crime, but if exceptions keep turning up its generality is obviously suspect. By the same token, successful tests of a general theory with a particular crime, say armed robbery, cannot be the basis for inferring that the theory applies equally well to embezzlement or even to other forms of robbery.

Only repeated tests of a theory with different people, places, or events will establish its degree of generality.

Crime varies in many ways. There are variations from one population, place, and time to another, and from one individual to another; there are variations in the frequency with which people commit crimes (called the "incidence" of crime), and variations in the proportion of people who commit those crimes (the "prevalence" of crime); there are variations in the way crimes are committed, and in the consequences that follow for offenders as well as for victims; there are variations in criminalization, from the declaration that certain activities are crimes all the way to the imposition of penalties.

A general theory that explains all these variations would be impressive indeed. In the first place, it would need to explain variations at the individual level as well as variations at the societal level. The things that account for differences among individuals may not account for differences among societies, and vice versa. As Braithwaite (1989a: 104) asserts: "There is some evidence, for example, that while unemployment is a strong predictor of individual criminality, societies with high unemployment rates do not necessarily have high crime rates." In the second place, a theory that accommodates all these variations would have to explain not only the behavior that constitutes crime but also the propensity of people to engage in that behavior and the propensity of others to apply criminal labels to those people and acts.

A third reason such an all-encompassing theory would be impressive relates to the conceptualization of crime as an event. One way to think of crime as an event is illustrated by the routine activities approach, discussed in chapter 2. In this conceptualization, crime occurs when opportunities and motivated offenders fortuitously come together in the absence of capable guardians. From this vantage point, a general theory of crime would have to explain variations in the situational matrix that gives rise to criminal events.

The central concepts of a theory usually reflect the training of its author(s). It comes as no surprise when a sociologist includes social variables in a theory of crime, nor when a psychologist includes personality variables, a biologist constitutional variables, or a geographer spatial variables. Yet some scholars see discipline boundaries as a hindrance to the development of a general theory of crime. Gottfredson and Hirschi (1990: 274) make this point, arguing that "much of the research generated by these disciplines is beyond the reach of their own explanations of crime." They "find no adequate positivistic theory that accounts for a range of well-documented facts about crime (e.g., the age curve [crime rates peak at age twenty to twenty-four and fall off rapidly thereafter], the gender gap, the disproportionate involvement of minorities, the high correlation between crime rates and rates of other "deviancy"), and the characteristics of crime itself" (Barlow, 1991: 231). And so Gottfredson and Hirschi claim to base their theory on a conception of human nature and of crime that escapes the fetters of disciplines.

If the disciplinary baggage theorists carry around restricts their ability to construct a general theory of crime, the competition among different theoretical perspectives within a discipline is surely more restrictive. This has led some criminologists to seek **integrated theories** that borrow from otherwise competing paradigms. In sociological criminology, for example, attempts have been made to unite control theory with rationality-opportunity theory, associational theory with strain theory, and cultural deviancy theory with control theory. These efforts expose some of the commonalities among ostensibly competing theories (Barlow and Ferdinand, 1992: 201–22), though tests of integrated theories (usually with juveniles) have had mixed success. To the extent that an integrated theory explains a wider range of phenomena, it is more general than the individual theories of which it is constructed, and that makes theoretical integration a worthwhile challenge. We examine integrated theories at the end of this chapter.

SIX GENERAL THEORIES OF CRIME

Our observations above might well evoke pessimism about the possibility of constructing a general theory of crime. Yet the challenge has now been taken up, although it should be said that Katz (1988) makes no claim that his work constitutes a general theory. In truth, his is as much method as theory, but the two are so intertwined as to be indistinguishable, as we shall see. Here, then, are the six theories. There is space to do only a superficial job, and readers are strongly advised to read the original sources in their entirety. Always remember that the further removed one is from the original author, the more likely it is that arguments and ideas will be misrepresented. This is another good reason to read the original works.

We begin with two theories that share a common grounding in sociobiology, although one is an evolutionary theory and the other is a behaviorist learning theory.

Wilson and Herrnstein's General Theory. Wilson and Herrnstein (1985: 42) offer an integrative theory of criminal behavior that combines sociobiological, psychological (behaviorist), and rationality-opportunity perspectives on crime. Their theory is about "the forces that control individual behavior," and it incorporates behavioral, biological, and environmental factors to explain why some people commit "serious" street crimes and others do not.

An underlying assumption of the theory is that when individuals are faced with choices of action, they evaluate them according to their consequences and will prefer those with the highest anticipated ratio of rewards to costs. To the extent that individuals act on this basis, their behavior is rational. Therefore, both stealing and bestiality can be rational. Wilson and Herrnstein believe that individuals can choose to commit or not commit a crime, and for any given level of internal restraint (the "bite of conscience"), they will select crime over noncrime whenever the reward-cost ratio is greater for the crime than for the noncrime.

What any given individual considers rewarding (or costly) is part human nature (i.e., it satisfies such primary drives as hunger and sex) and part learned. These rewards may be material or nonmaterial, certain or uncertain, and immediate or delayed. The evaluation of any particular action will be influenced by how well a person handles uncertainty and delay, which Wilson and Herrnstein believe is influenced by nature, temperament, and social environment. Aggressive individuals, for example, are inclined to be more impulsive and less able to delay gratification, a trait characteristic also of youth. The rewards of noncrime are often delayed, whereas the rewards of crime generally precede their costs and will therefore be preferred by less mature and more impulsive individuals. Finally, there is the important question of equity: Crime may be preferred to noncrime if it is perceived to correct an imbalance in distributive justice. Such an imbalance occurs when people feel that in comparison to them, others get more than they deserve on the basis of their contribution.

Wilson and Herrnstein's theory is controversial partly because of their claim that the theory is general enough to encompass most sociological theories of criminal behavior (1985: 63–66), partly because it is used to justify conservative crime control policies (528–29), and, perhaps most of all, because it links criminal behavior to constitutional factors. On the other hand, Wilson and Herrnstein have explored some new avenues and some old ones in a way that merits serious study.

A major criticism of their approach is its focus on "serious" street crime—murder, theft, rape—to the exclusion of other forms of criminality. A general theory of crime that explains only a small range of behaviors is not so general, and in any case it is certainly not established that embezzlers, con artists, organized criminals, fences, and pilferers are constitutionally different from noncriminals, or for that matter, from other criminals. It is also curious that despite their declared focus on serious street crime, the voluminous research that Wilson and Herrnstein bring to bear on their theory often does not make that distinction. Finally, Wilson and Herrnstein's approach manifests the ideology of conservative criminology in its thinly veiled search for the criminal type (for additional criticisms, see Gibbs, 1985).

Inferential support for Wilson and Herrnstein's theory (and also that of Gottfredson and Hirschi, discussed later) comes from a survey of college undergraduates by Nagin and Paternoster (1993). These authors asked students to describe their involvement in three distinctive offenses—drunk driving, sexual assault, and theft. Students were presented with various scenarios that were experimentally varied across the sample. They were asked to estimate the chances they would commit the act specified in the scenario, as well as the chances that they would be arrested; they were also questioned about their perceptions of the costs and benefits of committing the offense, and they were also given questions designed to measure their level of self-control.

Nagin and Paternoster found evidence of individual differences in the propensity to commit crime (individuals lacking self-control were more likely to say they would commit an offense), as well as evidence that students took vulnerability of the target and perceived benefits and costs of doing the crime in account. The authors thus concluded that individual differences and situational factors both influence the decision to commit crime—although in this case hypothetical crimes. The authors advocate more research along these lines, although less research has been conducted on Wilson and Herrnstein's theory as the years have passed since Nagin and Paternoster's study.

Cohen and Machalek's Evolutionary Theory. The evolutionary ecological theory proposed by Cohen and Machalek (1988) is also integrative, and what is remarkable is the simplicity of the result. The theory is heavily influenced by biological developments and is described as a general theory even though the authors apply it to a restricted range of crimes (although see Vila, 1994, for an attempt to extend the theory to all forms of criminal behavior). Even though the theory remains to be fully developed, it unites the perspectives of routine activity, structure, social psychology, and biology.

Cohen and Machalek (1988: 467) argue that variation in individual behavior is explained by the "alternative behavioral strategies" that are used as people try to meet their needs. Some of these strategies are *expropriative*, because they involve depriving others of valuable things. Many crimes are expropriative, and it is these crimes to which the theory is applied.

Behavioral strategies develop over time as people (like other organisms) strive to meet their needs. The successful strategies tend to become "major" ones. However, the more prevalent a strategy becomes within society, the more vulnerable the population is to "invasion" by alternative strategists, or to "nonconformists" who are willing to be creative. This is one way that new strategies evolve and behavior diversifies.

In addition, individuals differ in their physical and behavioral traits and resources. These differences may result in the selection (intentional or not) of different strategies, just as they may help or hinder a person's successful adoption of a preferred strategy. In this way, "conditional" strategies arise alongside major strategies, and again behavioral diversity grows.

Human beings possess intelligence, meaning they can think; however, people do not always act with conscious purpose. "It is thus unnecessary to assume that criminal acts are perpetrated by rational, calculating individuals who understand fully the strategic implications of their chosen actions" (Cohen and Machalek, 1988: 479). Indeed, people may have resource advantages that they do not realize or intend, and yet these advantages explain why they have adopted a strategy. If a strategy works well it will probably be tried again, although the individual may never question or realize why it worked.

Cohen and Machalek argue that property crimes, as expropriative strategies, are promoted by various factors, some pertaining to individuals, others to the type and mix of noncriminal strategies that exist in a time and place. Deficiencies in social, cultural, and physical resources may promote criminal strategies (such as burglary) that are employed as alternatives to inaccessible noncriminal strategies. However, criminal alternatives may also be promoted by resource advantages: "[An] individual who is rich in [resources] may be even more predisposed to commit a criminal act precisely because he or she commands the resources required to implement an expropriative strategy successfully" (Cohen and Machalek, 1988: 483).

If both resource deficiencies and advantages promote crime, it is difficult to see how resource differences can explain individual or group differences in the selection of expropriative crime. Cohen and Machalek get around this problem by taking a conventional and conservative approach: People who are socially and economically disadvantaged are more likely to be exposed to values and experiences that encourage criminal behavior. They do not tell us why this should be so. On the other hand, resource variability can explain the type of crime selected, for as seen repeatedly in chapter 3, access to criminal opportunities often requires the right combination of resources.

Because expropriative strategies arise as alternatives to legitimate production activities, they are promoted by the expansion and proliferation of noncriminal activities. For example, Cohen and Machalek (1988: 480) observe that "large-scale concentrations of producers offer rich and inviting opportunities" to both advantaged and conditional strategists. Once discovered, a particular theft strategy is likely to proliferate through conventional social-psychological processes such as imitation and social learning, and through independent discovery.

This brief sketch does not do justice to Cohen and Machalek's theory, which contains other elements and emphasizes the evolutionary dynamics that underlie the development and acquisition of behavioral strategies (see also Machalek and Cohen, 1991; Vila and Cohen, 1993; and Vila, 1994). Nevertheless, it is important to note again that none of the elements described above is new. One can find them in the theories reviewed in the last several chapters. A new idea that does emerge is the notion that crime is shaped by "strategy evolution" in general, and that the characteristics, frequency, and mix of behavioral strategies explain the amount and types of crime that exist in any particular place, time, or group. An evaluation of their theory using real-world data has not yet been accomplished; however, computer simulations have not disproved the theory (Vila and Cohen, 1993: 907).

Gottfredson and Hirschi's General Theory of Crime. * Crime can be thought of as a form of cheating, where one person or group extracts resources from another without compensating the victim (Machalek and Cohen, 1991: 223). What crimes have in common is the fact that they victimize. When crime is conceptualized this way, questions about the ubiquity and evolution of crime follow naturally enough, for how can societies survive in the face of such parasitic conduct? Gottfredson and Hirschi (1990) take a different approach in conceptualizing crime, although they acknowledge that suffering occurs. Much of the account that follows is taken from a critical review of their theory (Barlow, 1991).

Taking classical (rational choice) theory as a starting point, Gottfredson and Hirschi argue that crime, as any other behavior, turns on the likelihood that it will bring pleasure. Its characteristics must in general be consistent with that result irrespective of the specific motives, interests, or talents of the people doing it. Gottfredson and Hirschi observe that most crimes are in fact attempts, and this implies something about the nature of crimes: they are unlikely to be carefully thought out, skillful acts involving special expertise, technology, or organization. Criminal acts are relatively easy and simple to commit, involve little skill or planning, and tend to be exciting, risky, or thrilling.

What makes crimes distinct from analogous acts is that they entail the use of force and fraud, and this helps make gratification immediate. On the other hand, force and fraud also threaten the self-interests of victims and are therefore universally resisted. Like Machalek and Cohen (1991) and Durkheim ([1893] 1964a) before them, Gottfredson and Hirschi see potential retaliation as the inseparable other side of crime. And so we have three other characteristics of crimes: they provide immediate gratification but also produce pain and suffering for victims and the risk of long-term costs for offenders.

---

*Parts of this section are from Barlow (1991).

Beyond the commonalities already noted, crimes will not occur unless an appropriate opportunity exists. That opportunity is defined by the logical structure of the crime itself, and therefore will vary from one specific offense (embezzlement) to another (rape). Gottfredson and Hirschi describe the "typical or standard" characteristics and the logical structures (necessary elements or conditions) of burglary, robbery, homicide, auto theft, rape, embezzlement, and drug use. The characteristics and elements of the offenses are strikingly similar. However, it is also apparent that the likelihood of any particular crime being committed is influenced by the availability of opportunities and a person's access to them, issues the authors do not explore. Presumably, the characteristics of situations and the personal properties of individuals jointly affect the use of force or fraud in pursuit of self-interest.

Gottfredson and Hirschi maintain that crimes are interchangeable not only among themselves but also with analogous acts that do not involve force or fraud. They call this the **versatility construct**. And so they end up rejecting traditional distinctions among crimes (e.g., petty and serious, personal and property, attempted and completed, street and suite) as "without import" and "a waste of time." They look for what crimes have in common as a basis for inferring what criminals have in common.

Criminality: Low Self-Control. If crimes differ in opportunities for their commission, individuals differ in the extent to which they are vulnerable to the temptations provided by those opportunities. Gottfredson and Hirschi use the notion of self-control to represent that vulnerability, and criminality is synonymous with low self-control. **Criminality** refers to the propensity to use force and fraud in the pursuit of self-interest. Its characteristics are inferred from the characteristics of crime. In this way Gottfredson and Hirschi ensure that the conception of criminality is consistent with their conception of crime.

The traits associated with **low self-control** include: short-time perspective; low diligence, persistence, and tenacity; a tendency to be "adventuresome, active, and physical"; a tendency to be "self-centered, indifferent, or insensitive to the suffering and needs of others"; and a tendency to have "unstable marriages, friendships, and job profiles." Since these traits are also implicated in many noncriminal acts (e.g., alcohol use, accidents, smoking, running away, truancy) "crime is not an automatic or necessary consequence of low self-control" (Gottfredson and Hirschi, 1990: 91). In other words, there is no theoretical basis for predicting which of many possible crimes and analogous acts will be committed by individuals with low self-control.

Gottfredson and Hirschi identify the major cause of low self-control as "ineffective parenting." However, individual differences among children (and parents) may affect the prospects for good parenting. Thus low intelligence tends to compromise the recognition of low self-control and the willingness or ability to do anything about it. Other factors affecting parental control and the prospects for effective socialization include parental criminality and anything that interferes with the monitoring and supervision of children. Gottfredson and Hirschi acknowledge that schools and other socializing institutions (marriage, work, Boy or Girl Scouts) may have a positive effect on self-control; but the further from early childhood one moves, the harder it is to make up for early deficiencies. Besides, the traits characteristic of low self-control are inconsistent with success at school, work, and interpersonal relationships. This fact explains, in their view, why delinquent youths end up in the company of each other ("birds of a feather") and why failure in school, marriage, and work correlates strongly with delinquency and crime (they all require diligence, hard work, and willingness to defer gratification).

The Stability Postulate. Central to the theory is the proposition that levels of self-control are relatively stable throughout the life course. Put another way, "differences between people in the likelihood that they will commit criminal acts persist over time" (Gottfredson and Hirschi, 1990: 107). This "stability postulate" is predicated on the belief that the early failure of control and socialization cannot readily be overcome later in life any more than effective control and socialization of a child can later be undone. Together with the notion that there are many noncriminal acts that are analogous to crimes, the stability postulate explains why the so-called age-curve of crime is invariant across space and across crimes, as well as why "[m]en are always and everywhere more likely than women to commit criminal acts" (p. 145).

To summarize, the central proposition of Gottfredson and Hirschi's general theory of crime is as follows: Crime rate differences among individuals are explained by the independent effects of variations in the characteristics of crime itself (i.e., the opportunity to pursue self-interest through the use of force or fraud) and variations in self-control (criminality, or the propensity to use force or fraud in the pursuit of self-interest). Criminal opportunities held constant, low self-control predicts relatively high rates of offending, low self-control earlier in life predicts criminality later in life, and criminality earlier in life predicts low self-control later in life.

Scope of the Theory. Despite continued reference to "ordinary" or "common" crimes, Gottfredson and Hirschi call their theory general, going so far as to claim that the theory "is meant to explain all crime, at all times, and, for that matter, many forms of behavior that are not sanctioned by the state" (p. 117). In short, the independent effects of crime opportunities and criminality explain bait-and-switch scams in appliance stores, police brutality, bid-rigging, employee theft, fraudulent advertising, insider trading, tax evasion, smuggling, gang crimes, labor racketeering, prison rape, armed robbery, arson, burglary, murder, rape, and shoplifting; and they also explain drug use, accidents, smoking, and eating between meals. No specialized theories are needed because all crimes and analogous acts "provide relatively quick and relatively certain benefit with minimal effort" (Gottfredson and Hirschi, 1990: 190).

Unfortunately, Gottfredson and Hirschi do not develop the opportunity (crime) side of their theory sufficiently well to predict which of all these varied acts individuals are likely to commit (at a high or low rate) at any given time, or when they might switch from one crime to another or from crime to a noncriminal but analogous act. Nor do they provide a basis for deducing what kind of social or cultural setting would experience a high (or low) rate of any particular crime or analogous act. Their treatment of these issues as theoretically irrelevant or inconsequential hardly lessens the theory's vulnerability to attack. In fact, it is quite clear that Gottfredson and Hirschi have a very unique, and in our view, myopic understanding of crime, especially those committed in the context of an organization or institution.

The theory is most vulnerable in its application to white-collar crime, both organizational and occupational. Gottfredson and Hirschi present FBI arrest data on embezzlement and fraud to show that correlates of "white collar" crime are similar to those of murder (and therefore other common crimes), and they also refer to "good research" that shows just how mundane, simple, and easy occupational crimes are and that the people who commit them also tend to commit analogous acts (drug and alcohol use, for example).

The evidence is at the very least inconclusive about these issues, and at most contrary to the claims of Gottfredson and Hirschi. Indeed, much research into organizational and occupational crime clearly challenges another assertion of their theory—that crime is more prevalent among those outside the occupational structure than among those in it (see Barlow, 1991). The lack of consistent evidence of a relationship between unemployment and crime is one challenge, but another comes from abundant evidence that employee fraud and theft, though often mundane, are widespread in all sectors of the U.S. economy as well as in those of other countries. Furthermore, evidence of widespread crime in the fields of health, real estate, banking, insurance, defense contracting, and politics hardly supports the contention that high-end occupations are inconsistent with criminality (Reed and Yeager, 1996; Yeager and Reed, 1998).

Gottfredson and Hirschi do not assert that criminality is absent among corporate executives or other high-level employees, merely that it is less prevalent the higher one climbs the occupational ladder. Even if this is true, many of the crimes committed at the high end display characteristics opposite to those indicative of low self-control. Compared to low-end crime, high-end crime is much more likely to involve planning, special expertise, organization, delayed gratification, and persistence—as well as considerably larger potential gains with arguably less long-term cost. Such distinctions are also apparent when comparing the activities of fences with thieves, "good" burglars with "kick-it-in men," pickpockets with purse snatchers. Gottfredson and Hirschi's theory can accommodate these observations in only one of two ways: Either temptations to commit force and fraud in the pursuit of self-interest overwhelm the resistance associated with self-control, or (many) individuals with low self-control manage somehow to become managers, professionals, and entrepreneurs.

If their stability postulate is wrong, however, it is possible for people with low self-control early in life to develop it later and for individuals with self-control early in life to lose it later. Braithwaite's theory of reintegrative shaming (discussed below) presumes this to be true, while Gottfredson and Hirschi's theory requires that it not be. Recall that low self-control is inconsistent with effective control and socialization, and that includes socialization into as well as out of crime. Hence the groups and organizations to which offenders belong are regarded as facilitating crime among people who already lack self-control. Gottfredson and Hirschi thus dismiss as misguided (or poor) research suggesting that the social and cultural milieu of an organization generates criminality among its members. Besides, they argue, there is little social support of white-collar offenders because their offenses usually victimize the organizations in which they work and are detrimental to fellow employees.

Our reading of wide-ranging research is very different. Whether the subject is police corruption, employee pilfering, the ethics of corporate managers, antitrust violations, city politics, or state crime, one finds social support of criminality through subcultures of criminality—accommodating norms, goals, means, and values and networks of cooperation. Gottfredson and Hirschi's view that such support relates to the nature and context of crime itself rather than to the propensity of individuals to commit it would perhaps constitute a fatal counterattack if they could also show that self-control cannot be undermined by external (group) influence. This has not been established, however, and contrary to the general theory, rational choices are "far from being self evident and stable"; rather, they are "socially constructed in group interaction" (Yeager and Reed, 1998: 894).

Minority Crime. Among the facts about crime in America are these: African Americans constitute roughly 14 percent of the population, yet nearly 50 percent of those arrested for violent crime are black, as are 33 percent of those arrested for property crimes, 40 percent of those serving jail time, and 47 percent of those in state prisons (Sourcebook of Criminal Justice Statistics, 2006). How would the general theory of Gottfredson and Hirschi explain these facts?

They reject traditional explanations of minority involvement in crime (e.g., inequality and subcultural theories) and resort to an emphasis on the self-control component of their theory. In their view, parental management of children is the key to understanding racial variations in crime; and within the realm of parenting, discipline is considered more important than supervision, which affects access to criminal opportunities. However, Gottfredson and Hirschi cite no evidence, saying only that "[p]artitioning race or ethnic differences into their crime and self-control components is not possible with currently available data" (p. 153).

On Gottfredson and Hirschi's side, the relationship between parenting and delinquency is one of the strongest in the literature, and evidence is piling up that the impact of structural factors (e.g., family composition, socioeconomic status) on delinquency is mediated by parental management. Nevertheless, if poverty, community disorganization, large family size, and family instability impact negatively on parental management, rates of crime and delinquency will be affected. Such structural conditions are prevalent in inner-city African American communities (Anderson, 1999; Wilson, 1987), where rates of victimization by force and fraud are also high (Stewart and Simons, 2006). Gottfredson and Hirschi do not explore the implications of this for their theory.

In rejecting inequality theories of race differences in crime, Gottfredson and Hirschi point out that "[offenders] tend to victimize people who share their unfortunate circumstances" (p. 152). True, but then this question arises: Are there race differences in the tendency for offenders to victimize people who are like themselves? According to their theory, crime is a matter of "proximity, ease, and convenience of rewards"; hence, there is no a priori basis for predicting such differences. Nevertheless, studies of the urban distribution of crime indicate that African American offenders have a more restricted image of the city than white offenders, who can move around more freely and need not concentrate their criminal activities in areas close to home, thereby foregoing "easy marks" (Carter and Hill, 1979; Boggs, 1964). This suggests that while most crime tends to be intraracial, crimes committed by whites are likely to be more dispersed and hence potentially more rewarding—but also more costly and risky—than crimes committed by blacks. If access to profitable criminal opportunities is skewed in favor of whites, Gottfredson and Hirschi are silent on the issue and its implications for their theory.

Gottfredson and Hirschi's general theory of crime has come under considerable empirical scrutiny since its publication. An example of the most common approach to testing the theory is a study of drunk driving and self-control. Here a composite measure of low self-control was found to relate to DUIs for both men and women, and the authors found a strong risk-taking component to drunk driving, for example, not wearing seat belts.

However, they also found that teenagers did not have higher blood-alcohol levels than others and speculate that a minimum drinking age of nineteen might have been a factor. Furthermore, "it may be that teenagers express more of their criminality in other and more demanding [i.e., physical] ways" (Keane, Maxim, and Teevan, 1993: 40). A more recent study finds support for the theory but suggests that inclusion of routine activity theory concepts (reviewed in chapter 2) would make the theory stronger. The authors found that the relationship between low self-control and delinquency is mediated by the amount of time children are unsupervised by adults as well as the time they spend with friends (Hay and Forest, 2008).

As seems fairly typical of tests of this general theory to date, self-control is found to relate to crime or analogous acts and therefore has become an important contribution to criminology (Gibbs, Giever, and Higgins, 2003; Piquero, MacDonald, Dobrin, Daigle, and Cullen, 2005; Winfree, Taylor, He, and Esbensen, 2006; Vazsonyi, and Klanj, 2008).

Braithwaite's Theory of Reintegrative Shaming. Like Gottfredson and Hirschi, Braithwaite (1989a: 1) believes that "there is sufficient in common between different types of crime to render a general explanation possible." However, Braithwaite explicitly rejects the idea that crimes are inherently similar, arguing instead that they are qualitatively similar by virtue of the stigma attached to them and by the fact that the offender makes a "defiant choice" in grasping the opportunity to perpetrate a crime:

> The homogeneity presumed between disparate behaviors such as rape and embezzlement in this theory is that they are choices made by the criminal actor in the knowledge that he is defying a criminal proscription which is mutually intelligible to actors in the society as criminal (Braithwaite, 1989a: 3).

Braithwaite excludes acts that are formally crimes but whose criminalization is without support in the society at large, for example, "laws against marijuana use in liberal democracies or laws that create political crimes against the state in communist societies" (3). Braithwaite's theory applies to predatory crimes, acts that involve victimization of one person or group by another.

We encountered some of the ideas in Braithwaite's theory in previous chapters. But the theory is much more than this. Braithwaite offers yet another integrative theory, one that incorporates elements of major sociological theories of crime and delinquency: control theory, labeling theory, subcultural theory, associational theory, strain theory, and social learning theory.

Braithwaite's diagram of his theory is reproduced in figure 7.1. The arrows indicate the direction or flow of influence between linked variables, and the signs indicate whether the relationship between them is positive (i.e., a plus sign indicates the more of one, the more of the other) or negative (i.e., a minus sign indicates the more of one, the less of the other). On

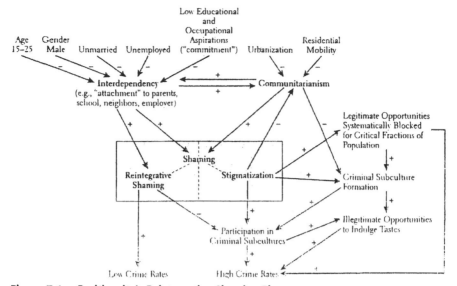

Figure 7.1. Braithwaite's Reintegrative Shaming Theory
Source: John Braithwaite, Crime, Shame, and Reintegration, Cambridge University Press, 1989. Reprinted
   with the permission of Cambridge University Press.

the integrative and original aspects of his theory, Braithwaite (1989a: 107)
has this to say:

> The top left of [the figure] incorporates the key variables of control theory;
> the far right—opportunity [strain] theory; the middle and bottom right—
> subcultural theory; the right side of the middle box—labeling theory. With
> one crucial exception (reintegrative shaming), there is therefore no originality
> in the elements of this theory, simply originality of synthesis.

The central proposition of the theory is this: Crime rates of individuals
and groups are influenced directly by processes of shaming. High-crime
rates result from shaming that stigmatizes, because rule-breakers who are
shamed but not forgiven are more likely to become "outlaws" and to participate in subcultures of crime. This is referred to as **disintegrative shaming**, a stigmatizing approach that involves:

- Disrespectful disapproval and humiliation;
- Ceremonies to certify deviance but no ceremonies to decertify devi-
  ance;
- Labeling the person, not just the deed, as evil; and
- Deviance is allowed to become a master status trait (Braithwaite,
  1989a: 194).

On the other hand, when rule-breakers are shamed but then forgiven and welcomed back to the fold, the unpleasant, punitive experience of being shamed is offset by the pleasant relief of discovering that one is still accepted (loved, wanted, cared about) despite the transgression. This what Braithwaite refers to as **reintegrative shaming**. The process of reintegrative shaming confirms the validity of the rules and reestablishes the transgressor's place as a member in good standing. This process involves:

- Disapproval while sustaining a relationship of respect;
- Ceremonies to certify deviance terminated by ceremonies to decertify deviance;
- Disapproval of the evil of the deed without labeling the persons as evil; and
- Deviance not being allowed to become a master status trait (Braithwaite, 1995: 194).

While Braithwaite hypothesizes that either kind of shaming is likely to be more successful at combating predatory crime than "punishment without associated moralizing and denunciation" (p. 86), systems of punishment that encourage reintegration should experience the lowest crime rates.

As a mechanism of social control, shaming works best among closely connected people whose fortunes, reputations, and futures are interdependent—as in families, for example, or among workmates, colleagues, and friends. Justice officials in Western industrialized societies are at a decided disadvantage: "Most of us will care less about what a judge (whom we meet only once in our lifetime) thinks of us than we will care about the esteem in which we are held by a neighbor we see regularly" (Braithwaite, 1989a: 87). Interdependence among individuals has a societal correlate—**"communitarianism"**—which has three elements:

> (1) densely enmeshed interdependency, where interdependencies are characterized by (2) mutual obligation and trust, and (3) are interpreted as a matter of group loyalty rather than individual convenience. Communitarianism is therefore the antithesis of individualism. (Braithwaite, 1989: 86)

Western industrialized societies, with their high rates of urbanization and residential mobility, are more individualistic than less-developed agrarian societies. The model in figure 7.1 shows that communitarianism has a positive effect on shaming but is itself undermined by shaming that is merely stigmatizing. This is because shaming without reintegration makes criminal subcultures more attractive and encourages their formation "by creating populations of outcasts with no stake in conformity" (Braithwaite, 1989a: 102). Criminal subcultures are also fostered by blocked legitimate opportunities, and once formed they encourage crime directly by providing illegitimate opportunities and incentives to deviate from the norms of conventional society.

At the individual level, **interdependency** is associated with age, marital status, gender, employment status, and aspirations within societal-wide approved opportunity systems. More so than other people, older teenagers and young adults—especially if they are male—are freed from the constraints and obligations of interdependency, as are single people, those without work, and those with low commitment to legitimate ways of "getting ahead." Absent the close ties of interdependency, such people are less likely to be exposed to or affected by shaming. They are more susceptible to crime because controls are weak.

Evaluation of the Theory. Braithwaite's work is an important contribution to criminological theory. Not only does he show how "old" competing theories can be integrated into one model but also his addition of the social-psychological variable, shaming, is a major innovation. Along with associational theories, his theory is one of the few that can be applied to occupational and organizational crimes. Other notable accomplishments are that the theory of reintegrative shaming can be applied at both individual and societal levels of analysis and that it incorporates background and foreground variables, although discussion of the lived experience of shaming is largely limited to the mechanics of gossip (see Braithwaite, 1989a: 75–77). The latter is certainly an area for future research and elaboration and will be considered when we discuss Katz.

Braithwaite suggests ways his theory could be tested and even mentions modifications that could be made to accommodate additional variables. Few specific tests of the theory have been conducted to date, but at least a dozen or so studies have found some empirical support of some of Braithwaite's theses (Botchkovar and Tittle, 2005; Chaplin and Cochran, 1997; Losoncz and Tyson, 2007; Makkai and Braithwaite, 1994; Vagg, 1998; Zhang and Zhang, 2004). Despite the absence of focused tests, Braithwaite confidently asserts the merits of his theory by claiming that it accounts for the thirteen best-established findings in criminology, which no other existing theory can do. Among these findings are the high rates of crime among males, people living in large cities, certain categories of young people (e.g., those with low aspirations, poor school performance, weak attachments to school or parents, or strong attachments to delinquent peers), and among disadvantaged people. The theory also accounts for the low rate of crime in Japan—an industrialized nation—when compared with other industrialized nations such as the United States (see Braithwaite, 1989a, especially pages 61–66).

One of the theory's most interesting aspects is its implications for criminal justice policy in highly individualized societies such as our own. Given that reintegrative shaming works best in the informal contexts of family, friends, and neighborhood, a justice policy aimed at preventing or reducing crime should be a community-based, largely informal system that uses traditional process and punishment as a last resort. Such an approach has come to be known in recent years as **restorative justice**. Box 7.1 provides some information on restorative justice practices that are consistent with Braithwaite's theory.

Expanding on the policy implications of the theory, Braithwaite and Pettit (1990) advocate a "republican" approach to criminal justice in which formal interventions are minimized and in which subjective assurances of liberty, equality, fraternity, and dialogue are guaranteed all citizens (also see Braithwaite, 1991; 1995). In such a setting, the reintegrative prospects of community shaming are enhanced and the likelihood is greater that the offender will recognize his offense and shame himself. In this manner, shaming becomes conscience-building, the essence of crime prevention in Braithwaite's view.

Despite its originality, broad scope, and impressive integration of existing theories, the theory of reintegrative shaming leaves at least one important issue unresolved. For example, Braithwaite (1989a: 13) claims his theory accommodates the existence of "multiple moralities" in modern societies, whereas some others do not. He argues, "[A] severe limitation of theories that deny this, like Hirschi's control theory, is that they give no account of why some uncontrolled individuals become heroin users, some become hit men, and others price-fixing conspirators." This is fair enough, but aside from identifying criminal subcultures as the milieu in which crime is learned and via which tastes may be indulged in illegitimate ways, it is by no means clear how one would derive predictions about variations in the prevalence and incidence of particular types of crime, or about crime selection by predisposed individuals.

Tittle's Control Balance Theory. Recall from chapter 5 that Hirschi's social control theory holds that people who are not strongly bonded to conventional society are those most likely to commit crime. Hirschi's argument, then, is that this *lack of control* produces criminal outcomes. But what about people who have a lot of control or those who are overcontrolled? Are they likely to commit crimes as well? Would they commit different types of crime than those who are undercontrolled?

Charles Tittle (1995) has produced an integrative *control balance theory* of deviance that addresses these and other questions. First, Tittle intends for his theory to explain deviance, not just crime. Deviance, according to Tittle (1995: 124), is "any behavior that the majority of a given group regards as unacceptable or that typically evokes a collective response of a negative type."

The central thesis of control balance theory is that the "amount of control to which people are subject relative to the amount of control they

Box 7.1. Restorative Justice

Restorative justice involves a holistic approach to criminal justice and crime prevention that promotes the healing of the victim, offender, and community. It is inspired by a genuine desire to right a wrong (crime), but in a fair and humane way. Restorative justice differs from traditional criminal justice in several ways. First, its focus is on the future. Healing requires an understanding of the past harm, but recovering from the injury, rebuilding the community, and forging interdependencies should be paramount. Second, the process by which justice is to be achieved is through dialogue, mediation, and negotiation, not through adversarial "warlike" techniques. Healing is the goal, not the amount of people who can be sent away to prison. Third, the offender takes responsibility for the crime and repentance is encouraged. This is crucial for reintegration, as traditional punishment and revenge philosophies generally do not facilitate healing. Fourth, restorative justice carries a concern not only for the victims of crime but also a sincere concern for the well-being of the offender. Historically, offenders were considered violators of the abstracted "society" and unfit for membership in the community.

There are many types of restorative justice practices in Australia, New Zealand, and in the United States. Here are some that are consistent with Braithwaite's shaming theory:

- Victim-offender, community accountability, and family group conferences where offenders, victims, and communities come together to reintegratively shame and restore community and victim health.
- Community and neighborhood advisory boards, which offer input and advice for the handling of deviance and deviants in the community.
- Peer mediation and conferencing, where the offender is shamed by peers and intimates and then reintegrated into the group.
- Victim services and victim impact statements, where victims can be heard by state officials, special victims agents, and the offender.
- Offender community service, in which the offender gives back to the community harmed.
- Offender competency development, such as the teaching of life, civic, and parenting skills.

Many county courts, prosecutor's offices, and probation departments in the United States have embraced the philosophy of restorative justice. To the many practitioners who have seen the failures of traditional justice, restorative justice is seen as an attractive approach, but it is still unclear whether the restorative justice movement will become the dominant form of doing justice in the years to come.

Sources: Coates, Umbreit, and Vos (2006), Minnesota Department of Corrections (1998), and the Restorative Justice Institute (1999).

can exercise" affects the probability of deviance more generally, as well as the *type* of deviance (Tittle, 1995: 142). Being controlled or experiencing control means that a person is subject to the will of others through, for example, rewards and punishments. If a teenager is not free to stay out all night, drink beer, choose her friends, or go to concerts, one might say they are experiencing control. When people *exercise* control, they have the ability to limit the options, choices, and behaviors of others. The parent who sets the limits in the above example is exercising control.

The relationship of control to deviance is found in the **control ratio**, which is the overall level of control people have in their lives. The ratio is calculated by weighing the total level of control a person exercises against the total level of control that the person is subject to. People who control more than they are controlled by others have a **control surplus**, while those who are controlled more than they control others have a **control deficit**. Tittle (1995: 266) provides the following example:

> a man may have a control surplus in the domestic realm but a control deficit in the work environment, a youth may have a control deficit in the society as a whole, but a control surplus in the recreational domain, and a woman may have a control surplus in the realm of interpersonal relations, but a control deficit with respect to the physical environment.

Another example is in order. Think of the class for which you are reading this book. How much control do you have over the course? How much control are you subject to in the course? You have probably been subject to control in the following ways: You must meet the class requirements, such as passing grades on papers and examinations, even the number, nature, and length of the papers and examinations is generally out of your control. You may also be required to attend lectures and participate in classroom discussions. You must also earn a certain amount of points or a certain overall grade to have this class "count" for credit. You have probably had little if any control over the textbook used, whether class is canceled, or if it is dismissed early. Clearly you are subject to great amounts of control and regulation in a typical college classroom. Now, what kinds of things *can* you control in the course? Unless the class is extremely unfair, most students have some control over their performance on exams and the relative content of their papers. You may also have some control in group discussions and by making observations or raising questions to the professor. You also, of course, have the ability to drop the course, be more or less interested in the course, and express your views about the course and instructor on teaching evaluations. All told, however, you can see how most students probably have a control deficit when it comes to the typical college course. Can you think of how this control deficit might lead to deviance in the

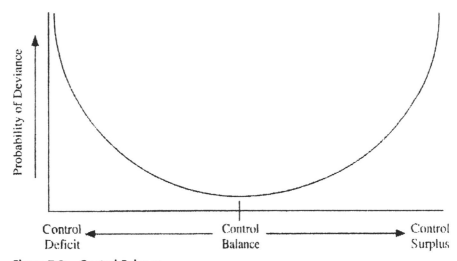

Figure 7.2. Control Balance
A. R. Piquero and M. Hickman (1999), "Empirical Test of Tittle's Control Balance Theory," *Criminology* 37, p. 321. Reprinted with permission of the American Society of Criminology.

form of cheating, plagiarism, and lying to the professor? How might the professor act deviantly as a result of his or her control surplus? Are there professors who sexually harass, discriminate, or use psychological "warfare" to intimidate students?

According to Tittle (2004; 1995), those who have a **control balance** are least likely to engage in deviance, but the probability and seriousness of deviance rises with the degree of control deficit and surplus (see figure 7.2). This is straightforward enough, but Tittle goes one step further by theorizing the *type* of resulting deviance will differ depending on whether one has a surplus or deficit. Those with a control deficit seek to escape or rectify their problem through deviance, while those with a surplus seek to extend their control.

Critical Variables. Surely a control imbalance is not by itself sufficient for the deviant act to take place. Tittle rightly acknowledges that other independent variables play a role in the genesis and persistence of deviant behavior:

1. The *predisposition* toward deviant motivation,
2. The situational stimulation of deviance (*provocation*),
3. The likelihood of *constraint* in the face of deviance, and
4. The *opportunity* to commit deviance.

Let us briefly review each of these variables.

Tittle argues that the predisposition to deviance is rooted in a fundamental aspect of human nature: the desire for autonomy. This means that people generally want to escape the control of others as well to extend their control over others. This universal drive for freedom and power is likely to result in deviance when control is imbalanced. Thus, while the theory is called control balance, a major *motivation* for deviance is the elimination of the control imbalance. Tittle also suggests that autonomy and control are embedded not only in the personal, individual context but also within organizational contexts, such as family and work.

While motivation is a necessary component of the deviant act, certain events and circumstances trigger the behavior. This is what Tittle (1995: 163) calls *provocation*, which includes "contextual features that cause people to become keenly cognizant of their control ratios and the possibilities of altering them through deviant behavior." Examples of provocation include being insulted, dismissed from employment, and any number of threats or challenges which can then trigger an attempt to balance the control ratio.

Constraint refers to the "probability or the perceived probability that control will actually be exercised" (Tittle, 1995: 167). Constraint, then, could be manifested in the form of the probability that the deviant act would result in, for example, arrest or discovery by a significant other. It also can be generally understood to be a calculation of the *risk* associated with deviance.

The last major variable in control balance theory is opportunity. Like the rational-opportunity theories reviewed in chapter 2, Tittle agrees that a situation or circumstance must be available for the performance of deviance. This means that there must be, for example, available victims, people to rob and assault, drugs to sell and use, and things to steal and destroy. Finally, in a refinement of the theory, Tittle (2004) has proposed integrating insights from Hirschi and Gottfredson's self-control theory.

Evaluation of the Theory. There are many strengths of control balance theory. First, the theory is truly *general*. It provides us with sound ways of understanding both white-collar and traditional street crime and deviance. Unlike Gottfredson and Hirschi's theory, Tittle does a splendid job of dealing with the conceptually difficult issues that distinguish occupational from organizational crime. Indeed, Tittle understands that there is more to white-collar crime than simple embezzlement.

Second, Tittle's theory is intended to explain deviance, not just those things that legislators happen to define as crime. While Hirschi and Gottfredson claim they transcend a narrow definition of crime, they do it poorly. Tittle's sociological approach to crime and deviance provides a measure of breadth and depth not found in many other theories of crime.

Third, control balance theory weaves many of the most well-supported findings in criminological theory into the novel idea of control ratio. Tittle's specificity and attention to detail to these matters in many ways breaks the mold. While Braithwaite (1989a) also explains the relationship of his novel concept (shame) to other well-tested variables in criminology, Tittle does it more meaningfully, with keen attention to how the theory may be empirically tested in the future.

It usually takes several years for a theory in criminology to undergo rigorous testing. Tittle's theory has been tested in several studies (Baron and Forde, 2007; Piquero and Hickman, 1999; Piquero and Piquero, 2006). While some support was found in the Piquero and Hickman (1999) study for the notion that control imbalance leads to deviance, the types of deviance predicted by Tittle were not supported. More specifically, it was found that predation and defiance were significantly related to those with a control surplus, not just a control deficit. This finding confirms the suspicion voiced by Braithwaite (1997) that it would be better to collapse the types of deviance categories into simpler, broader constructs (e.g., reducing the types of autonomous deviance into a larger "predation" category). Tittle (1997) has agreed with a few of Braithwaite's suggestions along these lines. Indeed, Tittle (2004) has revised the theory to take into account some of the mixed empirical findings on the theory and some conceptual flaws. One of the main ways Tittle changed the earlier version of the theory was to admit that the qualitative categories of deviance expected as results of a control imbalance are not especially valid. Instead, Tittle (2004) now proposes that a person's control balance desirability, that is the long-term usefulness and resolutive capacity of a deviant act, is a central predictor of the type of deviant outcome.

Katz's Seductions of Crime. A fascinating book hit the shelves in the late 1980s, Jack Katz's *Seductions of Crime: Moral and Sensual Attractions in Doing Evil*. In this book, Katz explores the relationship between doing crime and the emotional states of the offender. His focus is the foreground of crime as opposed to the background variables traditionally emphasized in positivistic criminology. It is an analysis of the seductions and compulsions that are felt by people as they engage in criminal activity and that draw them into and through criminal "projects." To understand (and explain) crime as action, it is first necessary to reconstruct criminal events as they are experienced by participants. Criminology, Katz argues, should move from the inside of crime outward, rather than the other way around.

For Katz (1988: 9), the commonality among such diverse crimes as pilfering, robbery, gang violence, and apparently senseless robbery-murders is the "family of moral emotions" that are subjectively experienced by offenders: "humiliation, righteousness, arrogance, ridicule, cynicism, defilement, and vengeance. In each [crime] the attraction that proves to be most fundamentally compelling is that of overcoming a personal challenge to moral—not material—existence." The following passage illustrates Katz's central argument:

The closer one looks at crime, at least at the varieties examined here, the more vividly relevant become the moral emotions. Follow vandals and amateur shoplifters as they duck into alleys and dressing rooms and you will be moved by their delight in deviance; observe them under arrest and you may be stunned by their shame. Watch their strutting street display and you will be struck by the awesome fascination that symbols of evil hold for the young men who are linked in the groups we often call gangs. If we specify the opening moves in muggings and stickups, we describe an array of "games" or tricks that turn victims into fools before their pockets are turned out. The careers of persistent robbers show us, not the increasingly precise calculations and hedged risks of "professionals," but men for whom gambling and other vices are a way of life, who are "wise" in the cynical sense of the term, and who take pride in a defiant reputation as "bad." And if we examine the lived sensuality behind events of cold-blooded "senseless" murder, we are compelled to acknowledge the power that may still be created in the modern world through the sensualities of defilement, spiritual chaos, and the apprehension of vengeance. Running across these experiences of criminality is a process juxtaposed in one manner or another against humiliation. In committing a righteous slaughter, the impassioned assailant takes humiliation and turns it into rage; through laying claim to a moral status of transcendent significance, he tries to burn humiliation up. The badass, with searing purposiveness, tries to scare humiliation off; as one ex-punk explained to me, after years of adolescent anxiety about the ugliness of his complexion and the stupidity of his every word, he found a wonderful calm in making "them" anxious about his perceptions and understandings. Young vandals and shoplifters innovate games with the risks of humiliation, running along the edge of shame for its exciting reverberations. . . . Against the historical background of a collective insistence on the moral nonexistence of their people, "bad niggers" exploit ethically unique possibilities for celebrating assertive conduct as "bad" (Katz, 1988: 312–13).

Katz's "empirical" theory is, then, a theory of moral self-transcendence constructed through examination of the doing of crime as experienced and understood by its participants. Crime becomes a "project" through which offenders transcend the self that is caught up in the mundane routines of modern life. Crime embodies a creative exploration of emotional worlds beyond the realm of rational controls—it is spiritual, nonrational, self-fulfilling, and self-proclaiming. The lure of crime is, inter alia, its promise of providing "expanded possibilities of the self . . . ways of behaving that previously seemed inaccessible" (Katz, 1988: 73).

Katz (1988: 9) argues that there are three necessary and sufficient steps through which the construction of crime takes place: "(1) a path of action—distinctive practical requirements for successfully committing the crime; (2) a line of interpretation—unique ways of understanding how one is and will be seen by others; and (3) an emotional process—seductions and compulsions that have special dynamics."

If there is a link between the foreground and background in Katz's theory, the path of action is one obvious place to look. Observe:

> As a consequence of the inequality of resources in society, some of the ways of transcending mundane life are more open to some groups of people than to others. Sky diving, for example, may offer a transcendent experience, but it is unlikely to be available to many young black members of the urban under-class. Crack, on the other hand, may provide a similarly transcending experience . . . but unlike sky diving is available to all, rich and poor. Moreover, the poor, perhaps more than any others in modernity, are faced with lives in which meaninglessness and the destruction of the self are ever present possibilities (O'Malley and Mugford, 1991: 16).

O'Malley and Mugford make this observation in the face of criticism that Katz cannot explain the shape of crime, that is, its distribution among social classes, between cities, or among racial or ethnic groups, because he rejects structural perspectives, particularly strain theory. Yet one strength of Katz's work lies precisely in the fact that it begins with no assumptions about how predispositions to crime might be distributed and concludes that only through examination of the experience of elite (or white-collar) crime can we construct the necessary comparative picture (Katz, 1988: 313–24). However, Katz is not confident of criminology's ability to study the foreground of white-collar crime:

> Now, where would we get the data? With white-collar crime, we have a special problem in locating facts to demonstrate the lived experience of deviance. Despite their presumably superior capacity to write books and the healthy markets that await their publication efforts, we have virtually no "how-I-did-it-and-how-it-felt-doing-it" autobiographies by corrupted politicians, convicted tax frauds, and chief executive officers who have been deposed by scandals over inside trading (Katz, 1988: 319).

Katz goes on to suggest that what will turn out to be distinctive about elite crime is not its motivations or consequences but its emotional quality: Feelings of shame often attend its discovery. In contrast, "[s]tickup men, safecrackers, fences, and drug dealers often wear the criminal label with pride, apparently relishing the opportunity to tell their criminal histories in colorful, intimate detail" (Katz, 1988: 319).

Bringing up the issue of shame returns us to the central element in Braithwaite's (1989a) theory of crime. We noted that Braithwaite is largely silent on the emotional process involved in shaming except to say that people find shaming a humiliating experience that provokes fear and anxiety and, consequently, avoidance behavior on the part of the person shamed. The avoidance may come in the form of conformity (most likely if the shamed also experience pangs of conscience), or it may come in the form of withdrawal from the group and participation in deviant subcultures—behavior that provoked shaming now becomes behavior that is rewarded. If the shaming is followed by forgiveness and other reintegrative processes, it becomes a particularly powerful mechanism for reinforcing cultural (group) values and identity.

Katz complements Braithwaite in his documentation of the emotions moving around the edge of shame. His analysis of the process of transcendence may help criminologists understand more completely the dynamics of shaming, especially when it fails. The humiliating subordination that shaming is (when there is no self-participation or reintegration) represents a moral affront that must be "put right" through a transcendent process of self-reaffirmation, of reconstruction that salvages honor, identity, and worth. The formation and persistence of criminal subcultures, crucial to understanding the forms that deviance takes, and an important criminogenic source in Braithwaite's model, can be explored within the framework of foreground analysis of the kind Katz has demonstrated.

Importantly, Katz's (1988: 52–79) analysis of *sneaky thrills*—shoplifting, pilfering, vandalism, joyriding (some of which were discussed in chapter 5)—also shows how shaming can act as a stimulus for crime as well as a reaction to be avoided. It is precisely the people who have some emotional investment in the conventional order (especially their standing in it) who are likely to be responsive to shaming—otherwise, who cares if a parent, teacher, police officer, or judge bawls you out? Yet the euphoria or thrill of sneaky theft—the seduction of the crime itself—lies precisely in the risk that one will be shamed if caught:

> Thus, the other side of the euphoria felt from being successful is the humiliation from being caught. What the sneak thieves are avoiding, or getting away with by not being caught, is the shame they would feel if they were caught. . . . The thrills of sneaky thefts are metaphysically complex matters. On the one hand, shoplifters and vandals know what they are doing is illegal; the deviant character of the practice is part of the appeal. On the other hand, they typically register a kind of metaphysical shock when an arrest induces a sense that what they are doing might be treated as real crime. . . . Once an arrest occurs, the shoplifting career typically ends in response to an awareness that persistence would now clearly signal a commitment to a deviant identity (Katz, 1988: 64–66).

INTEGRATED THEORY

As we explained in chapter 5, social process theories deal with the dynamic aspects of the relationship between individuals and their immediate social environments. They explain how it is that certain people learn criminal behavior patterns and how they acquire criminal status. Where social structural theories (discussed in chapter 4) focus on the relationship of organization and culture to values, norms, resources, and opportunities, social process theories consider how the actions of individuals and groups influence what people do and become.

Even though process has been separated from structure in this review of prominent theories, the two are in reality intimately connected. One way to think of that connection is to visualize structure as setting the stage for process, which in turn brings structure to life. When thinking about crime, structure promotes and restrains criminal activity among different segments of the population, while process determines which individuals within those segments will become criminally active (or be singled out for criminal labeling), and which will not.

Two questions are therefore relevant when considering why crime varies from place to place or from group to group: (1) How do social structures compare? and (2) How do the activities and experiences of individuals compare? Often it is not possible to answer both questions at the same time because the kinds of information or methodologies needed are not available or not used. Sometimes the criminologist who engages in research is simply not interested in process questions, for example, but wants to evaluate the relationship between structure and crime, perhaps at a class or societal level.

It is helpful, nevertheless, to illustrate how structure and process can be linked in research. While there are many integrated theories, one fairly recent study assesses the criminal behavior of individuals who live in different family and neighborhood environments (structure) and are exposed to different interactional experiences (process). The study is by John Laub and Robert Sampson (1988), and it is based on a reanalysis of data compiled by Sheldon and Eleanor Glueck some forty years ago.

The Gluecks (1950) collected data on 500 officially defined delinquents and 500 nondelinquents. All subjects were white males growing up in poor, deteriorated neighborhoods close to the industrial and commercial zones of Boston. Their average age was just under fifteen. Data on all sorts of social, psychological, and biological variables were collected in a multifactor design. Despite a variety of criticisms leveled at the Gluecks' research design, the study remains a classic in the field (Laub and Sampson, 1988: 357–61).

The reanalysis of the Gluecks' data by Laub and Sampson focused primarily on the relationship between family factors and delinquency. The family factors were divided into two categories that reflect the distinction between structure and process. Structural factors included household crowding, economic dependence, residential mobility, and parental criminality. Process variables included parental discipline and supervision of a child and emotional rejection.

Laub and Sampson hypothesize that parental child-rearing practices and other family management skills would be most directly related to the delinquent behavior of a child since they constitute the emotional atmosphere and control environment to which the child is exposed while growing up. Basing their argument on work by Hirschi (1983) and others, Laub and Sampson predict that good parenting skills and a supportive emotional climate help prevent the emergence of delinquency in a child because they enhance family social control.

The authors also predict, however, that parental discipline and family emotional climate are directly influenced by background factors such as economic dependency, irregular employment, and parental criminality. Thus, the structural variables influence delinquency through their impact on family process. "For instance, it is likely that residential mobility and irregular employment by mothers are related to difficulties in supervising and monitoring children. Similarly, family disruption not only affects supervisory capacity, but also attachment and disciplinary practices" (Laub and Sampson, 1988: 367–68).

In this manner, Laub and Sampson show how structure and process can be linked in the explanation of delinquency. When they reanalyzed the Gluecks' data to test this model, they found that the quality of family social control was indeed directly and strongly related to serious and persistent delinquency among boys. Equally important, however, was the finding that the social structural variables helped set the stage by directly influencing the ways in which parents supervise and discipline their children and the quality of the emotional relationship between parent and child.

The relationship between family life and delinquency, it must be said, is one of the most researched issues in criminology. Yet a review of nearly 300 studies came up with few clear-cut conclusions, except to reiterate that a relationship *does* exist—deviance begins at home (Wright and Wright, 1994). The lack of definitive conclusions about the specifics of the link between family life and crime reflects in part the many inconsistencies plaguing the methods and findings of so much of the research. It also reflects problems in resolving the issue of causality:

> For example, when researchers observe an association between family conflict and delinquency, any one of three explanations may describe the actual relationship between the variables. Family conflict may, in fact, actually cause delinquency. Alternatively, having a delinquent child may create considerable conflict within the family. Or, perhaps family conflict and delinquency are unrelated, but increase or decrease in relation to one another because of their mutual relationship to yet a third variable, for instance, aggression proneness among family members. Researchers never prove causality but endeavor to eliminate alternative explanations by using more complex models and methods that allow them to rule out other possibilities (Wright and Wright, 1994: 2).

On the whole, one can safely say that family structure and family interaction *together with* external factors such as the economic condition, opportunity structure, quality of schools, and institutional stability of neighborhood and surrounding community go a long way toward explaining the antisocial behavior of youth. How relevant these same factors are for explaining adult crime, especially occupational and public order crimes, is another matter. The fact that most youths "mature" out of crime by their late teens and early twenties indicates that something is operating to halt or perhaps even reverse the impact of these factors for a majority of children once they reach adulthood.

Some criminologists believe that key adult roles such as spouse, full-time worker, and parent make continued criminality too costly. Perhaps people become concerned about losing their family's respect (e.g., Rowe, Lindquist, and White, 1989), or perhaps participation in family life bonds a person more closely to conventional society, including values and attitudes about marital, parental, and work responsibility (e.g., Thornberry, 1987; Sampson and Laub, 1990). On the other hand, Gottfredson and Hirschi (1990) argue that criminality reflects impulsivity, short-time perspective, and other characteristics of low self-control. Such individuals are unlikely to make successful marriage partners, parents, or workers as adults, just as they are unlikely to do well in school as children. Any relationship between marriage and family life and crime is therefore spurious, meaning that the three are related only through their association with low self-control.

Wright and Wright (1994) conclude that the research on this issue is inconclusive. But here is another thought: Some forms of crime—small business crime and perhaps some occupational and professional crimes—may actually thrive on strong family and work relationships. Since the emphasis in most criminological research is on street crime, it is easy to forget that robbery, burglary, drug pushing, rape, assault, and murder actually represent just the tip of the crime iceberg. An adequate description and explanation of the relationship between family life and crime must surely move beyond these crimes into the world of business crime, money laundering, fraud, and bribery—offenses not usually committed by children, nor by people whose backgrounds automatically suggest a delinquent childhood.

The Life Course Perspective. A very promising integrated theory of crime has been proposed by Sampson and Laub (1992; 1993b; 2003) who reanalyzed the Gluecks' (1950) data. Their theory centers on the notion of the life course, through which all individuals travel from birth to death. The **life course** consists of *trajectories*, which are long-term sequences and patterns of behavior (e.g., schooling, work life, marriage, parenthood, or criminal career), and *transitions*, which are specific life events within a trajectory, such as first job, first marriage, going to college, or joining a gang (Piquero and Mazerolle, 2001).

Sampson and Laub's review of research shows that there are fairly stable attributes of individuals that are established early in life and that provide continuity and consistency as individuals age; aggression might be one, with adult manifestations in the form of spousal abuse and harsh punishment of children. But they also find evidence that a childhood trajectory may be modified or even halted by key life course events, such as getting married or getting a job or moving from one town to another. Sampson and Laub believe that in the transition to adulthood, it is not so much the timing of discrete life events such as marriage but, rather, "the quality or strength of social ties" that result (Sampson and Laub, 1992: 73).

Sampson and Laub call for a deeper examination of how continuity and change work together in an individual's life course to inhibit or promote antisocial behavior. In proposing a dual focus on continuity and change within the individual life course, they nevertheless recognize that structural conditions, including social opportunities and the actions of social control agencies, impact on the life experiences of individuals and therefore the chances that an individual's criminal behavior will begin, end, continue, or undergo modification over time.

Perhaps the most interesting conclusion of Sampson and Laub's (2003) prodigious series of studies is that crime involvement for all persons, including serious, persistent offenders, declines significantly with age. This finding, although somewhat contested (e.g., Blokland, Nagin, and Nieuwbeerta, 2005) is that desistance from crime as one ages is a universal fact, regardless of the differences in individuals' early childhood experiences.

CHAPTER SUMMARY

Consistent with the goal of general theory, the theories reviewed in this chapter seek to identify the things diverse crimes have in common and to build explanations around them. Most of the theories are heavily indebted to existing ideas about crime, and what is new is more in the packaging than in the substance. On the other hand, Katz shows us a way of thinking about crime that departs significantly from the other approaches even as it complements Braithwaite's.

It is safe to say that criminologists will be examining these theories closely in the years ahead. Do not expect that one will emerge as *the* explanation of crime. For one thing, criminologists disagree on the definition of their subject matter. For another, the data and methodology for adequate tests of all theories do not yet exist. What is likely to happen is continued refinement and reshaping, so that the dominant theories a decade from now will show their indebtedness but will not be the same.

Remember, too, that the criminological enterprise is affected not only by the ideas and values of its participants but also by the ideology underlying public policy. That ideology affects the funding of research. Theories that challenge established paradigms tend in any case to be embraced with great caution, all the more so if they conflict with the funding priorities of governments and universities.

If the measure of criminology is its success at explaining crime, where do you think we stand? We certainly know a lot about the crime scene, and well we should after more than 100 years of research. We can also point to theories that have remained prominent for many, many years—differential association is perhaps the best example. Some of the general theories we have reviewed in this chapter address crime at both micro and macro levels of analysis, and some integrate theories that once appeared incompatible. Some also bring together behaviors that were once thought to be so different as to require different explanations—rape and shoplifting, for example. It is noteworthy, too, that an argument made long ago by French sociologist Emile Durkheim now seems more relevant than ever: that crime and punishment are two parts of an inseparable whole; that one cannot be explained without also explaining the other.

KEY TERMS

communtarianism
control balance
control deficit
control ratio
control surplus
criminality
disintegrative shaming
general theories
integrated theories
interdependency
life course
low self-control
reintegrative shaming
restorative justice
versatility construct

DISCUSSION QUESTIONS

1. Of the six major theories reviewed in this chapter, which do you find most helpful in explaining crime? Why or why not?

2. A major criticism of Wilson and Herrnstein's approach is its focus on "serious" street crime. Do you think the theory is as applicable to white-collar crime?
3. Cohen and Machalek argue that some people try to meet their needs through expropriative strategies. Under what conditions is this strategy likely to be chosen over others?
4. According to Braithwaite, shaming, or the fear of being shamed, is a powerful force in our lives. Is shame a universal feeling, and can it lead to lawful behavior as well as crime?
5. Gottfredson and Hirschi's self-control theory is more positioned to explain street crimes than white-collar offenses. However, are there instances of elite crime or deviance that do revolve around the interest in immediate or short-term gratification?

ACTIVITIES

1. Attend a local sentencing hearing. Are any themes voiced by lawyers or the judge that are consistent with shaming theory?
2. Conduct an informal poll with people you know and ask them what they think is the most important factor in the commission of crime. Analyze the responses and note which ones are related to any of the general and integrated theories discussed in this chapter.
3. Write down all the important things and people that you have control over, and likewise, those things and people who control you. Where do you fall on the various control levels, as discussed by Tittle? Would your involvement in crime be influenced by your control level?

Epilogue

Tools for Using Criminological Theory

At the very least, a course in criminological theory should enable students to offer the casual observer some insight into the character and causes of crime. However, as is true with many apparently simple questions, thoughtful answers rarely come easily. For one thing, there are dozens of theories of crime and the sheer variety of competing explanations can be overwhelming. For another, "crime" and "criminality" cover many different things, so an explanation of one may hardly touch another. And as we have seen in the preceding chapter, attempts to construct general theories of crime that apply to many forms are fraught with difficulties and pitfalls. Small wonder students who have completed this course often feel more confused about crime than when they started.

We believe that some of the confusion can be lessened if students keep the following seven points in mind when thinking about criminological theory.

1. There are many different types of crime. A cursory glance at annual crime statistics shows that while petty theft, vandalism, and simple assault make up the bulk of crimes known to the police, many other offenses are committed in a given year, among them: sexual assaults, forgery, liquor law violations, weapons violations, drug crimes, gambling offenses, disorderly conduct, robbery, auto theft, vagrancy, embezzlement, prostitution, fraud, and murder. There are also many types of crime that are not listed at all, from so-called white-collar offenses and state and governmental crimes to domestic violence. But you get the implication: a theory of crime that does well for one type may not do as well for another, or even be relevant (a simple example: a theory that explains barroom violence is hardly relevant for corporate price-fixing, or safecracking by professional thieves).

2. Criminality varies among individuals as well as among groups. This is an important distinction because the clues to variations among individuals may be different from those relevant for groups. Explaining individual differences draws us toward psychological and social-psychological theories, while variations among groups are better addressed with social-structural theories.

3. Variations in criminality are not the same as variations in crime. This important distinction has been addressed by Ron Clarke and Travis Hirschi, among others. "Criminality" can be thought of as the propensity to commit crime and is a property of individuals or groups. "Crime" refers to offenses as events that occur with greater or lesser frequency, duration, intensity, and so on. Crime is all about opportunities, while criminality is all about motivations. Theories designed to explain variations in criminality are unlikely to shed enough light to also explain variations in crime as an event—and vice versa.

4. Among the ways crimes differ is in the resources and ability needed to commit them. This means that even though an opportunity for crime exists, it must still be accessed (taken advantage of), and the ability to do this varies among individuals and groups. Almost anyone can punch someone else (a simple assault) or shoplift (a petty theft); safecracking is another story, as are price-fixing and bomb-making. To the degree that opportunities for crime and access to them vary independently, a promising theory will address both these aspects of crime.

5. Just as crimes differ objectively in opportunity and access, they also differ subjectively. Simply put, while an opportunity for crime must exist objectively for the offense to occur, subjective perceptions will influence whether the opportunity is seized. Just as objective opportunities for crime (and access to them) vary among places and times, as well as among individuals and groups, so do perceptions of those opportunities (and access to them). A promising theory will also address these variations.

6. Crime is a social construction. From a legalistic point of view, acts are not criminal until lawmakers say they are—and assign a penalty for violations. Generally speaking, the seriousness of offenses is gauged by the penalties assigned to them; the lighter the penalty, the less serious the crime. So crimes vary by seriousness, where seriousness is a judgment made by people with the legal authority to do so. Although by no means exact, there is a connection between the legal seriousness of an offense and its perceived wrongness among the public at large. The two tend to vary together, that is, if one is high so is the other. Thus, a person who plants a bomb that kills twenty people faces execution or life in prison without parole; this same act receives the highest severity scores in national surveys of the general public. On the other hand, vagrancy and trespassing are relatively minor crimes in terms of penalties; not surprisingly, they receive among the lowest severity scores from the general public.

This has bearing on the likelihood that crimes will be committed if only because the more serious a contemplated act is perceived to be, the less likely it will occur. There are two reasons for this: (1) more serious crimes carry higher penalties (or costs and risks); this is the core of the deterrence argument; and (2) more serious crimes incur greater moral objection; this is the "normative" or wrongness argument found in neutralization theory. A promising theory of crime will address both the legal and moral aspects of seriousness.

7. Finally, external counter-control may reduce both crime and criminality. By this we mean that criminal events and the propensity to participate in them are each susceptible to efforts by others (police, courts, parents, teachers, friends, neighbors, witnesses, etc.) to prevent them from occurring in the first place, or to lessen their impact if they do arise. At the level of events, effective counter-control works on the opportunities for crime and/or access to them—it makes a given *situation* less prone to crime; at the level of motivations, effective counter-control reduces the likelihood that an individual or group finds crime appealing—it makes people less prone to committing crime. A promising theory of crime will address the impact of counter-control on both events and people.

The primary goal of any theory is to predict differences; that is, when there will be more or less of something. In our case, theory should result in predictions about crime and criminality. Policymakers can then use these predictions to make strategic decisions in the effort to reduce crime and criminality.

Some scholars (e.g., Gibbs, 1972, 1994) believe that predictive power is the only appropriate criterion when assessing theories. But there is a hitch: To achieve such assessments it is necessary that theories be stated formally, so that their logical structures are exposed in a parsimonious way and their arguments made explicit. Unfortunately, this is rarely the case in social science theory, and criminology is no exception. If convincing is necessary, simply look back through the chapters you have read and try to derive testable predictions from the mostly discursive theories presented. In many cases it will be a difficult, if not impossible, task. Worse, just when you think you've nailed down a testable prediction derived from one of the theories, the author of the theory could very easily say, "That's not what I meant."

So when friends or acquaintances bemoan the "crime problem" and ask you to suggest solutions, you should first ask them to be more specific. What kind of crime are they talking about? Are they talking about criminal events or criminal people? If it is the latter, are they talking about individuals or groups of people? If the former, are they interested in the objective features of a situation or the subjective ones? An even more fundamental question you should ask is this: "What do they *mean* by the words 'crime' and 'criminal'? A legalistic answer would focus your attention on acts and situations defined as crime by legislatures and on the people who commit those acts. An answer that emphasized social harm or moral prohibitions would focus your attention on a much broader range of acts and potentially a broader range of people. The definition of "crime" and "criminal" thus has important implications for theory. Indeed, some criminologists (e.g., Black, 1976) believe that variations in crime and criminality are directly linked to the behavior of law itself.

AN ANALYTICAL FRAMEWORK

Textbooks such as this one provide a survey of the main theories in criminology, but how can beginning students of crime think more cogently about explaining crime in broader terms? We have thought long and hard about the numerous criminological theories reviewed in this book and have concluded that there is indeed a way to make better sense out of the causes of crime than having to consider every detail of criminological theory. In what follows, we lay out an analytical framework—not a causal theory—of crime that allows students to center on three main variables on three levels of analysis.

Drawing on an integrated theoretical model of organizational crime (Kauzlarich and Kramer, 1998; Kramer, Michalowski, and Kauzlarich, 2002), we propose that crime in general can be understood as a result of the coincidence of (a) pressure for goal attainment, (b) the availability and attractiveness of legitimate means for achieving those goals, and (c) the absence of effective social control. This proposition can be boiled down to three elements: motivation, opportunity, and control. *Motivation* refers to the factors that make one inclined to pursue goals. These goals are often rooted in the desire for money, status, power, or respect, concepts found in a variety of criminological theories previously reviewed. One who is highly motivated to achieve any of these goals is at greater risk for criminal behavior, but it should be remembered that many who pursue these goals do not engage in criminal behavior. Therefore, as Sutherland indicates in his ninth proposition of differential association theory, motivations alone cannot be the basis of a sufficiently general theory of crime. Indeed, all the motivation in the world is moot if the opportunity to realize those goals is blocked. Therefore, the second major element of our proposition is *opportunity*, which refers to the available resources one has to meet his or her goals. The ability to pursue goals is contingent on the amount of economic, cultural, and social capital one has so that people who are socially disadvantaged or otherwise unable to reach goals through legitimate means, a la Merton's anomie/strain theory, are more likely to resolve their strain through criminal activity. Finally, the notion of *control* refers to the degree of informal and formal regulation surrounding a person or group. Those who are not subject to effective social control are more likely to, in combination with strong goals and blocked legitimate means, find criminal behavior more attractive. This is consistent with control theories reviewed previously in this text.

We are not interested here in developing a formal theory of crime but rather ways for you, the student, to think more coherently about the variety of ways that crime can be understood within the parameters of motivation, opportunity, and control. Table E.1 provides a graphic illustration of our analytical framework and identifies key variables and concepts related to the causes of crime.

While motivation, opportunity, and control are the three key concepts, none of them can be understood as monolithic categories that operate on only one level of analysis. Recall from chapter 1 that levels of analysis are slices of reality that guide the degree of abstraction used in thinking about crime. There are two main levels of analysis: micro (small picture) and macro (big picture). Micro level theories focus on individuals and social processes, while the macro perspective is interested in large-scale social structures. To these levels we can add a third—*meso*, which refers to an intermediate or "in between" level of analysis. This level is concerned with more immediate factors than the macro level, but those that are still removed from the individual. For example, whereas a macro level of analysis might target inequality in a society as a contributing factor to increases in crime and a micro theory would look at the individual self-control levels, the meso level of analysis would focus on the neighborhood, family, or school environment. Indeed, not all people are equally affected by inequality, nor do they share the same levels of social control. We propose, as many criminologists do, that this is due to the mediating effects of their immediate social environment.

Motivation

As table E.1 indicates, motivation on the *macro* level of analysis sensitizes us to many of the key theoretical concepts reviewed earlier. Recall Merton, Messner, and Rosenfeld and Bonger's concerns about how competition and materialism produce conditions conducive to crime. The logic here is that larger cultural and structural elements of a society produce and reinforce norms and values that make criminality more attractive. For example, disproportionate pressure in any society for people to achieve material items, wealth, and recognition can become primary to one's life at the expense of family, neighborhood, and community bonds. Any complete analysis of crime should take into consideration these larger background factors.

Table E.1.   An Analytical Framework for Studying the Causes of Crime

	Motivation	*Opportunity*	*Control*
Macro	Competition, Materialism, Media, & Ideology	Inequality in Race, Gender, Class, Age, & Technology	Law & Criminal Justice
Meso	Status & Community Norms	Neighborhood, Community, School, & Family: Resources Culture Support	Police-Community Relations, Collective Efficacy, Family & School Structure, & Environmental Design
Micro	Individual Goals, Feelings of Relative Deprivation, Rational Choice, & Previous Victimization	Intelligence Skills/ Training Time & Ability	Coping,Skills, Neutralization, Hardened Targets, Self-control, & Shaming

At the *meso* level of analysis, the motivation for crime is thought to be rooted in local or community-based social structures or cultures. Some communities, such as those discussed by Anderson, Cohen, Cloward, and Ohlin, and Laub and Sampson (chapters 4 and 7) have unique cultures and norms that reward or expect some forms of behavior over others. Anderson, for example, found that in many lower-income communities, African Americans feel that adopting the "code of the street" provides them with both protection from victimization and the achievement of status within the community. Anderson further argues that higher rates of violent crime in inner cities are explained by this cultural response to structural conditions of isolation, alienation, and lack of economic opportunity (which we shall discuss under the concept of opportunity below).

At the micro level of analysis, motivation can be studied in terms of how individuals conceptualize their own personal and professional goals, whether they feel marginalized, how they intellectually process potential rewards and punishments, and whether they have been previously victimized. All of these variables are important to consider as similarly situated people (at the macro and meso levels of analysis) do not always act in identical ways. Indeed, most individuals from economically disadvantaged communities living in a wider culture of materialism do not engage in serious crime, so we must ask, what distinguishes those who do? One answer is through Classical and rational choice theoretical approaches (reviewed in chapter 2) that examine how individuals think differently about the possible punishments and rewards for engaging in crime. Another way to think about micro level motivations for crime is to consider the extent to which individuals vary in their exposure to negative treatment, as Agnew has proposed in his general strain theory, reviewed in chapter 4.

Opportunity

People need opportunities to accomplish anything. These opportunities may be self-created or a product of one's social position. While motivation for criminality is critical to understanding the causes of crime, we must also consider the range of opportunities for criminal behavior available to an individual or group in order to develop a fuller understanding of crime.

On the macro level of analysis, many criminological theories maintain that economic deprivation and racial and gender inequality are key variables in explaining who has the opportunity to live life without engaging in crime and who doesn't. In terms of rates of crime, high levels of violence in poor urban areas are thought to be related to the lack of good jobs and schools in communities. Elijah Anderson illustrated this point quite well in his studies of poor African American communities in U.S. cities. One can also see this line of reasoning in many other criminological theories, such as Braithwaite's reintegrative shaming approach (reviewed in chapter 7) and Currie's theory on crime in market societies, which was reviewed in chapter 6. Further, the level of supervision and physical security in neighborhoods impact how much opportunity there may be for criminality. Routine activities and situational crime prevention theories reviewed in chapter 2 are helpful in this way.

Opportunity is not only a macro level matter but also one that is operational at the meso level of analysis. Opportunities provided in more immediate social environments such as the schools, family, and neighborhood play key roles in the extent to which criminal behavior is attractive. If neighborhoods, families, and schools are close-knit—what Braithwaite calls interdependent—crime tends to be lower because of the internalization of social norms contrary to criminality (a la social disorganization theory and social control theory) and the potential fear that social and cultural capital (e.g., respect and friendship) can be lost.

On the micro level of analysis, opportunities for crime relate to variable individual perceptions. As we discussed earlier, some people may be intellectually incapable of figuring out how to engage in sophisticated crimes such as computer hacking, Internet fraud, or Ponzi schemes while others might be able to see these opportunities without much difficulty. Additionally, the amount of time a person has can be directly related to the ability to see and seize criminal opportunities. For example, those with demanding family or job responsibilities may find little time to think about criminal enterprises. Likewise, children who are busy with chores or homework after school and who are otherwise supervised by adults in their activities would have less opportunity to think about seizing criminal opportunities.

Control

Humans are socially regulated in a number of ways—and by a number of audiences. In a college classroom, for example, most students and professors alike are aware of norms that govern their behavior—and the potential costs of violating these rules (e.g., being reprimanded and losing respect or status). Likewise, parental, school, peer, community, and government control over the definition and enforcement of standards of conduct are thought to be critical for understanding why some people break rules and others do not. Why would some people never dare to commit a burglary, for example, while others do it routinely? Indeed, not all people succumb to regulation and control, nor do all societies and communities have the same degree of control over the people in their geographic area.

On the macro level, the regulation of behavior can be linked to large-scale social structures such as law and the criminal justice system. Recalling Classical criminological theory and modern-day rational choice approaches reviewed in chapter 2, the logic is quite simple: People inclined to engage in crime will not do so if they greatly fear the punishment for doing so. Thus, to control potential criminal inclinations, the possibility of arrest, prosecution, conviction, and sentencing to a prison or jail should be threatened in order to compel people to obey the law. Many federal and state laws are designed with the assumption that the threat of punishment can have a deterrent effect, although as we have discussed earlier in chapter 2, deterrence theory has several limitations. Additionally, sociological theories, like that proposed by Braithwaite, suggest that people not only want to avoid a criminal sentence, but many also fear the resulting shame and stigma that results from criminal processing. Of course, this embarrassment takes place only if the individual actually cares about the opinions of others, and this is not as likely in noncommutarian societies.

On the meso level of analysis, local policing, community, neighborhood, and school networks also offer the potential for regulation and control. No matter what national or state laws exist, the immediate climate of control is a more significant factor impacting crime commission. Social disorganization theory and Laub and Sampson's notion of "collective efficacy" are particularly salient here. If people in a community are closely attached and dependent on one another, there is more to lose in the way of status and respect as a result of engaging in criminal behavior. Additionally, peacemaking criminologists would posit that these intimate relationships create more respect for others' property and life, thus making criminality less attractive.

On the micro level of analysis, Gottfredson and Hirsch's self-control theory (chapter 7) is helpful here as it points out that individuals have varying degrees of control over their own behavior. Those who pursue more clearly self-interested and short-term goals are more likely to commit crime, especially when other macro and meso controls are inoperable. Also on this level, Agnew's general strain theory is helpful because it suggests that those who do not have the coping skills to deal with negative treatment are more likely to resolve strain through crime. Therefore, the ability to control reactions to painful circumstances, such as child abuse, is something to look for when thinking about the causes of crime at this level of analysis.

This brief overview of an analytic framework was designed to help you think more clearly and integratively about crime and criminality. The framework borrows heavily from many of the theories of crime reviewed earlier in the text by integrating key concepts along various levels of intellectual analysis. We wish you good fortune in the development of your understanding of crime and criminality. It has been our lives' intellectual pursuit, and we all still have much to learn.

References

Adams, Mike S. (1996). "Labeling and differential association: Towards a general social learning theory of crime and deviance," *American Journal of Criminal Justice* 20(2): 147–64.

Adams, Mike S., and David T. Evans. (1996). "Teacher disapproval, delinquent peers, and self-reported delinquency: A longitudinal test of labeling theory," *Urban Review* 28(3): 199–211.

Adler, Freda. (1975). *Sisters in crime: The rise of the new female criminal*. New York: McGraw-Hill.

Agnew, Robert. (1985). "Social control theory and delinquency," *Criminology* 23: 47–60.

Agnew, Robert. (1992). "Foundation for a general strain theory of crime and delinquency," *Criminology* 30: 47–87.

Agnew, Robert. (1994). "The techniques of neutralization and violence," *Criminology* 32: 555–80.

Agnew, Robert. (1999). "A general strain theory of community differences in crime rates," *Journal of Research in Crime and Delinquency* 36(2): 123–55.

Agnew, Robert. (2001). "Building on the foundation of general strain theory: Specifying the types of strain most likely to lead to crime and delinquency," *Journal of Research in Crime and Delinquency* 38(4): 319–63.

Anderson, Elijah. (1999). *Code of the street*. New York: Norton.

Archer, Dane, and Rosemary Gartner. (1984). *Violence and crime in cross-national perspective*. New Haven, CT: Yale University Press.

Arrigo, Bruce. (1998). "Marxist criminology and Lacanian psychoanalysis: Outline for a general constitutive theory of crime," in Jeffrey I. Ross, ed., *Cutting the edge: Current perspectives in radical/critical criminology and criminal justice*. Westport, CT: Praeger. 40–62.

Arrigo, Bruce. (2003). "Postmodern justice and critical criminology: Positional, relational, and provisional science," in Martin D. Schwartz and Suzanne E. Hatty, eds., *Controversies in critical criminology*. Cincinatti: Anderson Publishing.

Bahr, Stephen J., John P. Hoffmann, and Xiaoyan Yang. (2005). "Parental and peer influences on the risk of adolescent drug use," *The Journal of Primary Prevention* 26(6): 529–51.

Bailey, Ronald H. (1976). *Violence and aggression*. New York: Time Life Books.

Bailey, William C. (1998). "Deterrence, brutalization, and the death penalty: Another examination of Oklahoma's return to capital punishment," *Criminology* 36: 711–33.

Baltagi, Badi. (2006). "Estimating an economic model of crime using panel data from North Carolina," *Journal of Applied Econometrics* 21(4): 543–47.

Bandura, Albert. (1973). *Aggression: A social learning analysis*. Englewood Cliffs, NJ: Prentice-Hall.

Barak, Gregg, Jeanne Flavin, and Paul Leighton. (2001). *Class, race, gender and crime: Social realities of justice in America*. Lanham, MD: Rowman & Littlefield.

Barlow, Hugh D. (1991). "Explaining crimes and analogous acts, or the unrestrained will grab at pleasure whenever they can," *Journal of Criminal Law and Criminology* 82: 229–42.

Barlow, Hugh D. (1995). *Crime and public policy: Putting theory to work*. Boulder, CO: Westview.

Barlow, Hugh D., and Theodore N. Ferdinand. (1992). *Understanding delinquency*. New York: Harper Collins.

Barlow, Melissa Hickman, David E. Barlow, and Theodore G. Chiricos. (1995a). "Economic conditions and ideologies of crime in the media: A content analysis of crime news," *Crime and Delinquency* 41: 3–19.

Barlow, Melissa Hickman, David E. Barlow, and Theodore G. Chiricos. (1995b). "Mobilizing support for social control in a declining economy: Exploring ideologies of crime within crime news," *Crime and Delinquency* 41(2): 191–202.

Barnett, Harold. (1981). "Corporate capitalism, corporate crime," *Crime and Delinquency* 27: 4–23.

Baron, Stephen W., and David R. Forde. (2007). "Street youth crime: A test of control balance theory," *Justice Quarterly* 24: 335–55.

Beccaria, Cesare. (1963). *Essay on crimes and punishments*, trans. by Henry Paolucci. Indianapolis, IN: Bobbs-Merrill.

Becker, Gary S. (1968). "Crime and punishment: An economic approach," *Journal of Political Economy* 76: 493–517.

Becker, Howard S. (1963). *Outsiders: Studies in the sociology of deviance*. New York: Free Press.

Bennett, Trevor, and Richard Wright. (1981). "Burglars' choice of targets: The use of situational cues in offender decision making." Presented at the annual meeting of the American Society of Criminology, Washington, D.C.

Bennett, Trevor, and Richard Wright. (1984). *Burglars on burglary*. Aldershot, UK: Gower.

Bentham, Jeremy. (1973). *The Principles of morals and legislation*. New York: Hofner Publishing.

Bernasco, Wim, and Floor Luykx. (2003). "Effects of attractiveness, opportunity, and accessibility to burglars on residential burglary rates of urban neighborhoods," *Criminology* 41: 981–1001.

Bernburg, Jon G., Marvin D. Krohn, and Craig J. Rivera. (2006). "Official labeling, criminal embeddedness, and subsequent delinquency," *Journal of Research in Crime and Delinquency* 43: 67–88.

Bernburg, Jon Gunnar, and Marvin D. Krohn. (2003). "Labeling, life chances, and adult crime: The direct and indirect effects of official intervention in adolescence on crime in early adulthood," *Criminology* 41(4): 1287–319.

Bjerregaard, Beth, and John K. Cochran. (2008). "A cross-national test of institutional anomie theory: Do the strength of other social institutions mediate or moderate the effects of the economy on the rate of crime? *Western Criminology Review* 9(1): 31–48.

Black, Donald J. (1976). *The behavior of law*. New York: Academic Press.

Blokland, Arjan, Daniel Nagin, and Paul Nieuwbeerta. (2005). "Life span offending trajectories of a Dutch conviction cohort," *Criminology* 43(4): 919–48.

Blumer, Herbert. (1969). *Symbolic interactionism: Perspective and method*. Englewood Cliffs, NJ: Prentice-Hall.

Boggs, Sarah Lee. (1964). "The ecology of crime occurrence in St. Louis: A reconceptualization of crime rates and patterns." PhD diss., Washington University, St. Louis, Missouri.

Bohm, Robert M. (1998). "Understanding crime and social control in market economies: Looking back and moving forward," in Jeffrey Ian Ross, ed., *Cutting the edge: Current perspectives in radical/critical criminology*. Westport, CT: Praeger.

Bonger, Willem. (1969). *Criminality and economic conditions, abridged version*. Bloomington, IN: Indiana University Press.

Borkin, Julie, Stuart Henry, and Dragan Milovanovic. (2006). "Constitutive rhetoric and constitutive criminology: The significance of *the virtual corpse*," in Walter S. DeKeseredy, Shahid Alvi, and Martin D. Schwartz, eds., *Advancing Critical Criminology: Theory and Application*. New York: Rowman & Littlefield.

Botchkovar, Ekaterina, and Charles R. Tittle. (2005). "Crime, shame and reintegration in Russia," *Theoretical Criminology* 9(4): 401–42.

Box, Steven. (1981). *Deviance, reality, and society*. 2nd ed. London: Holt, Rinehart, and Winston.

Braithwaite, John. (1978). "An exploratory study of used car fraud," in P. R. Wilson and J. B. Braithwaite, eds., *Two faces of deviance: Crimes of the powerless and powerful*. Brisbane: University of Queensland Press.

Braithwaite, John. (1989a). *Crime, shame and reintegration*. Cambridge, England: Cambridge University Press.

Braithwaite, John. (1989b). "Organizational theory and organizational shame," *Justice Quarterly* 6: 401–26.

Braithwaite, John. (1991). "Inequality and republican criminology." Presented at the annual meeting of the American Society of Criminology, San Francisco, November 18–23.

Braithwaite, John. (1997). "Charles Tittle's control balance and criminological theory," *Theoretical Criminology* 1(1): 77–97.

Braithwaite, John, and Philip Pettit. (1990). *Not just desserts: A republican theory of criminal justice*. Oxford, England: Oxford University Press.

Broidy, Lisa, and Robert Agnew. (1997). "Gender and crime: A general strain theory perspective," *Journal of Research in Crime and Delinquency* 34: 275–306.

Bruinsma, Gerben. (1992). "Differential association theory reconsidered: An extension and its empirical test," *Journal of Quantitative Criminology* 8(1): 29–49.

Buikhuisen, Wouter. (1988). "Chronic juvenile delinquency: A theory," in Wouter Buikhuisen and Sarnoff A. Mednick. eds., *Explaining criminal behavior*. Linden, Netherlands: E. J. Brill.

Burgess, Robert L. (1979). "Family violence: Some implications from evolutionary biology." Presented at the annual meeting of the American Society of Criminology, San Francisco.

Burgess, Robert L., and Ronald L. Akers. (1966). "A differential association-reinforcement theory of criminal behavior," *Social Problems* 14: 128–47.

Burgess, Robert L., and Patricia Draper. (1989). "The explanation of family violence: The role of biological, behavioral, and cultural selection," in Lloyd Ohlin and Michael Tonry, eds., *Family Violence*. Chicago: University of Chicago Press.

Bursik, Robert J., Jr. (1988). "Social disorganization and theories of crime and delinquency: Problems and prospects," *Criminology* 26: 519–51.

Bursik, Robert J., Jr. (2000). "The systematic theory of neighborhood crime rates," in Sally S. Simpson, ed., *Of crime and criminality: The use of theory in everyday life*. Thousand Oaks, CA: Pine Forge Press.

Bursik, Robert J., and Harold G. Grasmick. (1993). *Neighborhoods and crime: The dimensions of effective community control*. Lexington, MA: Lexington Books.

Bursik, Robert J. and Harold G. Grasmick. (1995). "Neighborhood-based networks and the control of crime and delinquency," in Hugh D. Barlow, ed., *Crime and Public Policy: Putting Theory to Work*. Boulder, CO: Westview.

Calder, James D., and John F. Bauer. (1992). "Convenience store robberies: Security measures and store robbery incidents," *Journal of Criminal Justice* 20: 553–66.

Carter, Ronald L., and Kim Q. Hill. (1979). *The criminal's image of the city*. New York: Pergamon.

Chambliss, William J. (1973). "The saints and the roughnecks," *Society* 11: 24–31.

Chambliss, William J. (1975a). "The political economy of crime: A comparative study of Nigeria and the U.S.A.," in Ian Taylor, Paul Walton, and Jock Young, eds., *Critical criminology*. London: Routledge and Kegan Paul.

Chambliss, William J. (1975b). *Criminal law in action*. Santa Barbara, CA: Hamilton.

Chambliss, William J. (1999). *Power, Politics, and Crime*. Boulder, CO: Westview.

Chambliss, William J., and Marjorie Zatz. (1993). *Making law: The state, the law, and structural contradictions*. Bloomington: Indiana University Press.

Chamlin, Mitchell B., and John K. Cochran. "Social altruism and crime," *Criminology* 35(2): 203–29.

Chapman, William R. (1986). "The role of peers in strain models of delinquency." Presented at the annual meeting of the American Society of Criminology, Atlanta, Georgia.

Cherry, T. and J. List. (2002). "Aggregation bias in the economic model of crime," *Economic Letters* 75(1): 81–6.

Chesney-Lind, Meda. (1987a). *Girls' crime and women's place: Toward a feminist model of female delinquency.* Honolulu: University of Hawaii Youth Development and Research Center.

Chesney-Lind, Meda. (1987b). "Female status offenders and the double standard of juvenile justice: An international problem." Presented at the annual meeting of the American Society of Criminology, Montreal, November 11–14.

Chesney-Lind, Meda, and Randall G. Shelden. (1992). *Girls, delinquency, and juvenile justice.* Pacific Grove, CA: Brooks/Cole.

Chodorkoff, Bernard, and Seymour Baxter. (1969). "Psychiatric and psychoanalytic theories of violence and its origins," in Donald J. Mulvihill, Melvin Tumin, and Lynn Curtis, eds., *Crimes of violence.* Washington, D.C.: U.S. Government Printing Office.

Christiansen, K. O. (1977a). "A preliminary study of criminality among twins," in Sarnoff A. Mednick and K. O. Christiansen, eds., *Biosocial basis of criminal behavior.* New York: Wiley.

Christiansen, K. O. (1977b). "A review of studies of criminality among twins," in Sarnoff A. Mednick and K. O. Christiansen, eds., *Biosocial basis of criminal behavior.* New York: Wiley.

Clarke, R. V., and M. Felson, eds. (1993). "Routine activity and rational choice," in *Advances in Criminological Theory,* Volume 5. New Brunswick, NJ: Transaction Publications.

Clarke, Ronald V., and Patricia Mayhew. (1988). "The British gas suicide story and its criminological implications," in Michael N. Tonry and Norval K. Morris, eds., *Crime and justice: A review of research, vol. 10.* Chicago: University of Chicago Press.

Clear, Todd, Dina Rose, Elin Waring, and Kristin Scully. (2003). "Coercive mobility and crime," *Justice Quarterly* 20: 33–63.

Cloward, Richard A., and Lloyd E. Ohlin. (1960). *Delinquency and opportunity: A theory of delinquent gangs.* New York: Free Press.

Coates, R., S. Umbreit, and B. Vos. (2006). "Responding to hate crimes through restorative justice dialog," *Contemporary Justice Review* 9(1): 7–21.

Cochran, John K., Mitchell B. Chamlin, and Mark Seth. (1994). "Deterrence or brutalization: An impact assessment of Oklahoma's return to capital punishment," *Criminology* 32: 107–34.

Cohen, Albert K. (1955). *Delinquent boys: The culture of the gang.* New York: Free Press.

Cohen, Lawrence E., and Marcus Felson. (1979). "Social change and crime rate trends: A routine activity approach," *American Sociological Review* 44: 588–608.

Cohen, Lawrence E., and Richard Machalek. (1988). "A general theory of expropriative crime: An evolutionary ecological approach," *American Journal of Sociology* 94: 465–501.

Cohen-Cole, E., S. Durlauf, J. Fagan, D. Nagin. (2008). "Model uncertainty and the deterrent effect of capital punishment," *American Law and Economics Review.* American Law and Economics Review Advance Access published online on April 15, 2008; accessed May 23, 2009.

Cornish, Derek B., and Ronald V. Clarke. (1986). "Situational prevention, displacement of crime and rational choice theory," in Kevin Heal and Gloria Laycock, eds., *Situational crime prevention.* London: H.M.S.O.

Cornish, Derek B., and Ronald V. Clarke. (1987). "Understanding crime displacement: An application of rational choice theory," *Criminology* 25: 933–47.

Cornwell, C., and W. Trumbull. (1994). "Estimating the economic model of crime with panel data," *Review of Economics and Statistics* 76(2): 360–66.

Costello, Barbara J., and Paul R. Vowell. (1999). "Testing control theory and differential association: A reanalysis of the Richmond Youth Project data," *Criminology* 37(4): 815–42.

Coupe, Timothy, and Laurence Blake. "Daylight and darkness targeting strategies and the risks of being seen at residential burglaries," *Criminology* 44(2): 431–64.

Cromwell, Paul F., ed. (1999). *In their own words: Criminals on crime.* 2nd ed. Los Angeles: Roxbury.

Cullen, Francis T. (1983a). "Paradox in policing: A note on perceptions of danger," *Journal of Police Science and Administration* 11: 457–62.

Cullen, Francis T. (1983b). *Rethinking crime and deviance theory: The emergence of a structuring tradition.* Totowa, NJ: Rowman and Allanheld.

Cullen, Francis T. (1994). "Social support as an organizing concept for criminology: Presidential address to the Academy of Criminal Justice Sciences," *Justice Quarterly* 11: 527–59.

Currie, Elliott. (1997). "Market, crime, and community: Toward a mid-range theory of post-industrial violence," *Theoretical Criminology* 1(2): 147–72.

D'Alessio, S. J., and L. Stolzenberg. (1998). "Crime, arrests, and pretrial jail incarceration: An examination of the deterrence thesis," *Criminology* 36: 735–61.

Daly, Kathleen, and Meda Chesney-Lind. (1988). "Feminism and criminology," *Justice Quarterly* 5: 101–43.

Daly, M., and M. Wilson. (1998). "The evolutionary social psychology of family violence," in C. B. Crawford and D. L. Krebs, eds. *Handbook of evolutionary psychology: Ideas, issues, and applications.* Mahwah, NJ: Lawrence Erlbaum. 431–56.

Daly, Martin, and Margo Wilson. (1988a). "Evolutionary social psychology and family homicide," *Science* 242: 519–24.

Daly, Martin, and Margo Wilson. (1988b). *Homicide.* New York: Aldine DeGruyter.

Davey, Jeremy, D. James, E. Freeman, Gavan R. Palk, Anita L. Lavelle, and Bevan D. Rowland. (2008). "Drug driving and deterrence: The impact of the new drug driving legislation and testing methods in Queensland," in *Proceedings Canadian Multidisciplinary Road Safety Conference* 18, Whistler, Canada.

Dekeseredy, W., S. Alvi, M. Schwartz, and A. Tomaszewski. (2003). *Under siege: Poverty and crime in a public housing community.* Lanham, MD: Lexington.

Dekeseredy, Walter, and Barbara Perry. (2006). *Advancing critical criminology.* Lanham, MD: Lexington.

Di Tella, R., and E. Schargrodsky. (2004). "Do police reduce crime? Estimates using the allocation of police forces after a terrorist attack," *American Economic Review* 94(1): 115–33.

Dollard, John, N. Miller, L. Doob, O. H. Mowrer, and R. R. Sears. (1939). *Frustration and aggression.* New Haven, CT: Yale University Press.

Downs, William R., Joan F. Robertson, and Larry R. Harrison. (1997). "Control theory, labeling theory, and the delivery of service for drug abuse to adolescents," *Adolescence* 32: 1–24.

Durkheim, E. (1938 [1895]). *Rules of Sociological Method.* New York: Free Press.

Durkheim, Emile. (1893). *De la division du travail social.* Paris: Alcan.

Durkheim, Emile. (1964). *The division of labor in society.* New York: Free Press.

Edwards, Willie J. (1993). "Constructing and testing a multiple-theory integrated model of juvenile delinquency," *Mid American Review of Sociology* 17(1): 31–43.

Ellis, Lee. (1991). "Monoamine oxidase and criminality: Identifying an apparent biological marker for antisocial behavior," *Journal of Research in Crime and Delinquency* 28: 227–51.

Ellis, Lee, and Anthony Walsh. (1997). "Gene-based evolutionary theories in criminology," *Criminology* 35(2): 229–76.

Erikson, Kai T. (1966). *Wayward puritans: A study in the sociology of deviance.* New York: Wiley.

Farley, John. (2005). *Minority-majority relations.* 5th ed. Upper Saddle River, NJ: Prentice Hall.

Feagin, Joe R. (2006). *Systemic racism: A theory of opression.* New York: Routledge.

Felson, Marcus. (1998). *Crime and everyday life.* 2nd ed. Thousand Oaks, CA: Pine Forge.

Felson, Marcus. (2002). *Crime and everyday life.* 3rd ed. Thousand Oaks, CA: Sage.

Ferrell, J. (1993). *Crimes of style: Urban graffiti and the politics of criminality.* New York: Garland.

Ferrell, Jeff. (1999). "Cultural criminology," *Annual Review of Sociology* 25: 395–418.

Ferrell, Jeff. (2001). *Tearing down the streets: Adventures in urban anarchy.* New York: Palgrave.

Ferrell, Jeff. (2003). "Cultural criminology," in Martin D. Schwartz and Suzanne E. Hatty, eds., *Controversies in critical criminology.* Cincinnati: Anderson Publishing. 71–84.

Ferrell, Jeff. (2004). "Boredom, crime, and criminology," *Theoretical Criminology* 8(3): 287–302.

Ferrell, Jeff. (2005). *Empire of scrounge: Inside the urban underground of dumpster-diving, trash-picking and street-scavenging.* New York: New York University Press.

Ferrell, Jeff, Keith Hayward, and Jock Young. (2008). *Cultural Criminology: An Invitation.* Thousand Oaks, CA: Sage.

Finley, Laura L. (2002). "The lyrics of rage against the machine: A study in radical criminology," *Journal of Criminal Justice and Popular Culture* 9(3): 150–66.

Fishbein, Diana H. (1990). "Biological perspectives in criminology," *Criminology* 28: 27–72.

Flavin, Jeanne. (1998). "Razing the wall: A feminist critique of sentencing theory, research, and policy," in Jeffrey I. Ross, ed., *Cutting the edge: Current perspectives in radical/critical criminology and criminal justice.* Westport, CT: Praeger. 145–64.

Fraser, S. (1995). *The bell curve wars.* New York: Basic Books.

Friedrichs, David O. (1996). *Trusted criminals: White collar crime in contemporary society.* New York: Wadsworth.

Friedrichs, David O. (1998a). "New directions in critical criminology and white collar crime," in Jeffrey I. Ross, ed., *Cutting the edge: Current perspectives in radical/critical criminology and criminal justice.* Westport, CT: Praeger. 77–94.

Friedrichs, David O. (1998b). *State crime. Volumes I and II.* Aldershot, UK: Dartmouth.

Friedrichs, David O. (2009). *Trusted criminals: White collar crime in contemporary society.* 4th ed. New York: Wadsworth Publishing.

Fuller, John. (2003). "Peacemaking criminology," in Martin D. Schwartz and Suzanne E. Hatty, eds., *Controversies in Critical Criminology.* Cincinnati: Anderson. 85–95.

Garland, David. (1985). "The criminal and his science," *British Journal of Criminology* 28: 109–37.

Gibbs, Jack. (1985). "Review essay," *Criminology* 23: 381–88.

Gibbs, Jack P. (1972). *Sociological theory construction.* Hinsdale, IL: Dryden.

Gibbs, Jack P. (1988). "Reply to Michalowski," *Criminologist* 13(4): 4–5.

Gibbs, Jack P. (1994). *A theory about control.* Boulder, CO: Westview.

Gibbs, Jack P., and Glenn Firebaugh. (1990). "The artifact issue in deterrence research," *Criminology* 28: 347–67.

Gibbs, John J., Dennis Giever, and George E. Higgins. (2003). "A test of Gottfredson and Hirschi's general theory using structural equation modeling," *Criminal Justice and Behavior* 30: 441–58.

Gilligan, James. (1996). *Violence: Our deadly epidemic and its causes.* New York: Grosset/Putnam.

Giordano, P. C., S. A. Cernkovich, and D. D. Holland. (2003). "Changes in friendship relations over the life course: Implications for desistance from crime," *Criminology* 41: 293–327.

Giordano, Peggy C., Toni J. Millhollin, Stephen A. Cernkovich, M. D. Pugh, and Jennifer L. Rudolph. (1999). "Delinquency, identity, and women's involvement in realtionship violence," *Criminology* 37(1): 17–40.

Glaser, Daniel. (1956). "Criminality theories and behavioral images," *American Journal of Sociology* 61: 433–44.

Glueck, Sheldon, and Eleanor Glueck. (1950). *Unraveling juvenile delinquency.* New York: Commonwealth Fund.

Glueck, Sheldon, and Eleanor Glueck. (1955) "Early detection of future delinquents," *Journal of Criminal Law, Criminology, and Police Science* 47(2): 174–82.

Gordon, David M. (1971). "Class and the economics of crime," *Review of Radical Economics* 3: 51–75.

Gordon, David M. (1973). "Capitalism, class and crime in America," *Crime and Delinquency* 19: 163–86.

Gorman, D. M., and Helene Raskin White. (1995). "You can choose your friends, but do they choose crime? Implication of differential association theories for crime prevention policy," in Hugh D. Barlow, ed., *Crime and public policy: Putting theory to work.* Boulder, CO: Westview. 131–56.

Gottfredson, Michael R., and Travis Hirschi. (1988). "Science, public policy, and the career paradigm," *Criminology* 26: 37–55.

Gottfredson, Michael R., and Travis Hirschi. (1990). *A general theory of crime.* Stanford, CA: Stanford University Press.

Green, Edward. (1993). *The intent to kill.* Baltimore: Clevedon Books.

Greenberg, David F. (1977). "Crime and deterrence research and social policy," in Stuart S. Nagel, ed., *Modeling the criminal justice system.* Beverly Hills, CA: Sage, 281–95.

Greenberg, David F. (1999). "The weak strength of social control theory," *Crime and Delinquency* 45(1): 66–81.

Greenleaf, Richard G., and Lonn Lanza-Kaduce. (1995). "Sophistication, organization, and authority-subject conflict: Rediscovering and unraveling Turk's theory of norm resistance," *Criminology* 33(4): 565-73.

Greer, C., and Y. Jewkes. (2005). "Extremes of otherness: Media images and social exclusion," *Social Justice* 32(1): 20-38.

Guay, J., M. Ouimet, and J. Proulx. (2005). "On intelligence and crime: A comparison of incarcerated sex offenders and serious non-sexual violent criminals," *International Journal of Law and Psychiatry* 28(4): 405-17.

Hagan, John. (1985). *Modern criminology: Crime, criminal behavior and its control.* New York: McGraw-Hill.

Hakim, Simon, and George F. Rengert, eds. (1981). *Crime spillover.* Beverly Hills, CA: Sage.

Hamlin, John E. (1988). "The misplaced role of rational choice in neutralization theory," *Criminology* 23: 223-40.

Hay, C., and W. Forrest. (2008). "Self-control theory and the concept of opportunity: The case for a more systematic union," *Criminology* 46(4): 1039-73.

Hayward, Keith. (2002). "The vilification and pleasures of youthful transgression," in J. Muncie, G. Hughes, and E. McLaughlin, eds., *Youth justice: Critical readings.* London: Sage.

Heimer, Karen. (1997). "Socioeconomic status, subcultural definitions, and violent delinquency," *Social Forces* 75: 799-833.

Heimer, Karen, and Stacy De Coster. (1999). "The gendering of violent delinquency," *Criminology* 37(2): 277-318.

Henry, Stuart, and Dragan Milovanovic. (1996). *Constitutive criminology: Beyond postmodernism.* Thousands Oaks, CA: Sage.

Henry, Stuart, and Dragan Milovanovic. (1999). *Constitutive criminology at work: Applications to crime and justice.* Albany: State University of New York Press.

Henry, Stuart, and Dragan Milovanovic. (2003). "Constitutive criminology," in Martin D. Schwartz and Suzanne E. Hatty, eds., *Controversies in critical criminology.* Cincinnati: Anderson Publishing. 57-70.

Herrnstein, R. J., and C. Murray. (1994). *The bell curve: Intelligence and class structure in American life.* New York: Free Press.

Hindelang, Michael J. (1978). "Race and involvement in common law personal crimes," *American Sociological Review* 43: 93-109.

Hindelang, Michael J., Travis Hirschi, and Joseph G. Weis. (1979). "Correlates of delinquency: The illusion of discrepancy between self-report and official measures," *American Sociological Review* 44: 995-1014.

Hipp, J., D. Bauer, P. Curran, and K. Bollen. (2004). "Crimes of opportunity: Testing two explanations of seasonal change in crime," *Social Forces* 82(4): 1333-72.

Hirschi, Travis. (1971). *Causes of delinquency.* Berkeley: University of California Press.

Hirschi, Travis. (1983). "Crime and the family," in James Q. Wilson, ed., *Crime and public policy.* San Francisco: Institute for Contemporary Studies.

Hirschi, Travis, and Michael J. Hindelang. (1977). "Intelligence and delinquency: A revisionist view," *American Sociological Review* 42: 572-87.

Hochstetler, A., H. Copes, and M. DeLisi. (2002) "Differential association in group and solo offending," *Journal of Criminal Justice* 30(6): 559-66.

Hollinger, Richard C. (1991). "Neutralization in the workplace: An empirical analysis of property theft and production deviance," *Deviant Behavior* 12: 169–202.

Hooton, Earnest A. (1939). *Crime and the man*. Cambridge, MA: Harvard University Press.

Horney, Julie, and Ineke Haen Marshall. (1992). "Risk perceptions among serious offenders: The role of crime and punishment," *Criminology* 30: 575–92.

Iadicola, Peter, and Anson Shupe. (1998). *Violence, inequality, and human freedom*. Dix Hills, NY: General Hall, Inc.

Jamieson, Ruth, and Kieran McEvoy. (2005). "State crime by proxy and juridical othering," *British Journal of Criminology* 45(4): 504–33.

Jang, Sung Joon. (1999). "Age-varying effects of family, school, and peers on delinquency: A multilevel modeling test of interactional theory," *Criminology* 37(3): 643–86.

Janssen, P., T. Nicholls, R. Kumar, H. Stefankis, A. Spidel, and E. Simpson. (2005). "Of mice and men: Will the intersection of social science and genetics create new approaches for intimate partner violence?" *Journal of Interpersonal Violence* 20(1): 61–71.

Jeffery, C. Ray. (1959). "An integrated theory of crime and criminal behavior," *Journal of Criminal Law, Criminology, and Police Science* 49: 533–52.

Jeffery, C. Ray. (1994). "Biological and neuropsychiatric approaches to criminal behavior," in Gregg Barak, ed., *Varieties of criminology*. Westport, CA: Praeger. 15–28.

Jensen, A. R. (1969). "How much can we boost IQ and scholastic achievement?" *Harvard Educational Review* 39: 1–123.

Kandel, Denise, and Mark Davies. (1991). "Friendship networks, intimacy, and illicit drug use in young adulthood: A comparison of two competing theories," *Criminology* 29: 441–69.

Katz, Jack. (1988). *Seductions of crime: Moral and sensual attractions of doing evil*. New York: Basic Books.

Kauzlarich, David, and Ronald C. Kramer. (1998). *Crimes of the American nuclear state: At home and abroad*. Boston: Northeastern University Press.

Kauzlarich, David, Rick A. Matthews, and William J. Miller. (2001). "Toward a victimology of state crime," *Critical Criminology: An International Journal* 10(3): 173–94.

Keane, Carl, Paul S. Maxim, and James J. Teevan. (1993). "Drinking and driving, self-control, and gender: Testing a general theory of crime," *Journal of Research in Crime and Delinquency* 30: 30–46.

Kennedy, Leslie W., and David R. Forde. (1990). "Routine activities and crime: An analysis of victimization in Canada," *Criminology* 28: 137–52.

Klockars, Carl B. (1974). *The professional fence*. New York: Free Press.

Kramer, R., R. Michalowski, and D. Kauzlarich. (2002). "The origins and development of the concept and theory of state-corporate crime," *Crime & Delinquency* 48(2): 263–82.

Kubrin, C., and R. Weitzer. (2003). "New directions in social disorganization theory," *Journal of Research in Crime and Delinquency* 40(4): 374–402.

Lasley, Jim. (1988). "Toward a control theory of white-collar offending," *Journal of Quantitative Criminology* 4: 347–62.

Laub, John H., and Robert J. Sampson. (1988). "Unraveling families and delinquency: A reanalysis of the Gluecks' data," *Criminology* 26: 355–80.

Lemert, Edwin M. (1951). *Social pathology.* New York: McGraw-Hil

Lemert, Edwin M. (1972). *Human deviance, social problems and social control.* 2nd ed. Englewood Cliffs, NJ: Prentice-Hall.

Lemert, Edwin M. (1974). "Beyond Mead: The societal reaction to deviance," *Social Problems* 21: 457–68.

Linden, E., and J. C. Hackler. (1973). "Affective ties and delinquency," *Pacific Sociological Review* 16: 27–47.

Link, Bruce, and Francis T. Cullen. (1983). "Reconsidering the social rejection of ex-mental patients: Levels of attitudinal response," *American Journal of Community Psychology* 11: 261–73.

Lombroso, Cesare. (1911). *Crime, its causes and remedies.* Boston: Little, Brown.

Lorenz, Konrad. (1971). *On aggression.* New York: Bantam Books.

Losoncz, Ibolya, and Graham Tyson. "Parental shaming and adolescent delinquency: A partial test of reintegrative shaming theory," *Australian and New Zealand Journal of Criminology* 40(2): 161–78.

Lunde, Donald T. (1970). *Murder and madness.* San Francisco: San Francisco Book Co.

Lyng, Stephen. (1990). "Edgework: A social psychological analysis of voluntary risk taking," *American Journal of Sociology* 95: 851–86.

Lyotard, J. (1984). *The postmodern condition: A report on knowledge.* Minneapolis: University of Minnesota Press.

Machalek, Richard, and Lawrence E. Cohen. (1991). "The nature of crime: Is cheating necessary for cooperation?" *Human Nature* 2: 215–33.

Maher, Lisa. (1997). *Sexed work: Gender, race, and resistence in a Brooklyn drug market.* Oxford: Clarendon Press.

Makkai, Toni, and John Braithwaite. (1991). "Criminological theories and regulatory compliance," *Criminology* 29: 191–217.

Makkai, Toni, and John Braithwaite. (1994). "Reintegrative shaming and compliance with regulatory standards," *Criminology* 32: 361–83.

Martínez, Ramiro, Jr., Richard Rosenfeld, and Dennis Mares. (2008). "Social disorganization, drug market activity, and neighborhood violent crime," *Urban Affairs Review* 43: 846–74.

Marx, Karl ([1859] 1971). *A contribution to the critique of political economy.* London: Lawrence and Wishart.

Marx, Karl, and Friedrich Engels. ([1846] 1947). *The German ideology.* New York: International Publishers.

Matsueda, Ross L. (1982). "Testing control theory and differential association: A causal modeling approach," *American Sociological Review* 47: 489–504.

Matsueda, Ross L., and Kathleen Anderson. (1998). "The dynamics of delinquent peers and delinquent behavior," *Criminology* 36(2): 269–308.

Matsueda, Ross L., and Karen Heimer. (1987). "Race, family structure, and delinquency: A test of differential association and social control theories," *American Sociological Review* 52: 826–40.

Matsueda, Ross L., Derek A. Kreager, and David Huizinga. (2006). "Deterring delinquents: A rational choice model of theft and violence," *American Sociological Review* 71(1): 95–122.

Matthews, Rick A. (2004). "Marxist criminology," in Martin D. Schwartz and Suzanne E. Hatty, eds., *Controversies in critical criminology*. Cincinnati: Lexisnexis/ Anderson.

Matthews, Rick A., and David Kauzlarich. (2000). "The crash of Valujet flight 592: A case study in state-corporate crime," *Sociological Focus* 3.

Matthews, Roger. (1986). "Policing prostitution," in Roger Matthews and Jock Young, eds., *Confronting crime*. Beverly Hills, CA: Sage.

Matza, David. (1964). *Delinquency and drift*. New York: Wiley.

Mauer, Marc. (2000). "The racial dynamics of imprisonment," in John P. May, ed., *Building violence: How America's rush to incarcerate creates more violence*. Thousand Oaks, CA: Sage.

Mauer, Marc, and Ryan King. *Uneven justice: State rates of incarceration by race and ethnicity*. Washington, DC: The Sentencing Project.

Maume, M. O., and M. Lee. (2003). "Social institutions and violence: A sub-national test of institutional anomie theory," *Criminology* 41(4): 1137–72.

Mayhew, P., R. V. G. Clark, J. N. Burrows, J. M. Hough, and S. W. Winchester. (1979). "Crime in public places," *Home Office Research Study* 49, London: H.M.S.O.

Mayhew, P., R. V. Clarke, and J. M. Hough (1992). "Steering column locks and car theft," in R. V. Clarke, ed., *Situational crime prevention: Successful case studies*. New York: Harrow and Heston.

Mayhew, Patricia, Ronald V. Clarke, and David Elliott. (1989). "Motorcycle theft, helmet legislation and displacement," *Howard Journal* 28: 1–8.

Mayhew, Patricia, Ronald V. Clarke, and Ike Hough. (1992). "Steering column locks and car theft," in R. V. Clarke, ed., *Situational crime prevention: Successful case studies*. New York: Harrow and Heston.

Mazerolle, Paul. (1997). "Delinquent definitions and participation age: Assessing the invariance hypothesis," *Studies on Crime and Crime Prevention* 6: 151–67.

Mazerolle, Paul. (1998). "Gender, general strain, and delinquency: Empirical examination," *Justice Quarterly* 15: 65–91.

McCarthy, Bill, John Hagan, and Todd S. Woodward. (1999). "In the company of women: Structure and agency in a revised power-control theory of gender and delinquency," *Criminology* 37(4): 761–88.

McCord, Joan. (1991). "Family relationships, juvenile delinquency, and adult criminality," *Criminology* 29: 397–417.

McIver, John P. (1981). "Criminal mobility: A review of empirical studies," in Simon Hakim and George F. Rengert, eds., *Crime spillover*. Beverly Hills, CA: Sage.

McNulty, T. L., and P. E. Bellair. (2003). "Explaining racial and ethnic differences in adolescent violence: Structural disadvantage, family well-being, and social capital," *Justice Quarterly* 20: 1–31.

Merton, Robert K. (1938). "Social structure and anomie," *American Sociological Review* 3: 672–82.

Merton, Robert K. (1957). *Social theory and social structure*. New York: Free Press.

Messerschmidt, James W. (1986). *Capitalism, patriarchy, and crime*. Totowa, NJ: Rowman & Littlefield.

Messerschmidt, James W. (1994). *Masculinities and crime*. Totowa, NJ: Rowman & Littlefield.

Messerschmidt, James. (1997). "From patriarchy to gender: Feminist theory, criminology, and the challenge of diversity," in Nicole Hahn Rafter and Frances Heidensohn, eds., *International feminist perspectives in criminology: Engendering a discipline*. Buckingham: Open University Press, 176–88.

Messerschmidt, James. (2000). *Nine lives: Adolescent masculinities, the body, and violence*. Boulder, CO: Westview.

Messner, Steven F., and Richard Rosenfeld. (2000). *Crime and the American dream*. 3rd ed. Belmont, CA: Wadsworth.

Messner, Steven F., and Richard Rosenfeld. (2007). *Crime and the American Dream*. 4th ed. Belmont, CA: Wadsworth.

Michalowski, Raymond J. (1985). *Order, law, and crime*. New York: Random House.

Michalowski, Raymond J. (1988). "Response to Nettler," *Criminologist* 13(4): 4.

Michalowski, Raymond J., and Susan Carlson. (1999). "Unemployment, imprisonment and social structures of accumulation: Historical contingency in the Rusche-Kirchheimer hypothesis," *Criminology* 37(2): 217–50.

Michalowski, Raymond, and Erdwin H. Pfuhl. (1991). "Technology, property, and law," *Crime, Law and Social Change* 15: 255–75.

Miller, Jody. (1998a). "Gender and victimization risk among young women in gangs," *Journal of Research in Crime and Delinquency* 35(4): 429–53.

Miller, Jody. (1998b). "Up it up: Gender and the accomplishment of street robbery," *Criminology* 36(1): 37–65.

Miller, Jody. (2003). "Feminist criminology," in Martin D. Schwartz and Suzanne Hatty, eds., *Critical Criminology* (Controversies in Crime and Justice Series). Cincinnati, OH: Anderson Publishing. 15–28.

Miller, Walter B. (1958). "Lower class culture as a generating milieu of gang delinquency," *Journal of Social Issues* 14: 5–19.

Minor, William. (1980). "The neutralization of criminal offense," *Criminology* 18: 103–20.

Minor, William. (1981). "Techniques of neutralization: A reconceptualization and empirical examination," *Journal of Research in Crime and Delinquency* 18: 295–318.

Moon, Byongook, Merry Morash, Cynthia Perez McCluskey, and Hye-Won Hwang. (2009). "A comprehensive test of general strain theory: Key strains, situational- and trait-based negative emotions, conditioning factors, and delinquency," *Journal of Research in Crime and Delinquency* 46: 182.

Morris, Allison. (1987). *Women, crime and criminal justice*. Oxford: Basil Blackwell.

Morris, Terrence. (1958). *The criminal area*. New York: Humanities Press.

Mullins, C. W., and R. Wright. (2003). "Gender, social networks, and residential burglary," *Criminology* 41(3): 813–40.

Mulvihill, D., M. Tumin, and L. Curtis. (1969). *Crimes of violence*. Washington, D.C.: U.S. Government Printing Office.

Mustaine, Elizabeth, and Richard Tewksbury. (1997). "Predicting risks of larceny theft victimization: A routine activity analysis using refined lifestyle measures," *Criminology* 36(4): 829–58.

Muzzatti, Stephen L. (2006). "Cultural criminology: A decade and counting of criminological chaos," in Walter S. Dekeseredy and Barbara Perry, eds., *Advancing Critical Criminology Theory and Application*. Lanham, MD: Lexington, 63–82.

Nagin, Daniel S., and Raymond Paternoster. (1993). "Enduring individual differences and rational choice theories of crime," *Law and Society Review* 27: 467–96.

O'Malley, Pat, and Stephen Mugford. (1991). "Crime, excitement and modernity." Presented at the annual meeting of the American Society of Criminology, San Francisco, November 18–23.

Osgood, D. Wayne, Martin Gold, and Carolyn Miller. (1986). "For better or worse? Peer attachment and peer influence among incarcerated adults." Paper presented at the annual meeting of the American Society of Criminology, Atlanta, Georgia.

Parker, Howard J. (1974). *View from the boys.* London: David and Charles.

Paternoster, Raymond, and Paul Mazerolle. (1994). "General strain theory and delinquency: A replication and extension," *Journal of Research in Crime and Delinquency* 31: 235–63.

Paternoster, Raymond, Linda E. Saltzman, Gordon P. Waldo, and Theodore G. Chiricos. (1983). "Perceived risk of social control: Do sanctions really deter?" *Law and Society Review* 17: 457–79.

Paternoster, Raymond, Linda E. Saltzman, Gordon P. Waldo, and Theodore G. Chiricos. (1985). "Assessments of risk and behavioral experience: An exploratory study of change," *Criminology* 23: 417–33.

Paternoster, Raymond, and Ruth Triplett. (1988). "Dissaggregating self-reported delinquency and its implications for theory," *Criminology* 26: 591–620.

Pearce, F., and S. Tombs (1998). *Toxic capitalism: Corporate crime and the chemical industry.* Aldershot, UK: Ashgate.

Pepinsky, Hal. (1999). "Peacemaking criminology and social justice," in Bruce A. Arrigo, ed., *Social justice/criminal justice: The maturation of critical theory in law, crime, and deviance.* Belmont, CA: West/Wadsworth.

Peterson, Ruth D., and William C. Bailey. (1991). "Felony murder and capital punishment: An examination of the deterrence question," *Criminology* 29: 367–95.

Pettit, Becky, and Bruce Western. (2004). "Mass imprisonment and the life course: Race and class inequality in U.S. incarceration," *American Sociological Review* 69: 151–69.

Pfohl, Stephen J. (1985). *Images of deviance and social control.* New York: McGraw-Hill.

Piquero, A., and M. Hickman. (1999). "An empirical test of Tittle's control balance theory," *Criminology* 27(2): 319–34.

Piquero, A., J. MacDonald, A. Dobrin, L. Daigle, and F. Cullen. (2005). "Self-control, violent offending, and homicide victimization: Assessing the general theory of crime," *Journal of Quantitative Criminology* 21(1): 55–81.

Piquero, Alex, and Paul Mazerolle. 2001. *Life-course criminology.* Wadsworth: Belmont, CA.

Piquero, Alex, and Raymond Paternoster. (1998). "An application of Stafford and Warr's reconceptualization of deterrence to drunk driving," *Journal of Research in Crime and Delinquency* 35(1): 3–39.

Piquero, N., S. Tibbetts, and M. Blakenship. (2005). "Examining the role of differential association and techniques of neutralization in explaining corporate crime," *Deviant Behavior: An Interdisciplinary Journal* 26(2): 159–88.

Piquero, Nicole Leeper, and Alex R. Piquero. (2006). "Control balance and exploitive corporate crime," *Criminology* 44: 397–430.

Pogarsky, Greg. (2002). "Identifying 'deterrable' offenders: Implications for research on deterrence," *Justice Quarterly* 19(3): 431–532.

Pratt, T. C., F. T. Cullen, K. R. Blevins, L. Daigle, and T. D. Madensen. (2006). "The empirical status of deterrence theory: A meta-analysis," in F. T. Cullen, J. P. Wright, and K. R. Blevins, eds., *Taking stock: The empirical status of criminological theory—Advances in criminological theory*. New Brunswick, NJ: Transaction.

Pratt, T. C., and T. W. Godsey. (2003). "Social support, inequality, and homicide: A crossnational test of an integrated theoretical model," *Criminology* 41: 611–43.

Pratt, Travis C. "Rational choice theory, crime control policy, and criminological relevance," *Criminology & Public Policy* 7(1): 43–52.

Presdee, Mike. (2000). *Cultural criminology and the carnival of crime*. London: Routledge.

Presser, Lois. (2003). "Remorse and neutralization among violent male offenders," *Justice Quarterly* 20(4): 801–25.

Quetelet, A. (1969 [1835]). *Sur l'homme et le development de ses facultes*. Paris: Hayez.

Quinney, Richard. (1979). *Criminology*. 2nd ed. Boston: Little, Brown.

Quinney, Richard. (1991). *Journey to a Far Place*. Philadelphia: Temple University Press.

Radzinowicz, Leon. (1966). *Ideology and crime*. New York: Columbia University Press.

Rafter, Nicole. (2000). *Shots in the mirror: Crime films and society*. New York: Oxford University Press.

Rafter, Nicole Hahn, and Frances Heidensohn. (1997). *International feminist perspectives in criminology: Engendering a discipline*. Buckingham: Open University Press.

Reckless, Walter. (1973). *The crime problem*. 5th ed. Englewood Cliffs, NJ: Prentice-Hall.

Reckless, Walter C., and Simon Dinitz. (1967). "Pioneering with self concept as a vulnerability factor in delinquency," *Journal of Criminal Law, Criminology, and Police Science* 58: 515–23.

Reed, Gary, and Peter Yeager. (1996). "Organizational offending and neoclassical criminology: Challenging the reach of a general theory of crime," *Criminology* 34(3): 357–82.

Reiman, Jeffrey. (2001). *The Rich Get Richer and the Poor Get Prison: Ideology, Class, and Criminal Justice*. 6th ed. Boston: Allyn and Bacon.

Reppetto, Thomas A. (1974). *Residential crime*. Cambridge, MA: Ballinger.

Restorative Justice Institute. (1999). "Restorative justice," www.doc.state.mn.us/rj, retrieved August 10, 2009.

Reuter, Peter, Jonathon Rubinstein, and Simon Winn. (1983). *Racketeering in legitimate industries: Two case studies*. Washington, D.C.: U.S. Department of Justice.

Rose, Dina R., and Todd R. Clear. (1998). "Incarceration, social capital, and crime: Implications for social disorganization theory," *Criminology* 36(3): 441–80.

Ross, J. I. (2009). *Cutting the edge*. 2nd ed. New Brunswich, NJ: Transaction Publishers.

Rountree, Pamela Wilcox, Kenneth C. Land, and Terance D. Miethe. (1994). "Macro-micro in the study of victimization: a hierarchal logistic model analysis across Seattle neighborhoods," *Criminology* 32(3): 387–409.

Rowe, Alan, John H. Lindquist, and O. Z. White. (1989). "A note on the family and crime in the United States," *Psychological Reports* 65: 1001–2.

Sampson, Robert J. (1986). "Crime in cities: The effects of formal and informal social control," in Albert J. Reiss and Michael Tonry, eds., *Communities and crime*. Chicago: University of Chicago Press, 271–311.

Sampson, Robert J. (1987a). "Communities and crime," in Michael R. Gottfredson and Travis Hirschi, eds., *Positive criminology*. Beverly Hills, CA: Sage, 91–114.

Sampson, Robert J. (1987b). "Urban black violence: The effect of male joblessness and family disruption," *American Journal of Sociology* 93: 348–82.

Sampson, Robert J., and John Laub. (1990). "Crime and deviance over the life course: The salience of adult social bonds," *American Sociological Review* 55: 609–27.

Sampson, Robert J., and John Laub. (1992). "Crime and deviance in the life course," *Annual Review of Sociology* 18: 63–84.

Sampson, Robert J., and John Laub. (1993). *Crime in the making*. Cambridge, MA: Harvard University Press.

Sampson, Robert J., and John H. Laub. (1997). "Life-course desisters? Trajectories of crime among delinquent boys followed to age 70," *Criminology* 41(3): 555–93.

Sampson, Robert J., and John H. Laub. (2003). "Life-course desisters? Trajectories of crime among delinquent boys followed to age 70," *Criminology* 41(3): 301–39.

Sampson, R. J., S. W. Raudenbush, and F. Earls. (1997). "Neighborhoods and violent crime: A multilevel study of collective efficacy," *Science* 277: 918–24.

Schwartz, Martin D., and David O. Friedrichs. (1994). "Postmodern thought and criminological discontent: New metaphors for understanding violence," *Criminology* 32(2): 221–46.

Schwartz, Martin D., and Dragan Milovanovic, eds. (1999). "Race, gender and class," in *Criminology: The Intersections*. New York: Garland Publishing, paperback edition.

Schwendinger, Herman, and Julia Siegel Schwendinger. (1985). *Adolescent subcultures and delinquency*. New York: Praeger.

Sellin, Thorsten. (1937). "The Lombrosian myth in criminology," *American Journal of Sociology* 42: 898–99.

Shannon, Lyle W. (1991). *Changing patterns of delinquency and crime*. Boulder, CO: Westview Press.

Shaw, Clifford R. (1931a). *Delinquency areas*. Chicago: University of Chicago Press.

Shaw, Clifford R. (1931b). *The natural history of a delinquent career*. Chicago: University of Chicago Press.

Shaw, Clifford R., and Henry D. McKay. (1942). *Juvenile delinquency and urban areas*. Chicago: University of Chicago Press.

Sheldon, William. (1949). *Varieties of delinquent youth*. New York: Harper.

Sherman, Lawrence W. (1993). "Defiance, deterrence, and irrelevance: A theory of the criminal sanction," *Journal of Research in Crime and Delinquency* 30: 445–71.

Shoham, Shlomo. (1970). *The mark of Cain*. Dobbs Ferry, NY: Citadel.

Shover, Neal, and David Honaker. (1992). "The socially bounded decision making of persistent property offenders," *Howard Journal of Criminal Justice* 31: 276–93.

Shover, Neil, and David Honaker. (1999). "The socially bounded decision making of persistent property offender," in Paul Cromwell, ed., *In their own words: Criminals on crime*. Los Angeles: Roxbury.

Shover, Neal, and Carol Y. Thompson. (1992). "Age, differential expectations, and crime desistance," *Criminology* 30: 601–16.

Simon, David R. (1999). *Elite deviance*. 6th ed. Boston: Allyn and Bacon.

Simon, Rita J. (1975). *Women and crime*. Lexington, MA: Lexington Books.

Simons, R. L., Yi-Fu Chen, E. A. Stewart, and G. H. Brody. (2003). "Incidents of discrimination and risk for delinquency: A longitudinal test of strain theory with an African American sample," *Justice Quarterly* 20: 827–54.

Simpson, Sally S., M. Lyn Exum, and N. Craig Smith. (2000). "The social control of corporate criminals: Shame and informal sanction threats," in Sally S. Simpson, ed., *Of crime and criminality: The use of theory in everyday life*. Thousand Oaks, CA: Pine Forge Press, 141–58.

Slocum, L., S. Simpson, and D. Smith. (2005). "Strained lives and crime: Examining intra-individual variation in strain and offending in a sample of incarcerated women," *Criminology* 43(4): 1067–11.

Sourcebook of Criminal Justice Statistics (2006). http://www.albany.edu/sourcebook/.

Spitzer, Steven. (1975). "Toward a Marxian theory of deviance," *Social Problems* 22: 638–51.

Stafford, Mark C., and Mark Warr. (1993). "A reconceptualization of general and specific deterrence," *Journal of Research in Crime and Delinquency* 30: 123–35.

Stanko, Elizabeth. (1990). *Everyday violence*. London: Pandora.

Stanko, Elizabeth. (1995). "A gendered criminological policies: Femininity, masculinity, and violence," in Hugh D. Barlow, ed., *Crime and public policy: Putting theory to work*. Boulder, CO: Westview. 207–26.

Stark, Rodney. (1987). "Deviant places: A theory of the ecology of crime," *Criminology* 25: 893–909.

Stewart, E., and R. Simons. (2006). "Structure and culture in African American adolescent violence: A partial test of the code of the street thesis," *Justice Quarterly* 23(1): 1–34.

Stewart, Eric A. (2003). "School social bonds, school climate, and school misbehavior: A multilevel analysis," *Justice Quarterly* 20(3): 575–604.

Surratt, Hilary L., James A. Inciardi, Steven P. Kurtz, and Marion C. Kiley. (2004). "Sex work and drug use in a subculture of violence," *Crime and Delinquency* 50(1): 43–71.

Sutherland, Edwin H., and Donald R. Cressey. (1974). *Criminology*. 9th ed. Philadelphia: Lippincott.

Sykes, Gresham M., and David Matza. (1957). "Techniques of neutralization: A theory of delinquency," *American Sociological Review* 22: 664–70.

Takaki, Ronald T. (1993). *A different mirror: A history of multicultural America*. Boston: Little Brown.

Tannenbaum, Frank. (1938). *Crime and the community*. New York: Columbia University.

Thornberry, Terence P. (1987). "Toward an interactional theory of delinquency," *Criminology* 25: 863–91.

Thornberry, Terence P., and Marvin D. Krohn. (2001). "The development of delinquency: An interactional perspective," in Susan O. White, ed., *Handbook of youth and justice*. New York: Plenum, 289–306.

Tifft, Larry, and Lynn Markham. (1991). "Battering women and battering Central Americans: A peacemaking synthesis," in Richard Quinney and Hal Pepinsky, eds., *Criminology as peacemaking*. Bloomington: Indiana University Press, 114–153.

Tifft, L., and D. Sullivan. (1980). *The struggle to be human: Crime, criminology, and anarchism*. Sanday, Orkney, UK: Cienfuegos Press.

Tittle, Charles R. (1980). *Sanctions and deterrence*. New York: Praeger.

Tittle, Charles R. (1995). *Control balance: Toward a general theory of deviance*. Boulder, CO: Westview.

Tittle, Charles R. (1997). "Thoughts stimulated by Braithwaite's analysis of control balance theory," *Theoretical Criminology* 1(1): 99–110.

Tittle, Charles R. (2004). "Refining control balance theory," *Theoretical Criminology* 8(4): 395–428.

Topalli, V. (2005). "When being good is bad: An expansion of neutralization theory," *Criminology* 43(3): 797–836.

Trasler, Gordon. (1986). "Situational crime control and rational choice," in Kevin Heal and Gloria Laycock, eds., *Situational crime prevention: From theory into practice*. London: H.M.S.O.

Triplett, Ruth. (2000). "The dramatization of evil: Reacting to juvenile delinquency during the 1990s," in Sally S. Simpson, ed., *Of crime and criminality: The use of theory in everyday life*. Thousand Oaks, CA: Pine Forge Press.

Trivizas, Eugene, and Philip T. Smith. (1997). "The deterrent effect of terrorist incidents on the rates of luggage theft in railway and underground stations," *British Journal of Criminology* 37(1): 63–75.

Tseloni, Andromachi, Karin Wittebrood, Graham Farrell, and Ken Pease. (2004). "Burglary victimization in England and Wales, the United States and the Netherlands; A cross-national comparative test of routine activities and lifestyle theories," *British Journal of Criminology* 44(1): 66–92.

Tucker, Robert C. (1978). *The Marx-Engels reader*. 2nd ed. New York: W. W. Norton Company.

Tunnell, Kenneth D. (1990). "Choosing crime: Close your eyes and take your chances," *Justice Quarterly* 7: 4.

Tunnell, Kenneth D. (1992). *Choosing Crime: The criminal calculus of property offenders*. Chicago: Nelson-Hall.

Turk, Austin T. (1966). "Conflict and criminality," *American Sociological Review* 31: 338–52.

Turk, Austin T. (1969). *Criminality and legal order*. Chicago: Rand McNally.

Vagg, Joon. "Delinquency and shame: Data from Hong Kong," *The British Journal of Criminology* 38(2): 247–65.

van den Berghe, Pierre L. (1974). "Bringing beasts back in: Toward a biosocial theory of aggression," *American Sociological Review* 39: 777–78.

Vaughan, Diane. (1996). *The Challenger launch decision: Risky technology, culture, and deviance at NASA*. Chicago: University of Chicago Press.

Vazsonyi, Alexander T., and Rudi Klanjšek. (2008). "A test of self-control theory across different socioeconomic strata," *Justice Quarterly* 25(1): 101–31.

Velez, Maria B., Lauren J. Krivo, and Ruth D. Peterson. (2003) "Structural inequality and homicide: An assessment of the black-white gap in killings," *Criminology* 41(3): 645–73.

Vila, Bryan J. (1994). "A general paradigm for understanding criminal behavior: Extending evolutionary ecological theory," *Criminology* 32: 311–59.

Vila, Bryan J., and Lawrence E. Cohen. (1993). "Crime as strategy: Testing an evolutionary ecological theory of expropriative crime," *American Journal of Sociology* 98: 873–912.

Walker, Samuel. (1998). *Sense and nonsense about crime and drugs: A policy guide.* 4th ed. New York: West/Wadsworth.

Walsh, Anthony, and Lee Ellis. (1999). "Political ideology and American criminologists' explanations of criminal behavior," *Criminologist* 24: 1–27.

Walsh, Dermot. (1980). *Break-ins: Burglary from private houses.* London: Constable.

Ward, D., M. Stafford, and L. Gray. (2006). "Rational choice, deterrence, and theoretical integration." *Journal of Applied Social Psychology* 36(3): 571–98.

Warr, Mark, and Mark Stafford. (1991). "The influences of delinquent peers: What they think or what they do?" *Criminology* 29: 851–66.

Warner, Barbara D. (2007). "Directly intervene or call the authorities? A study of forms of neighborhood social control within a social disorganization framework," *Criminology* 45: 99–129.

Weisburd, David, Laura A. Wyckoff, Justin Ready, John E. Eck, Joshua C. Hinkle, Frank Gajewski. "Does crime just move around the corner? A controlled study of spatial displacement and diffusion of crime control benefits," *Criminology* 44(3): 549–92.

Weitzer, Ronald, and Charis Kubrin. (2004). "Breaking news: How local TV news and real-world conditions affect fear of crime," *Justice Quarterly* 21(3): 497–523.

Wellford, Charles. (1975). "Labeling theory and criminology: An assessment," *Social Problems* 22: 332–45.

Welsh, B., and D. Farrington. (1999). "Value for money? A review of the cost and benefits of situational crime prevention," *British Journal of Criminology* 39(3): 345–69.

White, H., and R. Agnew. (1992). "An empirical test of general strain theory," *Criminology* 30: 475–99.

Whitehead, Tony L. (2000). "The epidemic and cultural legends of black male incarceration: The socialization of African American children to a life of incarceration," in John P. May, ed., *Building violence: How America's rush to incarcerate creates more violence.* Thousand Oaks, CA: Sage.

Wilson, James Q., and Richard J. Herrnstein. (1985). *Crime and human nature.* New York: Simon and Schuster.

Wilson, William Julius. (1987). *The truly disadvantaged: The inner city, the underclass, and public policy.* Chicago: University of Chicago Press.

Winfree, L., T. Taylor, N. He, and F. Esbensen. (2006). "Self-control and variability over time: Multivariate results using a 5-year, multisite panel of youths," *Crime and Delinquency* 52(2): 253–79.

Wolfgang, Marvin E. (1961). "Pioneers in criminology: Cesare Lombroso (1835–1909)," *Journal of Criminal Law, Criminology, and Police Science* 52: 361–91.

Wolfgang, Marvin E., and Franco Ferracuti. (1967). *The subculture of violence.* London: Tavistock.

Wright, B., A. Caspi, and T. Moffitt. (2004). "Does the perceived risk of punishment deter criminally prone individuals? Rational choice, self-control, and crime," *Journal of Research in Crime and Delinquency* 41(2): 180–213.

Wright, Kevin N., and Karen E. Wright. (1994). *Family life, delinquency, and crime: A policymaker's guide*. Washington, DC: Office of Juvenile Justice and Delinquency Prevention.

Wright, Richard T. (2000). Comments made at a presentation at Southern Illinois University, Edwardsville, March.

Wright, Richard T., and Scott H. Decker. (1994). *Burglars on the job: Street life and residential break-ins*. Boston: Northeastern University Press.

Wright, Richard T., and Scott H. Decker. (1997). *Armed robbers in action*. Boston: Northeastern University Press.

Yeager, P., and G. Reed, (1998). "Of corporate persons and straw men: A reply to Herbert, Green, and Larragoite," *Criminology* 36(4): 885–97.

Young, Jock. (1986). "The failure of criminology: The need of radical realism," in Roger Matthews and Jock Young, eds., *Confronting crime*. Beverly Hills, CA: Sage, 4–30.

Young, Jock (1997). "Left realism: The basics," in Brian MacLean and Dragan Milovanovic, eds., *Thinking critically about crime*. Vancouver, BC: The Collective Press, 28–36.

Zhang, Lening, and Sheldon Zhang. "Reintegrative shaming and predatory delinquency," *The Journal of Research in Crime and Delinquency* 41(4): 433–57.

Index

About the Authors

Hugh D. Barlow is emeritus professor of sociology at Southern Illinois University, Edwardsville. He is coauthor with David Kauzlarich of *Introduction to Criminology*, 9th edition (2009), and author of *Dead for Good: Martyrdom and the Rise of the Suicide Bomber* (2007). Barlow is recipient of the Herbert Bloch Award given by the American Society of Criminology for services to the profession. He resides in Albuquerque, New Mexico.

David Kauzlarich is professor and chair of sociology and criminal justice studies at Southern Illinois University, Edwardsville. He is coauthor with Hugh D. Barlow of two other criminology textbooks and several other books including *Crimes of the American Nuclear State: At Home and Abroad* (with Ronald C. Kramer). Kauzlarich has recently received major awards from the American Society of Criminology's Critical Criminology Division and Southern Illinois University, Edwardsville for his research and teaching.